Globalisation and the Challenge to Criminology

There is no doubt that globalisation has profound effects on crime, justice and our feelings of security, identity and belonging. Many of these affect both the making of laws and the breaking of laws. It has been argued however that criminology has been too provincial, focusing as it often does on national laws and issues, whilst others have said that globalisation is the stuff of international relations, global finance and trade, not of criminology. This book disputes this by asserting that criminology has a firm place in this arena and globalisation offers the discipline a challenge that it should relish.

Some of the field's top scholars from the UK, the USA, Canada, Australia and New Zealand consider these challenges and present cutting-edge analysis and debate. Topics covered include transnational organised crime, international policing and a range of other issues involving global harm such as genocide, the workings of international financial institutions, the fate of international migrants and the impact of anti-immigration sentiments in Europe. A particular focus is on borders and arrangements that deal with migration and populations that are excluded and adrift.

This book highlights criminology's analysis and engagement in new understandings of globalisation, in particular its harmful and unethical manifestations, and offers a mode of scrutiny and vigilance. *Globalisation and the Challenge to Criminology* will be of particular interest to those studying criminology, criminal justice, policing, security and international relations as well as those who seek to understand globalisation, and in particular, its harmful outcomes.

Francis Pakes is Director of the Research Centre for Comparative and International Criminology at the University of Portsmouth. His more recent work has a strong focus on the nature of globalisation, and its consequences for crime and justice in general and for criminology in particular. He is a former treasurer of the British Society for Criminology and has also published on the intersections of psychology, mental health and criminal justice.

LIVERPOOL JMU LIBRARY

3 1111 01526 1447

Globalisation and the Challenge to Criminology

Edited by
Francis Pakes

Routledge
Taylor & Francis Group

LONDON AND NEW YORK

First edition published 2013
by Routledge
2 Park Square, Milton Park, Abingdon, Oxon OX14 4RN

Simultaneously published in the USA and Canada
by Routledge
711 Third Avenue, New York, NY 10017

Routledge is an imprint of the Taylor & Francis Group, an informa business

© 2013 Francis Pakes, selection and editorial material

The right of Francis Pakes to be identified as editor of this work has been asserted by him in accordance with sections 77 and 78 of the Copyright, Designs and Patents Act 1988.

All rights reserved. The purchase of this copyright material confers the right on the purchasing institution to photocopy pages which bear the photocopy icon and copyright line at the bottom of the page. No part of this book may be reprinted or reproduced or utilised in any form or by any electronic, mechanical, or other means, now known or hereafter invented, including photocopying and recording, or in any information storage or retrieval system, without permission in writing from the publishers.

Trademark notice: Product or corporate names may be trademarks or registered trademarks, and are used only for identification and explanation without intent to infringe.

British Library Cataloguing in Publication Data
A catalogue record for this book is available from the British Library

Library of Congress Cataloging-in-Publication Data
Globalisation and the challenge to criminology / edited by Francis Pakes.
p. cm.
1. Crime and globalization. I. Pakes, Francis J. II. Title: Globalization and the challenge to criminology.
HV6252.G556 2012
364—dc23
2012021435

ISBN: 978-0-415-68607-5 (hbk)
ISBN: 978-0-415-64352-8 (pbk)
ISBN: 978-0-203-43685-1 (ebk)

Typeset in Times New Roman
by Book Now Ltd, London

Contents

Illustrations

Figures

Table

Contributors

Mathieu Deflem, University of South Carolina, USA

David O. Friedrichs, University of Scranton, USA

B.K. Greener, Massey University, New Zealand

Samantha Hauptman, University of South Carolina at Union, USA

Susanne Karstedt, University of Leeds, UK

Ben Muller, University of Western Ontario, Canada

David Nelken, University of Macerata, Italy

Francis Pakes, University of Portsmouth, UK

Sharon Pickering, Monash University, Australia

Dawn L. Rothe, Old Dominion University, USA

Daniel Silverstone, London Metropolitan University, UK

Juliet P. Stumpf, Lewis & Clark Law School, USA

Leanne Weber, Monash University, Australia

1 Globalisation and criminology

An agenda of engagement

Francis Pakes

It is not easy to come to the essence of globalisation. For starters, it refers to notions of global finance, branding and migration. We also think of global institutions such as the United Nations or Cable News Network (CNN), and global fame embodied in stars like Usain Bolt, Lady Gaga or Oprah Winfrey. Global brands come to mind. We may consider politicians with global fame such as Barack Obama and Vladimir Putin. But we also cannot help to be reminded of apocalyptic terms such as global meltdown, pandemics and genocide. We might be forced to ponder global resources, from fossil fuel to precious metals and rain forests. There is much to challenge, much to protect, much to celebrate and much to fight against, it seems, when it comes to some of globalisation's most obvious manifestations. It is therefore no wonder that globalisation invokes feelings of profound and intense ambiguity.

Essential descriptions of globalisation involve talk of contradictions. Globalisation is frequently referred to as a set of contradictory processes consisting of both flows and counterflows; efforts to open up the world for trade, production and consumption go hand in hand with measures to constrict this through fences, borders and other types of barriers.

Simple descriptions of globalisation tend to run as follows. Globalisation refers to the growing interconnectedness and integration of people, goods and finance (Held, 1995). Two principal drivers can be identified that explain its acceleration in the last few decades. The first is technology. Information and communication technology has allowed international trade and finance to become despatialised to a large extent. This has allowed outsourcing, for instance and the emergence of a truly global marketplace, increasing the value and prowess of multinational companies. It has never been quicker, easier and cheaper to transfer money, goods, ideas or people over the globe although not all of these 'commodities' travel with the same ease.

The second driver is in the realm of politics and policy. This, on the one hand, refers to the opening up of parts of the world for globalisation, notably the former Eastern Bloc after the fall of the Berlin Wall in 1989 and the collapse of the Soviet Union soon after. The second is ideological transformations in major emerging economies such as in China. That means that large parts of the world are now open for global business which has accelerated global competition in is of production, investment and increasingly, consumption. Other components of this driver include globally spread globalisation-friendly policies, furthering free trade (within certain limitations and constraints), competitive taxation of various sorts, and the furtherance of global consumption through global branding and marketing, and much of this is frequently discussed under the banner of neo-liberalism.

It is not difficult to portray both sets of processes as a picture of progress. Innovation in information and communication technology is easily framed within a narrative of advancement: we now have Skype, Facebook and Twitter to allow us to stay connected and informed. Information technology ostensibly serves as the antidote to isolation and ignorance. A plethora of websites including Amazon and Paypal allow us to run our household to a large extent on line. No more queuing up at the post office as our affairs are sorted swiftly and effortlessly on line. Finally, through dedicated websites and chat rooms we find new friends, soul mates or a support network way beyond our street, village or country. The story here is that information and communication technology has enhanced our life beyond compare; a story of advancement and achievement.

There is a similar interpretation forced upon the latter driver which goes that the unlocking of large parts of the world represents genuine humanitarian progress. Peoples that previously were subdued and deprived of opportunity are now able to engage in the good things in life such as travel, consumption, education and career. For millions, perhaps billions, there is hope for a better life, owing to political change that allows them to free themselves from the strain of toxic ideology and state repression and totalitarianism.

But this is where the contradictions start. On the other hand, the degree and pace of globalisation has brought urgent issues to the fore. Two of these are directly related to these drivers. The negative effects of global finance are now plain to see for all further to the financial crisis of 2008 and the resulting fall out in much of the industrialised world. The ease and ubiquity of IT and our reliance on it brings with it the fear of cybercrime in many guises, from cyber bullying to attacks on IT infrastructure that supports state security and much in between. It makes for life and luxury to be regarded as perennially precarious.

The spread of globalisation-friendly policies is equally subject to heated debate and controversy. Whereas the talk is of spreading prosperity it is arguable that such policies fail to deliver to those on the receiving end. Stiglitz has made this argument for a number of years and in this volume, Friedrichs and Hauptman make a similar argument. This is due to several processes are at work that are at times difficult to disentangle. The first is that neoliberalist policies imposed on countries in financial need, through the World Bank and the International Monetary Fund (IMF) make in fact life harder for citizens in those countries (see Klein, 2007, for a fierce critique). Another is that within countries, both developed and developing, the differences between the 'have's' and the 'have nots' tend to increase. Whereas countries may be keen to brand themselves as 'open for business' and be attractive to investors and speculators, GDP may increase but unemployment may rise and wages may drop as workers find themselves competing in a global context. The third is that through outsourcing and the shifting of manufacturing to the areas of the world with the cheapest wages, local unemployment may soar in developed parts of the world where manufacturing jobs will disappear whilst at the same time in developing countries wages need to be kept low and the labour market as little regulated as possible. The upshot of this may be that workers worldwide fail to experience the benefits of globalisation. Fourth, these developments have enhanced the clout of international corporations from oil companies to banks. They have become 'too big to fail', which leads to levels of liability that are too big for most individual countries to bear. It brings the challenge of regulating such business and holding them accountable for harm. It raises the question of who is in charge in our globalised world. Fifth, issues of sovereignty have also been eroded through supranational institutions such as the United Nations, the European Union, the G8, G20, etcetera. If there is such a thing as global governance, it is probably is governance via summit, either at the United Nations, G8 or G20 meetings or the World Economic Forum in Davos. How effective and fair such governance is remains to be seen. At any rate, the narrative of progress (e.g. Friedman, 1999) looks bleaker a good decade later.

To add to all this there are the unwanted or unexpected consequences of globalisation. They frequently occur in the realms of culture, identity and community. These include undesirable flows and movement, none more so than of people, in particular those '*sans papiers*'. The chapters by Muller (this volume), and Weber and Pickering (this volume) consider policies that deal with the movement of bodies and the harm caused by these policies of exclusion. There are further sentiments brought about or intensified by globalisation to which governments have felt it imperative to respond to over and beyond strengthening borders. Quests for national identity have intensified and measures against those that threaten it have become harsher and at time no less than brutal. Pakes's (this volume) chapter considers such manifestations in several European countries.

Finally, there are overall aspects of globalisation that are difficult to evaluate: does globalisation lead to peace and prosperity as Friedman (1999) has argued in the past, or is globalisation is an accelerator of inequality and a harbinger of poverty and conflict? If the latter is the case and there are good arguments that it might be, then, as Bauman has argued, globalisation throws an ethical challenge (Bauman, 2001). The quest for global governance is, or at least must be, closely linked for the quest for global justice. This often is not conceptualised as criminal justice per se although issues of genocide and the absence of any sort of justice in weak or failed states is incorporated in a search for global modes, means and platforms to provide accountability and fairness. Conceptualisations of what global justice means and what it might look like are certainly emerging at the moment (e.g. Brock, 2009). Needless to say, globalisation is likely to put unsustainable strains on our natural environment that will produce human suffering. Shortages in food, fresh water, fuel and essential materials for industry may well bring out conflicts and movements on scales not seen before. Therefore the ethical challenge needs to incorporate issues of sustainability and a fair distribution of available resources.

Berberoglu (2009) is quite unequivocal in his assessment of the nature of globalisation: it is the highest stage of imperialism operating on a world scale in which processes of globalisation constitute the mechanisms to facilitate global plunder and oppression. Anti-globalisation is in effect the class struggle gone global (Berberoglu, 2009). His assessment represents an interesting antidote to the often-phrased notion that we need a new frame of reference in order to understand globalisation. Berberoglu's point seems to be that the old paradigm of class struggles and capitalism works just fine.

There is no doubt that globalisation at present plays out unevenly and often in disastrous ways. It leaves weaknesses in global regions there to be exploited by legitimate business, states, as well as organised criminals and terrorists. Part of the case for global governance is to tackle effectively transnational harmful behaviour resulting from exploiting criminogenic asymmetries between the regulated North and the less regulated South (Passas, 1999). The dumping of toxic waste is one such example whereas in the past, nuclear tests on far away atolls is another example of a tendency for legitimate and illegitimate actors to take hazardous conduct and goods to where they can be dealt with the least amount of cost, reputational damage and risk of litigation or other forms of enforcement. Global asymmetries are key globalisers and often not for the good.

Those who seek to study or even govern globalisation are chasing a moving target. The very nature of globalisation provides a real challenge to any sort of global governance whatever shape that might take: uncertainty about its nature and about what happens next requires great agility in making sense of it. There certainly is an argument to be made that globalisation is modern day colonialism. Others have argued that globalisation has led to a global class struggle only obscured by issues of nationality. The high visibility of American globalisation cannot be denied: we can listen to American artists anywhere where there is Internet, and McDonalds, Starbucks and Microsoft have a global reach through branding of incredible strength. American cultural hegemony is certainly identifiable world-wide. But there is a sense that the 2008 global economic crisis is accelerating a process of de-hegemonisation away from the United States towards several locations of which India, China and possibly South America are the main contenders. Others argue that considering hegemony or dominance in terms of geographic region is already underplaying the despatialising aspects of globalisation and that the emerging social and financial state is one in which global corporations are the defining force. At any rate, globalisation has no master plan and does not have a single direction. That makes governance particularly problematic: how can we control a set of processes so paradoxical, elusive yet ubiquitous?

Brock (2009) argues that, like it or not, we already have global governance given shape by agencies such as the United Nations, the World Trade Organisation, the International Monetary Fund. Nederveen Pieterse (2008), however, calls the 1990s institutional architecture of globalization around the IMF, World Bank and World Trade Organisation increasingly fragile. The IMF has reduced financial clout, whereas financing from Chinese sources has become globally popular. The influence of newly industrialised economies (e.g. China and India) is increasing and so is that of the G20 and G77. A new development he charts is not a widening gap between developed and developing countries but stronger bifurcations and inequalities within developing countries, of which he uses China and India as examples. Some areas will boom (e.g. Hyderabad, Friedman, 1999) but other rural areas and the urban poor will (continue to) suffer. Nederveen Pieterse puts it graphically:

> For every swank mall that will spring up in a booming Indian city, a neglected village will explode in Naxalite rage; for every child who will take wings to study in a foreign university there will be 10 who fall off the map without even the raft of a basic alphabet to keep them afloat; for every new Italian eatery that will serve up fettuccine there will be a debt-ridden farmer hanging himself and his hopes on a rope.
>
> (Nederveen Pieterse, 2008, p. 713)

It seems customary in many publications on globalisation to build it up and convince the reader that the world has changed profoundly only to subsequently emphasise that despite all the 'flow speak' (Bude and Dürrschmidt, 2010) we should not forget to appreciate the 'cultural thickness of everyday territoriality' (p. 482), i.e. that life for the most part remains rooted in locality. Despite email, smart phone and credit card I still am where I am. Bude and Dürrschmidt argue that too enthusiastic talk of globalisation loses sight of limits. Talk of borderless worlds and limitless choice is vacuous at least in light of the lived experience of the vast majority of people on earth. Our experience remains limited, not limitless. Instead, place has emerged or re-emerged as the most potent organiser of our fate. Being born on one or the other side of Fortress Europe, or in Mexico as opposed to Arizona makes a massive difference to life expectancy, entitlements to health care, education and social security. Where we ask 'what side or you on', it is perhaps most poignant in relation to borders, and less in terms of ideology.

So, globalisation matters but so does place. The new does not replace the old but somehow co-exists with it. That is perhaps what has prompted Savelsberg to argue for a 'process turn' in the study of globalisation. Global challenges interact with local conditions making the case of broader comparative analysis (Savelsberg, 2011; Pakes, 2010; also Bowling, 2011). Area studies and cross-national remain important: 'Global challenges and scripts encounter local cultural conditions, rooted in religion and collective memories, and distinct institutional arrangements' (Savelsberg, 2011, p. 82). How those play out is both difficult to predict and fascinating to observe.

That there is a role for criminology here should be obvious. First, we need to address our traditional subject matter, matters of crime, harm, power and justice as given shape in local conditions and global developments. This is a substantial challenge, although many top academics are leading the way (e.g. Bosworth and Hoyle, 2011; Aas, 2007; Drake *et al.*, 2010). Second, we need to identify the hot spots, the places where globalisation hurts. These spots can be specific geographic areas. One of those is the Isle of Lampedusa, a focal point of immigrants from North Africa into the European Union. In addition, hot spots can be conceptual in nature. Borders are the best example of such hot spots and subject to acute reconceptualisations (e.g. Muller, this volume; Zureik and Salter, 2005). Issues of 'crimmigration', citizenship and deportation are others (see Stumpf, this volume). Schinkel (2009) identifies the detention centre where '*homo sacer*', illegal residers, outsiders without entitlements, are held. The detention centre serves symbolically as heterotopias and physically as the affirmation of exclusion (Schinkel, 2009). Where Muller speaks of borderlands as a firing line of globalisation, Weber and Pickering (this volume) talk about death at the global frontier. It is clear that globalisation is forcing a drastic reconceptualisation of places of engagement for criminology. At the same time, we should join the quest for and critically examine manifestations of and claims to, global justice with the ambition to transcend time and place.

This volume contains a number of contributions that chart how the world of criminology is adapting to cope with globalisation. It is clear that strictly sticking to national boundaries, as if they were 'do not cross' crime scene tapes, is obscuring from our sight a lot of harmful behaviour. Several contributions take that transnational or global perspective and do so with verve. Others comment on how traditional criminology has adapted and its level of analysis comes to incorporate global developments. Yet others look at how policing or criminology inquiry is coping in the new landscape. Altogether, it brings a degree of optimism that a substantial part of criminology is truly global: follow the global harm, not the local law. Together they demonstrate that after a slow start, criminology is well and truly engaged with globalisation, and it is set to transform the discipline at its very core.

Together the contributions in this book show the vibrancy of international and global criminology. David Nelken looks at issues in method and content in comparative criminal justice, which is subject to much debate in the field currently (Pakes, 2010; Nelken, 2011). Daniel Silverstone looks at organised crime. His key message, refreshingly perhaps is that much of 'conventional' organised crime, at least in the United Kingdom, remains rather rooted in the local. David Friedrichs and Dawn Rothe in contrast look at harmful behaviour by global financial institutions, such as the World Bank and the IMF. They make a strong case that criminology should concern itself much more urgently with such forms of global harm doing. The role of policing in relation to globalisation is scrutinised by Mathieu Deflem and Samantha Hauptman, and also by B.K. Greener. Mathieu Deflem and Samantha Hauptman consider the policing of international terrorism, in particular in the aftermath of 9/11. B.K. Greener considers policing efforts in international peace keeping missions. Both chapters highlight some of the transformations of global policing and the ethical and practical challenges these pose.

Juliet Stumpf considers crimmigration, the increasing alignment of processes, aims and discourses of immigration law and criminal law, frequently to devastating effect. Leanne Weber and Sharon Pickering consider issues of deportation and the definite and at times harrowing consequences of deportation policy and practice in many Western countries. In doing so they highlight the importance of borders and citizenship, something Ben Muller takes on in his vivid description of Borderworld, an area governed by biometrics, drones, exclusion and division. In an evocative chapter Susanne Karstedt looks at the challenge to criminology posed by genocide and mass atrocities, an area of research that criminology traditionally has been reluctant to engage with. Finally, Francis Pakes looks at globalisation's counter processes, such as neo-nationalism, or parochialism often expressed in a desire to close borders. In particular he charts the rise of anti-immigration anti-Islamic parties in several European countries and their wider effects in policies on criminal justice, immigration and human rights and civil liberties. His message of vigilance is one to take further. There is no doubt that apart from many beneficial effects, globalisation causes or enhances inequality and suffering. That calls on criminology to be engaged, to place its finger where it hurts and expose new means of harm production. It is encouraging to see colleagues do exactly that. I would like to extend the invitation to others in the field of criminology and beyond. Globalisation has made the global struggle for justice and fairness perhaps harder but certainly more important. In that struggle it is important that the voice of criminology is heard.

References

Aas, K.F. (2007) *Globalization and Crime*. London: Sage.

Bauman, Z. (2001) The ethical challenge of globalization. *New Perspectives Quarterly*, *18*, 4–9.

Berberoglu, B. (2009) The class nature of globalization in the age of imperialism. *Critical Sociology*, *35*, 785–800.

Bosworth, M. and Hoyle, C. (2011) *What is Criminology?* Oxford: Oxford University Press.

Bowling, B. (2011) Transnational criminology and the globalization of harm production. In: M. Bosworth and C. Hoyle (eds) *What is Criminology?* Oxford: Oxford University Press.

Brock, G. (2009) *Global Justice: A Cosmopolitan Account*. Oxford: Oxford University Press.

Bude, H. and Dürrschmidt, J. (2010) What's wrong with globalization? Contra 'flow speak' – towards an existential turn in the theory of globalization. *European Journal of Social Theory*, *13*, 481–500.

Drake, D., Muncie, J. and Westmarland, L. (2010) *Criminal Justice: Local and Global*. Cullompton: Willan (with the Open University).

Friedman, T. (1999) *The Lexus and the Olive Tree*. New York: Farrar, Straus & Giroux.

Held, D. (1995) *Democracy and the Global Order*. Stanford, CA: Stanford University Press.

Klein, N. (2007) *The Shock Doctrine*. London: Penguin.

Nederveen Pieterse, J. (2008) Globalization the next round: Sociological perspectives. *Futures, 40,* 707–720.

Nelken, D. (2011) *Comparative Criminal Justice.* London: Sage.

Pakes, F. (2010) The comparative method in globalised criminology. *Australian and New Zealand Journal of Criminology, 43,* 17–30.

Passas, N. (1999). Globalization, criminogenic asymmetries and economic crime. *European Journal of Law Reform, 1,* 399–424.

Savelsberg, J.J. (2011) Globalization and states of punishment. In: D. Nelken (ed.) *Comparative Criminal Justice and Globalization.* Farnham: Ashgate.

Schinkel, W. (2009) 'Illegal aliens' and the state, or: Bare bodies vs the zombie. *International Sociology, 24,* 779–806.

Zureik, E. and Salter, M.B. (eds) (2005) *Global Surveillance and Policing: Borders, Security, Identity.* Cullompton: Willan.

2 The challenge of globalisation for comparative criminal justice[1]

David Nelken

This chapter is concerned with the extent to which globalisation can and should be taken into account in studying criminal justice comparatively. The questions it touches on include: Does it still make sense to think about criminal justice systems in terms of separable national jurisdictions at a time of global links between crime threats and criminal justice responses? In what ways do the nation-state or other, more locally based, justice practices shape or resist 'global' trends? To what extent is a global 'gaze' on crime threats possible and desirable? How can such a perspective avoid the risks of ethnocentrism or relativism by which what purports to be global is in fact local (Nelken, 2009b)?

There has been an undoubted rise of interest in global criminological issues.[2] But this has so far largely gone hand in hand with a continuation of older type of comparative enquiries. Even the best studies of comparative criminal justice devote themselves principally to explaining differences in national laws, ideas and practices across different jurisdictions (see, for example, the descriptive comparisons of juvenile justice in different jurisdictions in Muncie and Goldson (2006) or the cross-national collaborative efforts to test hypotheses on the organisational variables that affect police integrity and corruption in Klockars *et al.* (2004)). On the other hand, most studies of the best ways to respond to supposed transnational threats or to spread human rights pay little attention to the difficulties of comparative enquiries, except perhaps to lament the obstacles created by difference between places. These endeavours, to some extent, have different aims and audiences. But trying to keep comparative and globalisation issues strictly apart has little to recommend it other than to allow for the continuation of 'business as usual', and it risks, as will be seen, missing a variety of interesting interconnections.

It may seem at first sight that there is no obvious connection between the details of lower criminal court procedure and the problem of how to combat various threats posed by serious transnational crime. But even the world of 'high policing' is less often engaged in a strenuous life and death struggle with transnational organized crime than in developing a more technologically advanced response to traditional 'high volume crime' (Sheptycki, 2002). International law and conventions that seek to spread or enforce human rights have obvious implications for matters such as corruption, terrorism and immigration – but they are relevant also to the length of ordinary criminal trials (Nelken, 2008). More generally, responding to transnational phenomena such as irregular migration has profound effects on the provisions, temper and everyday practice of local systems of criminal justice. Conversely, for a wide range of questions regarding international relations, human rights, truth commissions, restitutive justice and transitional justice it is the proper role of international criminal justice as compared to more local means of handling conflict that is a matter of debate (Karstedt, 2009).

Certainly, there are still remarkable differences in the types of conduct for which people are punished in, say, the United States, China, Thailand or Saudi Arabia, as well as in the type of penalties used. Local conditions also have a lot to do with explaining the differing involvement of immigrants in crime in different European countries and the response to this (Solivetti, 2010). But decisions made by criminal justice actors here and elsewhere increasingly (have to) relate to their understandings about criminal justice elsewhere and the desire to be similar or be different to them. Finland's successful efforts to reduce its incarceration rates have been linked to its desire to come into line with published evidence of the rates in other Scandinavian countries (Lappi-Seppälä, 2007). Conversely, the introduction of international crime victimisation surveys had an influence on policy makers and (to a lesser extent) public opinion in the Netherlands where it produced 'a wholesale change in the philosophy of criminal justice policy' (Downes, 2011: 40). This does not mean of course that those doing the comparison have got it 'right'. Typically, actors construct ideas and practices in other societies in terms that reflect their own concerns and assumptions – even when they are seeking to collaborate with them. As scholars come to study these 'second-order' comparisons they will increasingly need to move from 'methodological nationalism' to more cosmopolitan approaches (Beck and Sznaider, 2006).

In seeking to throw more light on the relationship between globalisation and criminal justice I shall first summarise the 'state of the art', then move on to discuss the way globalisation affects the units we want to compare and how it is linked to the alleged decline of the nation-state. I shall point to the need to see globalisation as a contested process, and then consider its implications for social justice and for diversity. The aim will be to show the need for careful research into globalisation's significance for criminal justice at national, regional and local levels rather than simply taking it to be an unstoppable force for convergence.

Broadening a discipline

Comparative criminal justice textbooks and readers reveal considerable uncertainty about how best to integrate the effects of globalisation into traditional classificatory and descriptive schemes. Material that fits awkwardly into the normal comparative paradigm is sometimes relegated to a separate book (Reichel, 2007), to an early chapter (Reichel, 2008), or a closing one (Dammer *et al.*, 2006).

Titles such as Winterdyk and Cao's *Lessons from International/Comparative Criminology/Criminal Justice* also signal that a variety of related topics are being dealt with – but do not say how, if at all, they may be connected (Winterdyk and Cao, 2004). Sheptycki and Wardak distinguish 'area studies', 'transnational crime issues' and 'transnational control responses' (Sheptycki and Wardak, 2005). But they themselves admit that more needs to be said about when our account of a country's criminal justice system should focus more on internal factors or on external influences. It may be plausible that the account of criminal justice in Saudi Arabia in their book treats the country as autonomous (though more could have been said about its pan-Islamic mission). But it is less obvious why the chapter on South Africa focuses mainly on internal developments whereas the chapter on West Africa is all about its vulnerability to the outside world.

Some authors emphasise the limits of comparative criminal justice. Katja Aas, the author of a superb recent introduction to 'crime and globalisation', argues that 'one can no longer study, for example, Italy by simply looking at what happens inside its territory, but rather need to acknowledge the effects that distant conflicts and developments have on national crime and security concerns and vice versa' (Aas, 2007: 286; see also Aas, 2011). Not surprisingly, therefore, she devotes little energy in her textbook to problems of comparing individual countries and instead seeks to show us the complex processes by which the 'global' and 'the local' are intertwined. Nick Larsen and Russell Smandych likewise explain that the

> cross-cultural study of crime and justice has evolved from a 'comparative' or 'international' approach to what is now increasingly referred to as a 'transnational' or 'global' approach to crime and justice . . . the effects of rapid globalisation have changed social, political, and legal realities in such a way that comparative and international approaches to crime and justice are inadequate to capture the full complexity of these issues on a global scale.
>
> (2008: xi)

In particular they draw attention to 'global trends in policing and security, convergence and divergence in criminal justice and penal policy, and international criminal justice, war crimes and the global protection of human rights' (Larsen and Smandych, 2008: xi).

But Piers Beirne, in his preface to their collection, warns against going too far down this road. He concedes that

> globalisation and transnational crime do indeed tend to blur the relatively distinct boundaries and mobilities that exist between nations and between sovereign territories . . . it is thus increasingly moot whether it makes sense to talk of crime in 'Russia' or in 'India' or in 'Northern Ireland' or in the 'USA'.
>
> (Beirne, 2008: ix)

But he insists that

> comparative criminology still has a vital role to play, both in its own terms and also adjacent to global criminology and as one of its key constituents... the question of how globalisation and transnational crime affect different societies – similarly or differently, both similarly or differently at the same time, or somewhere in between – is first and foremost a comparative one.
>
> (Ibid.)

For example, he sees a valuable role for comparative criminology in identifying which (failed) states are more vulnerable to the penetration of transnational orga- nized crime – which he identifies as places where there are corrupt politicians, weak controls, lengthy borders and so on.

Francis Pakes too worries whether comparative criminal justice is now *passé*. The subject, he argues,

> is in the process of losing its relevance. Simply put, the reasoning is that the world has changed and comparative criminology has insufficiently changed with it. The charge against comparative criminology is that it tends to com- pare and contrast phenomena in distinct cultures or jurisdictions and that, by doing so, diffuse interrelations and complications brought about by globali- sation are ignored or understated.
>
> (Pakes, 2010b, 17ff)

He asks whether global criminology will supersede the field of what we currently think of as 'classic' comparative criminology so that before comparative crimin- ology gets its act together we will have moved on to doing 'international and transnational criminology' and replies that we should not embrace a 'vision of comparative criminology being abandoned as if it were a ghost town after the gold rush'. The comparative method will remain an influential tool in inquiries involving transnationalisation, globalisation, crime and control (ibid.).

Pakes suggests that the comparative approach could be seen as only a matter of methodology whereas globalisation is an 'object of study'. Globalisation, he says, concerns the 'what' not the 'how', describing something taking place in the world such as the trafficking of illegal goods – or people. Hence there cannot really be any contradiction. But he also concedes that the term 'globalising criminology' can be used as if it related to methodology. He therefore draws a further distinc- tion between two senses of global criminology that are 'subject to conceptual con- fusion'. 'Strong' global criminology, he claims, should probably take the world as its unit of analysis. It might address questions such as the relation between climate change and civil unrest, transgressions and control. Here, 'global' denotes object. In contrast, globalised criminology frequently refers to relations: those who advo- cate it frequently argue that we need to take the interconnectedness of the world into account (ibid.: 18–19).

In explaining his view of comparative criminology and global criminology as 'complementary projects' David Friedrichs agrees that there needs to be a careful division of intellectual labour (see also Roberts, 2007). 'A comparative criminology', he says,

> addresses the nature of the crime problem and the form and character of criminal justice systems in countries around the world; a transnational criminology is focused principally upon transnational or cross-border forms of crime, and endeavours on various levels to control and respond effectively to such crime; an international criminology focuses on international crime – or crime that is specifically recognized widely across nations as crime against humanity – and international law, as well as the institutions of international law; and a global criminology is best applied to the study of the evolving context within which crime and criminal justice now exists.
>
> (Friedrichs, 2011: 167)

For his part René Van Swaaningen (2011) argues that transnational comparative enquiry requires criminologists to be broadly interdisciplinary, catholic in taste and open to new insights in the pursuit of justice and humanity. He distinguishes topics in terms of branches of knowledge (cultural anthropology, green criminology etc.) that need to be called on if we are to answer questions such as: How do we compare the experience of crime and victimization across diasporic cultures and communities? How do we map the relationships between intra-group and inter-group crime and violence in multicultural contexts? How do we measure the social harm caused by different categories of crime (as various as hate crime; environmental crime; terrorist, political, or state crime; or financial and economic crime) and evaluate its impact on different types of individual, community or population? Approaches can be brought together, he suggests, in terms of 'levels of analysis'. Thus his 'fourth level of analysis', for example, examines 'global flows' and relates them to 'global power-relations, the North–South divide and basic capitalist economic laws' (p. 140). Here, neither the local consequences of globalisation nor the global implications of local developments are the central object of study, but the inter-connectedness of nodal societies and global cities (Van Swaaningen, 2011).

Globalisation, changing boundaries, and the state

But what is meant by globalisation? Much of what is so described, not least the trend towards neo-liberalism, is easily confused with Americanisation. It is also important not to attribute too much to globalisation. For many purposes we would also need to clarify its relation to modernity and post-modernity and to theoretical debates about the rise of the so-called 'risk society' or 'network' society. Obviously, processes of mutual contacts and influence did not start with what is now called globalisation and it would be reductive to describe them as such. The role of empire and colonialism has been fundamental in shaping criminal justice systems in much of the world. Given that ideas and practices of criminal justice have always circulated between countries and elites it is questionable how far penal systems were ever 'embedded' in given nation-state contexts (Melossi *et al.*, 2011). Any given national system will therefore be at least in part a reworking of ideas coming from elsewhere (we can think of the spread of Beccaria's or Lombroso's ideas from Italy). Italian criminal justice, for example, is currently moulded by scholarship that reflects, on the one hand, the importance of German penal doctrine, still unchallenged among law professors of substantive criminal law, and, by contrast, the more recent revolution in criminal procedure owing to the import of Anglo-American ideas.

At a minimum, however, we could think of globalisation as referring to the consequence of the greater mobility of capital (sometimes, but not always, willingly embraced by states as a political neo-liberal choice) and new forms of international interconnections that have grown at the expense of national ones as nation-states are incorporated into the world economy and informational cyberspace. Increasingly, as a result of globalisation, we inhabit a deterritorialised world where we can participate via the media in communities of others with whom we have no geographical proximity or common history (Coombe, 2000). Because national cultures are influenced by global flows and trends, their purported uniformity, coherence, or stability will often be no more than an ideological projection or rhetorical device.

With the advent of globalisation there is an increasingly wide gap between the (global) sites where issues arise and the places where they are managed (the nation-state). The consequences of globalisation for the economic fortunes of countries, cities or parts of them, means that the causes of ordinary crime problems, and not only those perpetrated by transnational criminal organisations, often have little to do with the unit in which they are located. This is so even if most crime – and even some so called transnational crime – remains in other respects a highly local phenomenon (Hobbs, 1998). Different kinds of units emerge as objects and as agents of control. As it increasingly blurs the differences between 'units', globalisation changes the meaning of place and the location and significance of boundaries (Appadurai, 1996; Shearing and Johnston, 2010). Likewise the use of cyberspace requires and generates a variety of new forms of control and resistance.

An ever more important role is played by international bodies such as non-governmental organizations and intergovernmental organizations and influential think-tanks. These formulate and spread what have been called 'global prescriptions' – including ideas about what to do about crime (Dezalay and Garth, 2002; Waquant, 2009a, 2009b; Nelken, 2010c). There is growing internationalization of policing or attempts by international courts of justice to enforce on states common minimal standards of conduct. On the one hand, new forms of 'soft law' characterise the way norms are produced, signalled and sanctioned. On the other, war-making, peacekeeping and criminal justice come to overlap – and even war is privatised (Klein, 2008).

The main criticism of traditional work in comparative criminal justice, however, is that it gives too much importance to one particular variable, the nation-state, at a time when the state is increasingly losing its monopoly over criminal justice (Drake *et al.*, 2009; Muncie *et al.*, 2009). Key crime initiatives for example now link regional or local centres of power (Edwards and Hughes, 2005) or are delegated to the private sector. As Muncie argues, state sovereignty in matters of criminal justice does indeed appear to be challenged by the likes of international courts, human rights conventions, multinational private security enterprises, cross border policing, policy networks and flows, and technologies of global surveillance. It is no longer clear what the scope of nation-state specific criminal justice is and who exactly constitutes the subject of its gaze. 'Governance' increasingly replaces government – and power is increasingly shared with other transnational and private actors. Innovation in crime control often happens not at the state level but below or above it (Muncie, 2011).

On the other hand, it would be premature to say that the nation-state has had its day as a source of ordering (Loader and Walker, 2007). Nation-state boundaries typically coincide with language and cultural differences and represent the source of criminal law and criminal statistics. The imposition of a common legal code and the common training of legal officials form part of attempts to achieve and consolidate national identity. And 'borders' continue to play important instrumental and symbolic roles, not least in responding to immigration. Even if sovereignty has become more difficult to exert in fiscal matters we have recently been seeing a process of de-globalisation after the economic crisis beginning in 2008 where national states had to step in to avoid the meltdown of the financial markets.

But even if we accept that the state is – in many respects – losing its centrality, it does not follow that what happens in the field of criminal justice necessarily follows this general logic. Criminal law continues to be a powerful icon of sovereignty and the nation-state persists as a key site where the insecurities and uncertainties brought about by globalisation are expected to be 'resolved'. It is even claimed that the state may 'act out' in responding to some crime problems precisely because it has lost power elsewhere (Garland, 1996). More functionally, some argue that states are obliged to enforce a new harsher type of order required because of the dismantling of welfare protections mandated by neo-liberalism (Waquant, 2009a, 2009b). Each country may also have its own reasons for increasing punitiveness. If the United States has seen 'governing through crime' in a range of domestic settings (Simon, 2007), in many European societies state power has been used mainly to criminalise non-citizen flows. In places such as South Africa the state has to underline its ability to provide public safety in order to convince the 'global economy' that it is a 'safe place' in which to do business.

Key issues in comparative criminal justice such as explaining different levels of imprisonment (e.g. Cavadino and Dignan, 2006; Lacey, 2008; Pratt *et al.*, 2005; Waquant, 2009a, 2009b; Whitman, 2005) require giving attention both to local specificities as well as to the way national policies and systems are affected by their location in larger networks of trade and communications. Reacting to Garland's account of the rise in late modernity of the 'culture of control' (Garland, 2000), Cavadino and Dignan seek to demonstrate very different responses at the level of nation-states (in accordance with their levels of enthusiasm for neo- liberal social policies). They are far from unaware of globalisation, indeed the point of their argument is to prove that differences 'persist' *despite* its influence. But we could just as well say that what they are describing are not just intrinsic policy differences in the way states choose to deal with marginal citizens but differential ways of responding to a similar trans-national trend (or the varying outcomes of the marketing and imitation of an American model of penality). Similar arguments could be made when seeking to explain the variety in the use of the death penalty (e.g. Hood, 2001; Johnson and Zimring, 2009).

But the state is not only an enforcer of criminal law, it can also can be a *victim* or a perpetrator of crimes. At the extreme the consequences of globalisation on nation-states can even lead to their unmaking. But if globalisation leads to a reduction in state sovereignty, why, asks Susanne Karstedt do we see failed states as a 'problem' rather than as the vanguard of globalisation (Karstedt, 2011)? Her answer is that such states pose a large threat because their implosion takes place in situations of violent ethnic and other conflicts. Regional powers try to take advantage of such weaknesses, international diasporas can fuel these conflicts, and multinational corporations engage directly for their own advantage with both elites and regional leaders.

This type of failed state thus signifies an aberrant pathway of globalisation. It is unable to meet the aspirations and expectations of its people with regard to what the state and governments should supply in terms of legitimacy, infrastructure, welfare and healthcare. The failure of state institutions to restrict exploitation and rent-seeking among elites, leads to grand corruption and misuse of resources. And many forms of trafficking and environmental crime, involving organised crime and terrorism have their origins more often in failed states than elsewhere. Karstedt points out that 'partial democracies' are at a higher risk of collapse, and suffer more than tenfold from political crises, as compared to outright autocracies, because they have only scantily developed mechanisms to deal with discontent. Globalisation exacerbates this because such states are caught between the interference of international actors and the questionable loyalties of their own populations. Such states turn out to be incapable of implementing the various international instruments against the types of organised crimes that affected them, even if they sign up to the relevant conventions and treaties.

Globalisation as a contested process

All this means that the outcomes of globalisation processes are not predetermined and that further progress in the direction of greater convergence or interdependence is not inevitable – even if it is often talked about as if it is (Nelken, 1997). Leading writers have been trying to develop the implications of this point. Joachim Savelsberg, for example, accepts that 'globalisation is a powerful process that affects criminal justice and penal policies in many countries. Comparative penal studies that treat countries as independent units of analysis can no longer be justified in light of this situation. While the institutional architecture of penal modernity with its courts and prisons may have remained in place, its deployment, strategic functions and social significance were radically altered' (p. 73) and 'global and national penal law and practice interact and partially "constitute" each other' (p. 69).

This makes it complicated to predict outcomes. The key to globalisation's effects, he argues,

> lie in nation-specific institutional arrangements through which knowledge about crime and punishment is produced and diffused, and in which legal and political decision-making is embedded. Distinct reactions are further advanced by country-specific historically rooted cultural sensitivities – that support some action strategies and delegitimise others.
>
> (Savelsberg, 2011: 75)

For Savelsberg, globalisation occurs along three paths:, norms and practices, including those on punishment; change as a consequence of global shifts in social structure and culture, there is a nation-specific processing of global scripts and nation-specific responses to the arrival of (late) modernity; and a new type of international criminal law has been gaining strength at the global level (ibid.). In particular he directs our attention to the importance of agents who, acting locally, use their transnational connections in strategic struggles to impose their authority on a particular field. 'Local actors', he says, 'generally interpret and process global challenges through historically-evolved institutions of knowledge production and political and legal decision making and through the lens of local cultural norms and cognitive frameworks' (p. 71). Hence the globalisation of the 'local' depends on the localisation of the (supposedly) global, and is not just a matter of impersonal macro-social forces.

For John Muncie too, economic forces are not uncontrollable, do meet resistance and have effects that are neither uniform nor consistent. As he sees it,

> globalisation as an analytical concept appears both seductive and flawed. It is seductive because it seems to offer some valuable means through which sense can be made of some widely recognised shifts in criminal justice policy, such as the retreat from welfare statism and a resurgence in authoritarianism.
>
> (Muncie, 2011: 99)

But we should not expect that policy transfer be direct or complete or exact or successful. Rather, it is mediated through national and local cultures, which are themselves changing at the same time. He argues that both the global and the national inform local identities, institutions, economic interactions and political processes. According to Muncie, globalisation is 'a combination of macro socio-economic developments, initiatives in international law and processes of policy flow and diffusion.' The key issue to be addressed is how globalisation activates diversity, as well as how it produces uniformity. The challenge is to articulate the dialectic between local specificities and transnational mobilities. For him 'the specificities of punishment remain embedded in specific geo-political contexts.... Even neo-liberal modes of governance find different modes of expression in conservative and social democratic *rationalities* and in authoritarian, retributive, human rights, or restorative *technologies*' (ibid.: 100).

Globalisation can produce both more convergence and greater divergence. Savelsberg tells us that 'Convergence in the purely formal sense often coincides with profound differences in the intent, content and, especially, implementation of legal frames and rules' (2011: 71). Even where there is evidence of growing commonalities we should not assume that the explanation lies in globalisation. Similar results do not have to be a result of worldwide trends, indeed they may have quite different causes – just as similar causes, whether global or otherwise and may, under different conditions, lead to different outcomes.

For Muncie likewise, 'The argument that criminal justice is becoming a standardised global product can be sustained only at the very highest level of generality' (Muncie, 2011, 99). In particular he stresses the way globalisation can produce 'contradictory' effects. Thus economic globalism may speak of the import, largely US inspired, of neo-liberal conceptions of the free market and community responsibilisation backed by an authoritarian state. However, legal globalism, largely UN inspired, unveils a contrary vision of universal human rights delivered through social democracies (ibid.).

He criticises globalisation theory for being over general and not recognising exceptions and argues that unravelling the impact of the 'global' and the 'exceptional' requires a level of analysis that neither elevates nor negates either but recognizes that each is realized only in specific localities, through which their meaning is inevitably reworked, challenged, and contested (Muncie, ibid.; see also Pakes, 2009).

To explore the role of the agents of globalisation we need to take a broad view of *who* is involved. The key actors include politicians, non-governmental organisations (NGOs) or pressure groups, regulatory bodies, journalists, and even academics themselves and not only judges, lawyers, police, probation officers or prison officers. They may also be representatives of businesses such as security providers or those who build and run private prisons. Attention needs to be given to the role of institutions, singly, collectively, or in competition. In Europe – but also beyond – EU institutions, the Council of Europe and the Equality and Human Rights Commission (EHRC) system are important players. The same crime threat may call forth responses from a variety of inter-governmental and non-governmental organisations, such as the UN commissioner for rights etc., the International Labour Organisation, or the International Organisation for Migration, Human Rights Watch, Amnesty etc. (see further Nelken, 2006). It is essential to study how agreement is achieved amongst the various signatories to conventions or those subject to regulatory networks (Merry, 2006). We also need to examine *what* it is that is being spread – scripts, norms, institutions, technologies, fears, ways of seeing, problems, solutions – new forms of policing, punitiveness, or conceptual legal innovations such as the 'the law of the enemy', mediation, restitutive or therapeutic justice? Finally, we can also ask *where* it is being spread, e.g. from or to national, sub-national and supra-national levels in europe, or more widely? and crucially – how widely?

Globalisation, social justice, and diversity

Apart from the empirical question of whether globalisation, as a matter of fact, is or is not producing harmonisation or convergence, there is also the fundamental normative question of when and why this should be pursued or accepted. The attempt to move towards a 'globalising' criminological perspective has the merit of bringing hitherto neglected crimes such as state crimes (including genocide) into better focus (Morrison, 2004; Hagan and Rymond-Richmond, 2008). There are many collective problems, from those regarding the environment to those that have to do with financial security, that cannot be solved by states acting alone, as well as many abuses suffered by individuals and groups which cannot safely be left only to the states responsible for them to deal with. And there is no doubt also that criminals can take advantage of legal and other differences between one state and another. But, on the other hand, the focus on a 'common threat' and the defence of national or international borders too easily pushes to one side the implications that developing such 'common' responses can have for questions of difference and diversity between and within various criminal justice jurisdictions.

Taking a Durkheimian view, we could say that changing forms of social and economic exchange both reflect and produce changing forms of 'moral' interdependence. If economic links and exchanges are now global, there must then be a 'moral' basis that makes this worldwide interdependence possible and which it furthers (Durkheim, 1893/1997). Hence globalisation could contribute to a new international solidarity, as already seen perhaps in the strengthening of international criminal justice, the increasing role of international human rights, as in the way that, by helping victims of human trafficking, as well as the victims of sex tourism abroad, nation-states are increasingly extending protections to non-nationals. On the other hand, from a neo-Marxist perspective, globalised exchange is too often itself a form of disguised exploitation; businesses and others find ways to avoid criminal penalties in the 'space between the laws', whilst international bodies impose neo-liberal recipes and financial straightjackets as the price for loans and assistance (Klein, 2008).

Globalisation is therefore best treated as a Janus-faced phenomenon whose effects are not easily classified as either 'good' or 'bad' (also because globalisation can communicate the knowledge that can be used to help counteract its (bad) effects). Muncie distinguishes between positive images of cultural exchange, free trade, advances in telecommunications and new opportunities, or conversely negative images of events being out of our, or national control, a 'world risk society'. In the sphere of youth justice for example, globalisation spreads both a harsher approach to youth but also more insistence on protecting their rights (Muncie, 2005, 2011). The extension of human rights is a largely positive development, especially for the protection of women and other vulnerable groups (Merry, 2006; Cain and Howe, 2008). But the development of global governance can also encourage an imaginary 'view from nowhere' and can also sap the social control potential of civic society (Nelken, 2003).

Some writers try to distinguish between hegemonic or counter-hegemonic globalisation, or globalisation 'from above' or 'from below', seeing this as the key to human rights that can be supported without reservation (e.g. Santos and Rodriguez-Garavito, 2005; Goodale, 2009). But, in practice, it can often be difficult to find fail-safe criteria for picking and choosing what is 'progressive' or not – especially as intentions and outcomes do not necessarily coincide. Merry tells us that the application of global protocols to reduce violence against women gains in legitimacy insofar as it is not enforced by dominating (and colonialist) nation-states but rather emerges in a fragmentary international agreement as a result of attempts at mutual persuasion. But it still faces a number of conundrums. It is difficult to find a way of both respecting cultural differences and protect women from violence. For such agreements to be accepted locally their implications for changing the status quo must be carefully disguised or blunted. But international support depends on credible programmes for real social change. Not least, those governments and courts least able or willing to help protect women's rights are those where such assistance is most needed (Merry, 2006).

The fight against transnational organised crime offers the best illustration of these points. On the one hand, there are a variety of extremely serious harms committed by such groups. On the other, the 'problems' and opportunities exploited by such criminals are usually linked to issues of demand and supply for illegal goods and benefits – and these problems are often exacerbated by prohibition. For almost every one of these activities there are at least two narratives that can be told. One stresses the noble fight of the state and/or NGOs to extend the scope and reach of human rights (e.g. Naim, 2005), the other the extent to which controllers selectively exploit the problems of given victim groups for their own interests (e.g. Van Schendel and Abraham, 2005; Nordstrom, 2007). The way such threats are characterised often tells us more about political and law-enforcement stereotypes than it does about their fluid and changing nature. The repeated scare claim – that criminal justice is strictly territorial whereas organized crime is not confined by national boundaries – tends to exaggerate the degree of collaboration between such groups and to underplay the growth of international collaboration in reply. And the powers given to enforcers to overcome organised crime can have effects on human rights that are in some ways as serious as those threatened by the criminals themselves (Nelken, 1997).

Paying more attention to the effects of globalisation also raises the question of whose interests are best represented by allegedly universal standards. Take, for example, the Palermo Protocol against human trafficking (a.k.a. 'the new slavery' for sexual, child or labour exploitation). This has been signed – and ratified – by a very large number of countries and has increased the possibility of providing relief to victims in a minority of extreme cases. But political elites, employers, workers and others have very different interests in the implementation of such conventions. There are also crucial divides between supply and demand countries. Supply countries have desperate need of the economic remittances of their migrants. Churches in some towns in Nigeria pray for the success of those who go abroad in one form or other of prostitution. Amongst demand countries, on the other hand, Germany and the Netherlands are basically concerned about having well-regulated systems of sex work, whereas Sweden, which is engaged in a determined effort to reduce commercial prostitution, makes little or no use of the Palermo protocol. The USA operates, for its own purposes, sanctions against countries it classifies as being reluctant to stop human trafficking – but it has learned to live with millions of unregistered Mexican migrants. In general, the crusade in favour of the rights of women (and others) not to be trafficked is often used as cover for blocking irregular migration projects and reaffirming the sacredness of national borders (Nelken, 2011b, 2012).

Shifting to the global level raises the question (crucial for the comparative scholar) whether there really can be a view from everywhere (or nowhere). Are types of crime really equally disapproved of across the world (Newman, 1999; Van Dijk, 2007)? Is the concept of human rights a universal (Donnelly, 2009)? Why is there apparently more difficulty in finding a common meaning for corruption than say acceptable prison conditions (see Twining, 2005; Nelken, 2010b)? The local sense of global initiatives aimed at transnational or other crimes needs to be carefully deconstructed. It can be difficult to judge whether or not a particular battle for rights is worthy of support. Transforming struggles over corruption into a question of human rights can be part of the problem and not only of the solution (Nelken, 2011a). The promotion of transparency as urged by Transparency International would seem to be an appropriate panacea. But closer familiarity with the phenomenon in specific contexts shows that transparency also has the effect of entrenching corruption – the more that is known about the use of underhand methods, the more others may feel they have to do the same (Nelken, 2009a).

Whether or not the source is always rightly described as globalisation, pressures for conformity do seem to be rising (Nelken, 2006). The implications of this for comparative criminal justice are important. Does it mean that local ways of doing things must and should give way? 'Globalisation', Pakes has argued, 'will diminish the variety of criminal justice systems. Common threats will invite common responses, which will increase the similarities in criminal justice systems around the world'. But, he goes on to say, 'on the one hand, this could be seen as a loss. But, on the other hand, 'criminal justice systems are not like the natural world, where we should celebrate diversity for its own sake. Increased requirements for communication and harmonisation provide rewards for convergence, and criminal justice systems will, after all, be judged on their effectiveness'. In any case, he concludes 'one can remain sure that as long as cultures, languages, public opinion, and social discourses differ, so will criminal justice systems and the way they operate' (Pakes, 2004: 178).

But these remarks, thoughtful as they are, do also beg a number of questions. Is there really no reason to value diversity 'for its own sake' just because 'criminal justice systems are not part of the natural world?' What of the benefits of maintaining a variety of forms of social experimentation? What of the need for procedure to seek to express a society's values and its traditions? What if, as we have seen, greater homogeneity often signifies imitation or imposition of a currently successful Anglo-American model that reflects and produces a certain sort of society (one, moreover, that requires a high level of punishment)?

It is not enough to say that 'the balance between fairness and effectiveness' will be worked out differently in different places. The issue is also what these terms mean – and how far the metaphor of 'balancing these values' is shared cross-culturally. In any case, we must be careful not to assume that the answer to what is desirable can be found simply by seeing what is likely to happen. If systems continue to operate differently[3] this will be at least in part because actors choose to do so for given reasons, and it is these reasons that can and should be appreciated or criticised. We should also be cautious about the claim that systems of criminal justice will 'after all, be judged on their effectiveness'. Who will be (who should be?) the judge of 'success' or effectiveness?

The methods used to measure the success of global initiatives also often blur the line between the normative and the descriptive (Merry, 2011). There can be confusion between what is 'normal' in the sense of not falling below a standard and the somewhat different meaning of what is normal or average. It can be instructive to ask how far the Strasbourg Court of Human rights is imposing 'universal' principles of good practice of criminal procedure on the signatories to the convention it enforces, and how far – as in imposing limits on acceptable court delays – it is (also) involved in a process of 'normalisation' to a European average (Dembour, 2006; Nelken, 2004, 2008). Why are trials that are very quick not considered a breach of human rights? Is it right to threaten Italy with exclusion from the European Convention on Human Rights – for conduct which follows from the fact that is an outlier in the times taken by its trials? The only other signatory treated in this way is Turkey, for its failure to comply over Cyprus and its continuing maltreatment of the Kurds. Italian court times do create suffering. Justice delayed is, too often, justice denied. But it is questionable whether excessive court delay is the same sort of breach of human rights as torture.

Notes

1 See Nelken (2011c), which develops in more detail many of the ideas referred to in this chapter.
2 As examples of recent textbooks, collections and readers see Crawford (2011); Dammer *et al.* (2006); Drake *et al.* (2009); Karstedt and Nelken (2012); Larsen and Smandych (2008); Muncie *et al.* (2009); Nelken (2010a); Pakes (2010a); Reichel (2008); Sheptycki and Wardak (2005); Tonry (2007); Winterdyk and Cao (2004); Winterdyk *et al.* (2009). On cross-national perspectives on crime and criminal justice, see Newman (1999); Van Dijk (2007); Van Dijk *et al.* (2007). On cross-national borrowing see, for example, Melossi *et al.* (2011); Newburn and Sparks (2004); Jones and

Newburn (2006); Nolan (2009). On criminal justice and criminal procedure see Findlay (2008) and Vogler (2005).

3 Even Pakes recognises that 'globalisation has not turned out to be the great leveller, but instead brought about highly localised responses' (Pakes, 2010b: 18).

References

Aas, K.F. (2007) *Crime and Globalization*. London: Sage.

Aas, K.F. (2011) Victimhood of the national? Denationalizing sovereignty in crime control. In: A. Crawford (ed.) *International and Comparative Criminal Justice and Urban Governance*. Cambridge: Cambridge University Press.

Appadurai, A. (1996) *Modernity at Large: Cultural Dimensions of Globalization*. Minneapolis: University of Minnesota Press.

Beck, U. and Sznaider, N. (2006) Unpacking cosmopolitanism for the social sciences: A research agenda. *British Journal of Sociology*, *57*, 1–23.

Beirne, P. (2008) Preface. In: N. Larsen and R. Smandych (eds) *Global Criminology and Criminal Justice: Current Issues and Perspectives*. Buffalo, NY: Broadview Press.

Cain, M. and Howe, A. (eds) (2008) *Women, Crime and Social Harm*. Oxford: Hart.

Cavadino, M. and Dignan, J. (2006) *Penal Systems: A Comparative Approach*. London: Sage.

Coombe, R.J. (2000) Contingent articulations: A critical cultural studies of law. In: A. Sarat and T. Kearns (eds) *Law in the Domains of Culture*. Ann Arbor: University of Michigan Press.

Crawford, A. (ed.) (2011) *International and Comparative Criminal Justice and Urban Governance, Convergence and Divergence in Global, National and Local Settings*. Cambridge: Cambridge University Press.

Dammer, H., Fairchild, E. and Albanese, J.S. (2006) *Comparative Criminal Justice*. Belmont, CA: Thomson.

Dembour, M.-B. (2006) *Who Believes in Human Rights? Reflections on the European Convention*. Cambridge: Cambridge University Press.

Dezalay, Y. and Garth, B.G. (2002) *Global Prescriptions: The Production, Exportation, and Importation of a New Legal Orthodoxy*. Ann Arbor: University of Michigan Press.

Donnelly, J. (2009) Human dignity and human rights. Research Project on Human Dignity. Available at: www.udhr60.ch/report/donnelly-HumanDignity_0609.pdf.

Downes, D. (2011) Comparative criminology, globalization and the 'punitive turn'. In: D. Nelken (ed.) *Comparative Criminal Justice and Globalisation*. London: Ashgate.

Drake, D., Muncie, J. and Westmarland, L. (eds) (2009) *Criminal Justice, Local and Global*. Milton Keynes: Willan/Open University Press.

Durkheim, E. (1893/1997) *The Division of Labour in Society*. New York: Free Press.

Edwards, A. and Hughes, G. (2005) Comparing the governance of safety in Europe. *Theoretical Criminology*, *9*, 345–363.

Findlay, M. (2008) *Governing Through Globalised Crime*. Cullompton: Willan.

Friedrichs, D. (2011) Comparative criminology and global criminology as complementary projects. In: D. Nelken (ed.) *Comparative Criminal Justice and Globalisation*. London: Ashgate.

Garland, D. (1996) The limits of the sovereign state: Strategies of crime control in contemporary society. *British Journal of Criminology*, *36*, 445–471.

Garland, D. (2000) *The Culture of Control*. Oxford: Oxford University Press.

Goodale, M. (2009) *Surrendering to Utopia: An Anthropology of Human Rights*. Stanford, CA: Stanford University Press.

Hagan, J. and Rymond-Richmond, W. (2008) *Darfur and the Crime of Genocide.* Oxford: Oxford University Press.

Hobbs, D. (1998) Going down the glocal: The local context of organized crime. *Howard Journal of Criminal Justice, 37*, 407–422.

Hood, R. (2001) The death penalty: A worldwide perspective. *Punishment and Society, 3*, 331–354.

Johnson, D. and Zimring, F. (2009) *The Next Frontier: National Development, Political Change, and the Death Penalty in Asia.* Oxford: Oxford University Press.

Jones, T. and Newburn, T. (2006) *Policy Transfer and Criminal Justice.* Milton Keynes: Open University Press.

Karstedt, S. (ed.) (2009) *Legal Institutions and Collective Memories.* Oxford: Hart.

Karstedt, S. (2011) Exit: The state, globalisation, state failure and crime. In: D. Nelken (ed.) *Comparative Criminal Justice and Globalisation.* London: Ashgate.

Karstedt, S. and Nelken, D. (2012) *Globalisation and Crime.* Aldershot: Ashgate.

Klein, N. (2008) *The Shock Doctrine: The Rise of Disaster Capitalism.* Toronto: Vintage Press.

Klockars, C.B., Ivkovich, S.K. and Haberfeld, M.R. (eds) (2004) *The Contours of Police Integrity.* London: Sage.

Lacey, N. (2008) *The Prisoners' Dilemma: Political Economy and Punishment in Contemporary Democracies.* Cambridge: Cambridge University Press.

Lappi-Seppälä, T. (2007) Penal Policy in Scandinavia. In: M. Tonry (ed.) *Crime, Punishment, and Politics in Comparative Perspective*, Volume 36 of *Crime and Justice.* Chicago: University of Chicago Press.

Larsen, N. and Smandych, R. (eds) (2008) *Global Criminology and Criminal Justice: Current Issues and Perspectives.* Buffalo, NY: Broadview Press.

Loader, I. and Walker, N. (2007) *Civilizing Security.* Cambridge: Cambridge University Press.

Melossi, D., Sozzo, M. and Sparks, R. (eds) (2011) *Travels of the Criminal Question: Cultural Embeddedness and Diffusion.* Oxford: Hart.

Merry, S. (2006) *Human Rights and Gender Violence: Translating International Law into Local Justice.* Chicago: University of Chicago Press.

Merry, S. (2011) Measuring the world: Indicators, human rights, and global governance. *Current Anthropology, 52*, 583–595.

Morrison, W. (2004) Criminology, genocide and modernity: Remarks on the companion that criminology ignored. In: C. Sumner (ed.) *Blackwell Handbook of Criminology.* Oxford: Blackwell.

Muncie, J. (2005) The globalization of crime control – the case of youth and juvenile justice: Neo-liberalism, policy convergence and international conventions. *Theoretical Criminology, 9*, 35–64.

Muncie, J. (2011) On globalisation and exceptionalism. In: D. Nelken (ed.) *Comparative Criminal Justice and Globalisation.* London: Ashgate.

Muncie, J. and Goldson, B. (eds) (2006) *Comparative Youth Justice: Critical Issues.* London: Sage.

Muncie, J., Talbot, D. and Walters, R. (2009) *Crime, Local and Global.* Cullompton/ Milton Keynes: Willan/Open University Press.

Naim, M. (2005) *Illicit: How Smugglers, Traffickers and Copycats are Hijacking the Global Economy.* New York: Arrow books.

Nelken, D. (1997) The globalization of crime and criminal justice: Prospects and problems. In: M. Freeman (ed.) *Current Legal Problems: Law and Opinion at the End of the 20th Century.* Oxford: Oxford University Press.

Nelken, D. (2003) Criminology: Crime's changing boundaries. In: P. Cane and M. Tushnet (eds) *The Oxford Handbook of Legal Studies*. Oxford: Oxford University Press.

Nelken, D. (2004) Using the concept of legal culture. *Australian Journal of Legal Philosophy*, *29*, 1–28.

Nelken, D. (2006) Signaling conformity: Changing norms in Japan and China. *Michigan Journal of International Law*, *27*, 933–972.

Nelken, D. (2008) Normalising time: European integration and court delays in Italy. In: H. Petersen, H. Krunke, A.L. Kjær and M. Rask Madsen (eds) *Paradoxes of European Integration*. Aldershot: Ashgate.

Nelken, D. (2009a) Corruption as governance. In: F. von Benda-Beckmann and K. von Benda-Beckmann (eds) *Rules of Law, Laws of Ruling*. Aldershot: Ashgate.

Nelken D. (2009b) Comparative criminal justice: Beyond ethnocentrism and relativism. *European Journal of Criminology*, *6*, 291–311.

Nelken, D. (2010a) *Comparative Criminal Justice: Making Sense of Difference*. London: Sage.

Nelken, D. (2010b) Anthropology, corruption and human rights. *Focaal: European Journal of Anthropology*, *58*, 124–130.

Nelken, D. (2010c) Denouncing the penal state. *Criminology and Criminal Justice*, *10*, 331–340.

Nelken, D. (2011a) Corruption and human rights: An afterword. In: H. Nelen and M. Boersma (eds) *Corruption & Human Rights*. Antwerp: Intersentia.

Nelken, D. (2011b) Human trafficking and legal culture. *Israel Law Review*, *43*, 479–513.

Nelken, D. (ed.) (2011c) *Comparative Criminal Justice and Globalisation*. London: Ashgate.

Nelken, D. (2012) Transnational legal processes and the (re)construction of the 'social': The case of human trafficking. In: D. Feenan (ed.) *The 'Social' in Social-Legal Studies*. London: Routledge.

Newburn, T. and Sparks, R. (2004) *Criminal Justice and Political Cultures: National and International Dimensions of Crime Control*. Cullompton: Willan.

Newman, G. (1999) *Global Report on Crime and Justice*. Oxford: Oxford University Press.

Nolan, J.L. (2009) *Legal Accents, Legal Borrowing: The International Problem-Solving Court Movement*. Princeton, NJ: Princeton University Press.

Nordstrom, C. (2007) *Global Outlaws: Crime, Money and Power in the Contemporary World*. Berkeley: California University Press.

Pakes, F. (2004) *Comparative Criminal Justice*. Cullompton: Willan.

Pakes, F. (2009) Globalisation and the governance of Dutch coffee shops. *European Journal of Crime, Criminal Law and Criminal Justice*, *17*, 243–257.

Pakes, F. (2010a) *Comparative Criminal Justice* (2nd edition). Cullompton: Willan.

Pakes, F. (2010b) The comparative method in globalised criminology. *Australian and New Zealand Journal of Criminology*, *43*, 17–34.

Pratt, J. *et al.* (2005) *The New Punitiveness*. Cullompton: Willan.

Reichel, P.L. (2007) *Handbook of Transnational Crime and Justice* (4th edition). New York: Sage.

Reichel, P.L. (2008) *Comparative Criminal Justice Systems* (5th edition). Upper Saddle River, NJ: Prentice Hall.

Roberts, P. (2007) Comparative law for international criminal justice. In: E. Orucu and D. Nelken (eds) *Comparative Law: A Handbook*. Oxford: Hart.

Santos, B. de Sousa and Rodriguez-Garavito, C. (2005) *Law and Globalization from Below: Towards a Cosmopolitan Legality*. Cambridge: Cambridge University Press.

Savelsberg, J. (2011) Globalization and states of punishment. In: D. Nelken (ed.) *Comparative Criminal Justice and Globalisation*. London: Ashgate.

Shearing, C. and Johnston, L. (2010) Nodal wars and network fallacies: A genealogical analysis of global insecurities. *Theoretical Criminology*, *14*, 495–514.

Sheptycki, J. (2002) *In Search of Transnational Policing: Towards a Sociology of Global Policing*. Aldershot: Ashgate.

Sheptycki, J. and Wardak, A. (eds) (2005) *Transnational and Comparative Criminology*. London: Glasshouse Press.

Simon, J. (2007) *Governing Through Crime*. Oxford: Oxford University Press.

Solivetti, L. (2010) *Immigration, Integration and Crime: A Cross-National Approach*. London: Routledge.

Tonry, M. (ed.) (2007) *Crime and Justice, Vol. 36: Crime Punishment and Politics in Comparative Perspective*. Chicago: University of Chicago Press.

Twining, W. (2005) Have concepts, will travel: Analytical jurisprudence in a global context. *International Journal of Law in Context*, *1*, 5.

Van Dijk, J. (2007) *The World of Crime*. London: Sage.

Van Dijk, J., Van Kesteren, J. and Smit, P. (2007) *Criminal Victimisation in International Perspective: Key Findings from the 2004–2005 ICVS and EU ICS*. The Hague: Ministry of Justice, WODC.

Van Schendel, W. and Abraham, I. (eds) (2005) *Illicit Flows and Criminal Things*. Bloomington: Indiana University Press.

Van Swaaningen, R. (2011) Critical cosmopolitanism and global criminology. In: D. Nelken (ed.) *Comparative Criminal Justice and Globalisation*. London: Ashgate.

Vogler, R. (2005) *A World View of Criminal Justice*. Aldershot: Ashgate.

Waquant, L. (2009a) *Prisons of Poverty*. Minneapolis: University of Minnesota Press.

Waquant, L. (2009b) *Punishing the Poor: The Neoliberal Government of Social Insecurity*. Durham, NC: Duke University Press.

Whitman, J. (2005) *Harsh Justice*. Oxford: Oxford University Press.

Winterdyk, J. and Cao, L. (2004) *Lessons from International/Comparative Criminology/ Criminal Justice*. Toronto: De Sitter.

Winterdyk, J., Reichel, P. and Dammer, H. (2009) *A Guided Reader to Research in Comparative Criminology/Criminal Justice*. Bochum: Brockmeyer Verlag.

3 Globalisation and criminology

The case of organised crime in Britain

Daniel Silverstone

This chapter will apply the lens of globalisation to the incidence of organised crime in the UK and ask: what are the limitations of criminology in researching this subject? If globalisation is 'a process (or set of processes), which embodies a transformation in the spatial organization of social relations and transactions – assessed in terms of their extensity, intensity, velocity and impact' (Held *et al.*, 1999: 16), then since its inception as a new paradigm of sociological and criminological thinking, globalisation has always incorporated the workings of organised crime as an example *par excellence*. On the one hand, globalisation theorists have looked to networks of drug cartels, cyber criminals and international 'gangs' who prey on the ubiquity of global demand for migrant labour and illicit commodities via the transformative power of new technologies to support their empirical claims (Castells, 1997), whilst on the other, the perceived threat from organised crime is a substantial building block in the argument that the globalised world is full of ontological insecurity and the 'fear of crime' is a key constituent of global governance (Sheptycki, 2008; Hallsworth and Lea, 2011).

Turning to the second argument, globally, there is a flurry of arguments over whether the threat from organised crime has been used by politicians in a functionalist way to justify the social control of the populace and, given the vagaries over defining the term, there cannot be a definitive answer to this question (Sheptycki, 2008). Nevertheless, in Britain the perceived level of threat from serious and organised crime has waxed and waned with the political seasons and it is at least arguable that more recently it has seemed to go up and down in inverse proportion to the perceived threat from terrorism. With the death of Bin Laden and the withdrawal from Iraq, the threat from Jihadi-inspired terrorism is seen to be declining but the perceived threat from organised crime is again reaching fever pitch. Indeed, during the summer and autumn of 2011, the threat from serious and organised crime emerged from the shadows to present not just an often boasted economic challenge but also a threat to the existence of the British state. This challenge has two very different dimensions which are likely, as Garland and others expect to shatter both our private and public equanimity and increase our reliance on the punitive state (Garland, 2002; Christie, 2000).

First, the risk from 'cyber crime' and 'cyber attack' graduated from a residual anxiety to overtake the fear of drugs and illegal immigration to become a tier-one national security priority and also to provide a key rationale for the expanding brief of the newly forming National Crime Agency. The threat is apparently already currently costing the UK an estimated £27 billion per annum, more than the damage done by the illegal drugs market at £13.9 billion (Cluely, 2011; Detica, Cabinet Office, 2011). As an emerging threat it not only invades our present but is projected to haunt our everyday mundane future as cyber criminals hijack those new technologies which big businesses have dreamt up to empower our future lives (Voas, 2011). Second, an old threat re-emerged, the threat of the 'grey gang', that is, the criminal gang (not innocent school-aged collectives), a gang that mirrors the definition of an organised crime group: 'Territorial, hierarchical and incredibly violent, they are mostly composed of young boys, mainly from dysfunctional homes. They earn money through crime, particularly drugs, and are bound together by an imposed loyalty to an authoritarian gang leader' (Cameron, 2011). First, these 'gangs' destroyed the public sense of security as they were initially identified by the Prime Minster as the key organisers and instigators of the nationwide riots which raged during the summer. Second, as if this was not sufficient, the gang is seemingly being re-labelled as an organised crime threat and gangs have become the number-one priority of the Metropolitan Police Service (Hogan-Howe cited in *The Guardian*, 2012).

This sudden increase in rhetoric ought to be due to some significant changes in the reach of serious and organised crime groups which perhaps has changed the United Kingdom's criminological landscape. However, within the academy, over the recent past, rather than revising the threat level up, academics have been arguing that the threat from large discrete serious and organised crime groups (or gangs) to and within the UK is exaggerated (Hallsworth and Young, 2008; Hallsworth and Silverstone, 2009). For instance, significant crime groups are seen to be less organised than previously believed and their international reach is seen as more limited (Morselli *et al.*, 2011). Indeed, as much as globalisation theorists have been emphasising that states and societies are experiencing a process of profound *change* as they try to adapt to a more interconnected but highly uncertain world (Held *et al.*, 1999: 2), it seems that there are also processes of profound continuity being experienced. These arguments will now be explored with reference to what criminology needs to do so that the gap between the claims of government and the academy's evidence is reduced in the near future.

British organised crime

The arguments over the globalisation of British organised crime started to develop in the mid-1980s at a time when it seemed that the crime threat was rapidly changing and, to modify Berman's citation of Marx and Engels, 'All that is solid melts into air' (1983). As others have commented the collapse of communism and the growth of industrialisation throughout the developing world meant that new global criminal opportunities arose (Aas, 2007; Seddon, 2008). The sheer scale of global financial transactions, the ease of migration from both the developing world to the developed world and vice versa, as well as unprecedented global developments in communication technologies, meant in the UK a transformation in the scale of old crimes such as drug and people trafficking, prostitution, fraud and the market in sexual images of children but also the emergence of new online crimes such as identity theft and the distribution of malware (Wall, 2007). In relation to the organisation of crime in the UK, local family firms embedded in working-class neighbourhoods metamorphosed into de-industrialised global networks enriched by the rewards of global labour and drug markets (Hobbs, 1998). And although the so-called threats from the Russian 'Mafia' and the 'Yardies' have been exposed as moral panics (Woodiwiss and Hobbs, 2009), there is no doubt that the map of British organised crime became more complicated as new criminal groups within previously law-abiding diasporas exploited their geographical position within the drug trade or within the international financial system.

Yet, defining organised crime is difficult as the UK definition is vague, 'those involved normally working with others, in continuing serious criminal activities for substantial profit, whether based in the UK or elsewhere',[1] and clearly this can encompass both a group of burglars and a transnational Triad. Within the academy, organised crime is normally expected to be interested in substantial profit but also to have an 'ontological dimension which refers to structure (durability, membership, hierarchy) and distinctive modalities of acting (serious criminal activity, use of violence, use of corruption)' (Longo, 2010: 1; Wright, 2006). Therefore here the term does at least provide an overarching category for all kinds of criminal groups – which in themselves have provoked fierce debates over definitions, such as those relating to 'Triads', 'Mafias', 'gangs' and cyber criminals (Chu, 1998; Hallsworth and Young, 2008; Levi, 2007). Second, in practice it is a term that law enforcement agencies use in determining their threat assessments and intelligence-gathering strategies and thus it is worth retaining. However, in practice the term 'organised crime' includes a wide range of criminal organisations from Chinese 'snakehead' groups, to London gangs such as the 'grey gang', to cyber groupings such as 'Dark market' and 'Mafias' such as the 'Camorra'. Therefore, there will necessarily be anomalies and exceptions to any summation of evidence. Nonetheless there are some general conclusions to be drawn.

First a word of warning: as if the first law of military conflict is to know your enemy, then there is a real problem concerning our knowledge around British organised crime (Waddington, 2010). The existing literature reveals the limits of criminology especially as globalisation theorists would be most interested in diaspora criminal groups to support their arguments. There are no studies of Turkish/Kurdish organised crime, little on South East Asian crime and nothing on the Russian or Albanian experience in the UK. Ruggerio and South (1997: 64) commented that 'compared to the US literature on the significance of the drug economy for ethnic minority communities, British work has been virtually non-existent and the death of sustained ethnographic work on black youth is remarkable'. Over the last fifteen years both Sanders (2005) and Gunter (2008, 2010) have provided ethnographic accounts of crime in predominantly black areas and of black offenders but their subjects have been mainly on the periphery of criminal markets rather than core participants within it. Instead, empirical work, pioneered by Dick Hobbs, has largely concentrated on the white working-class men or women involved in prostitution or working as bouncers or cigarette smugglers (Hornsby and Hobbs, 2007; Sanders, 2005). Outside this the Home Office has commissioned several interview-based studies with organised criminals which are more diverse but the results of which are constrained by the studies being undertaken in prison (Hales *et al.*, 2006; Matrix, 2007; Pearson and Hobbs, 2001; Webb and Burrows, 2009). Given the threat from cyber crime, it is instructive that despite the plethora of reports on the scale of the threat (Detica, Cabinet Office, 2011; Home Office, 2010; Symantec, 2008, 2011; Verizon, 2011), studies have little to say on who the offender actually is, as David Wall admits:

> They are the relatively small number of prosecutions compared with the apparently large volume of offending restricts the profiling of offenders. The little factual knowledge that does exist about cyber-offenders suggests that they tend not to be burly folk devils of the streets; rather they are more likely to display a much broader range of social characteristics.
>
> (Wall, 2010: 8)

Masterminds vs networks

Given the lack of empirical evidence, criminologists should be continually sceptical of any claims relating to the genius of criminal masterminds (the Moriarty or Blofeld hypothesis, Levi, 2004) and the international reach and criminal power of organised crime within the UK. The fear of the omnipotent criminal global organisation has a long history originating from Cressey's work on the Mafia in America, repeated in the cosmopolitan vision of Sterling's Pax Mafiosa, and reiterated most recently in the fears of the gang as the 'changing face of youth crime' (Pitts, 2008 cited in Hallsworth, 2011: 191), as well as the threat from cyber crime. No matter how often the criminal mastermind hypothesis is debunked, it keeps re-emerging, but it is worth reiterating that these exaggerated snippets are always the exception and not the norm and, furthermore, a recent review of the relevant academic literature cogently argues that it is not viable to see organised crime groups as 'large, omnipotent, hierarchically structured and smoothly functioning organisations that parallel the composition of legitimate firms' (McIntosh and Lawrence, 2011: 161; Morselli *et al.*, 2011).

Instead, organised criminal organisations within the UK consist, in the vast majority of cases, of networks[2] of some sort as the Serious Organised Crime Agency acknowledges in its annual threat assessment (2009-10: 1): 'Many groups are in practice loose networks of criminals that come together for the duration of a criminal activity, acting in different roles depending on their skills and expertise'. For example, a closer examination of the evidence on UK gangs (now being relabelled as organised crime, see above), whilst it shows the net-widening effect of defining groups of friends as organised gangs, does also support the existence of named groups with territory and some form of structure and allegiance which partly exist to generate illegal revenue. However, almost all of the literature also emphasises the fluid nature of these groups, their limited territorial control and the way personnel can move up and down the criminal hierarchy quickly due to imprisonment, injury or addiction (Hallsworth and Silverstone, 2009). If one moves away from the British gang and examines the Italian Mafia, which within Europe is still the most iconic of organised crime groups, and turns to the question of whether it has transplanted itself to the UK, evidence drawn from criminal investigations reveals networks of limited size with any illegal activity flowing through family personnel connected to legitimate businesses (Campana, 2011). This is similar to the emerging issue of Asian organised crime where familial structures, albeit in the widest sense, are at the heart of profitable criminal networks. For example in the Vietnamese, and indeed the Chinese, cases, those involved in organised crime are far from homogeneous. As well as career criminals, participants often include cross-generational family networks, some members of which are otherwise law-abiding. These symbiotic relationships are often in flux as criminals drift out of criminality and previously 'legitimate' people can become more involved (Silverstone, 2011; Silverstone and Savage, 2010).

Finally, this network structure continues rather than dissipates online within virtual criminal networks; David Wall (2007: 1) provides a useful threefold typology in relation to cyber criminals. The first is 'traditional organised criminal groups which make use of ICT to enhance their terrestrial criminal activities'; the second is 'organised cyber criminal groups which operate exclusively online'; the third is 'organised groups who both are ideologically and politically motivated individuals who make use of ICT to facilitate their criminal conduct'. There is emerging evidence (Detica, 2012) that there are organised crime groups (from each category) emanating from areas where the rule of law is less established and the state is either interested directly in supporting them or is corrupt, targeting the UK but there is little empirical research into the organisation or size of these groups in the UK. However, the relatively small network model still is still paradigmatic and in a more recent Government review it is admitted that while illegal online organisations

> can have several thousand members...they are usually run by a small number of experienced, specialist online criminals. The leading members of a network...often consist...of 10 to 30 online identities will divide the different roles between themselves.
>
> (Home Office, 2010: 12)

The few British studies that there are support this and show the usual kind of (dis)organised criminal impressed by the illusion of anonymity online and no longer available 'down the real' market (Treadwell, 2012). This analysis points to the existence of key personnel (who are targeted by law enforcement) and small networks and so far evidence from high-profile cases emerging in the UK reveals solitary eccentrics rather than online Godfathers.[3]

As argued above, these networks may include leaders and key personnel or specialists who may enjoy longevity[4] but they do not mirror their legitimate counterparts in size or structure. This means the participants vary in their motivations and skill sets. In typologies which have emerged from the literature on British organised crime, criminologists have been surprised that amongst business criminals who focus on personal enrichment and those who see crime as work there are also criminal adventurers who accept that risk is part of life. Whether it be the drug trafficker who enjoys the challenge, the gang member who enjoys the feeling of autonomy and power, or the EBay trader who likes to rip-off the big brands, there is evidence that the organised criminal is often a disorganised one, who if attracted to money goes about making it in an unstructured and often self-defeating way. There is also growing evidence of skilled amateurs who also participate in the illegal economy and although not well remunerated take pride in their expertise. For example, there is emerging evidence both in the UK and Canada of the professional amateur who takes pride in their illegal service provision, be it the way they cultivate cannabis plants or in the detail of their advice on how to do this, and interviews with smugglers, firearm suppliers and confessions of cyber criminals also reveal individuals who take great pride in their ability to excel at their criminal vocation (Bouchard, 2011).

The other key myth exploded in relation to organised crime groups is that they 'can move their members' illegal operations into a given geographic area with relative ease, assuming control over an abundance of lucrative illicit makers and infiltrating the licit commercial sector for money laundering purposes' (McIntosh and Lawrence, 2011: 161; Morselli *et al.*, 2011). The recent literature argues it is not only important to acknowledge the reduced size of the criminal organisations but also their reduced potency (Morselli *et al.*, 2011). The evidence from the UK is that it is not the case that any so-called 'Mc-Mafia' will be able to move from selling heroin to committing online fraud as easily as their legal counterparts move from selling high-fat burgers to low-fat salads. Clearly most organised crime groups commit multiple types of offences as by definition they will be committing some form of acquisitive crime and seeking to make a profit which they are extremely likely to bank. It is unsurprising that a significant amount of the criminal proceeds generated in the UK is laundered overseas, for example the most recent SOCA threat assessment (2009–10: 23) mentions the 'United Arab Emirates (UAE), the Far East and South East Asia (particularly Hong Kong, Singapore and Shanghai) and Spain' as attractive to money launderers. However, although organised crime groups have moved into the UK over time, this is often an unstructured process and not one driven by collective strategic vision of a coherent organisation.[5]

Indeed, unlike large American gangs such as the 'Bloods' and 'Crips', English gangs are renowned for being ephemeral (in that their names change frequently) and parochial and in London they are most often stuck in small parts of boroughs. Even the alleged fusion between radicalisation and gang threats in the form of the Muslim boys dissipated into an empirical black-hole (Hallsworth, 2011). Outside London there is evidence of gang members moving through areas but they are stymied by their lack of education and contacts in relation to moving into different crime types (Kintrea *et al.*, 2011). There is also evidence of movement into and from the world of cigarette smuggling but again the small pockets of research conducted in the UK seem to show individuals and small groups negotiating not just the available criminal opportunities but also reflecting on their own vulnerabilities and attitude to risk before changing criminal ventures (Hornsby and Hobbs, 2007). In relation to cyber crime, it was predicted that organised crime as it existed would move into the cyber world either by providing online pornography or sexual images of children or by entering the world of cyber fraud or identity theft. However, there does not seem to be any evidence of this in the UK either. Though the space is virtual rather than real, offenders who most often are the largest collectors of sexual images are paedophiles with peer-to-peer networks (Sullivan, 2012).

In relation to the online black economy, there is little evidence in the UK of organised crime groups moving from real crimes such as armed robbery into the creation of botnets or malware; rather the cyber world looks to consist of discrete criminal networks. As the head of the police central e-crime unit explains: 'There is no significant intelligence that old-fashioned "blaggers" have become cyber hackers. They wouldn't understand it. Nor have I evidence of old-fashioned gangsters commissioning cybercriminals'. The UK cyber criminals seem to be new criminals motivated by status or money, although it is inevitable that at some stages more established criminals might try to utilise them for their own purposes.

However, academic work elsewhere suggests that white-collar organised criminals are from different backgrounds from their more violent counterparts. In the USA, studies suggest that those involved in boiler-room scams often have chequered pasts but are very different from street criminals in their educational backgrounds and their associations if not in their spending habits (Shover *et al.*, 2003). Equally, though new groups do emerge, those groups who utilise new technologies to target the British public, such as groups from Nigeria and West Africa who were identified in the early 1990s in the use of so-called 419 frauds, are still a threat despite global access to the technologies. If we reverse the accusation and turn to the global reach of British organised crime groups, again the evidence is rather prosaic. British organised criminals undoubtedly take advantage of global travel and financial laws but there does not seem to be any evidence of their establishing centres outside of the UK. The closest to international domination is the existence of British crime groups operating in popular holiday destinations and drug markets in Ibiza and the Costa del Sol (SOCA, 2009–10).

Finally, in the UK, there is little evidence of organised crime groups working with political–military groups who support political objectives. Since Makarenko's article (2004) on the crime-terror continuum, with her typology linking organised crime with terrorist groups which has three types of relationships: 'convergence', 'alliance' and 'black hole', this purported linkage has had to be considered. However, in her article in 2004 there is no mention of any UK-based organised crime groups being linked to terrorism in any of her typologies. At the same time however, there are longstanding allegations that Turkish and Kurdish heroin deal-ers are connected to either the PKK or the Turkish army but these have not been subjected to academic scrutiny (Onay, 2008) Equally, the Sri Lankan community is subject to rumours linking credit-card fraud and gang criminality to the Liberation Tigers of Tamil Eelam (LTTE). However, again the evidence is thin, with the only piece of published evidence suggesting that Tamil gangs such as they are, are not a product of links with the LTTE 'but with a lack of access to education and employment' (Balasunderam, 2009: 9). Most recently, Norton-Taylor and Borger (2011) argue that it seems very likely that there are links between the Chinese security apparatus and Chinese cyber criminals and perhaps there are some links between Jihadi Islamists and the heroin trade. However, these links remain undefined. A recent research report into heroin dealing within the South Asian community proved inconclusive (Ruggerio and Khan, 2006). With regard to the Chinese security apparatus, there is no open source on how much support cyber criminals might get nor information on from what part of the their vast security apparatus derives. In summary, the political groups most often linked to organised crime (in relation to the supply of arms, drug dealing and money laundering) in Britain, the IRA and the Loyalist paramilitaries have not only disbanded and decommissioned but stayed this way. Therefore the terrorist organised crime nexus now looks less of a persuasive argument than ever as the main potential threat has disappeared. Overall, again in stark contrast to other parts of the world, Columbia and Afghanistan being the pre-eminent examples, in the UK organised crime lacks the links to political causes which might justify it being seen to be an existential threat to the UK.

Technology and equal opportunity

The third key myth is that new global technologies have abetted the organised criminal to fundamentally outwit law enforcement. In this regard, it is worth not-ing that globalisation theorists are right in stressing the transformative power of technologies, be it the ever growing speed in technological innovation from com-puters to mobile phones to smart phones, or the sheer speed of growth in their use. There is no doubt that the global reliance and use of technology is extraordi-nary, as one example illustrates: last year's mobile data traffic was three times the size of the entire global Internet in 2000, whilst global mobile data traffic in 2010 was over three times greater than the total global Internet traffic in 2000 (Cisco, 2011). However, we should be sceptical of the hypothesis that organised crime will gain a decisive technological advantage over law enforcement and new technological vulnerabilities will cause the end of the world as we see it now. New technologies provoke new anxieties, and the worries over the vulner-ability of 'smart phones' to hacking and the allegations that Blackberry's BB system enabled the UK riots[6] are merely the latest examples of this. However we might remember as Marx presciently observed, the burglar provides inspiration for the locksmith and this has happened with car security, internet security and border control; vulnerability inspires industries dedicated to prevention.

Again, as criminologists have been quick to point out, the advent of new technologies is not automatically a criminal goldmine. Rather, recent technologies such as the Internet provide exhaustive records of individual criminal movements which, supplemented by the advances in number plate recognitions and ability to locate and intercept mobile phones, mean criminal communication and movements are monitored more exhaustively than ever before. In the UK, it is extremely difficult for organised criminals to remain anonymous in their movements, consumption or communications patterns.

Therefore new criminal visibility should not be taken as a sign of renewed strength. The fact that a gang has posted pictures of themselves on YouTube, it does not mean that gangs are more powerful. The police now patrol social networking sites and these fora, as well as acting as advertising fora for gang names, have also led to arrests and prosecutions (Erhun, 2011). In fact, the Internet and other ICT technologies are also able to multiply the impact of law enforcement messages deliberately planted there (for example, crime prevention advice) or magnify the impact of successful law enforcement techniques as discussion boards digest the impact of raids and prosecutions. To conclude, what emerges from the evidence is a number of contradictory processes.

On the one hand there are moves by organised criminals to utilise state of the art ICT technologies to commit and enable crime, yet on the other, there is the continuity of old-fashioned technology, the use of cash couriers, the use of a hood to cover the face, the bicycle instead of a car[7] and high value placed on personal trust and reliability in both the virtual and real criminal worlds. Equally, law enforcement combines the high tech and low tech and it is still the low-tech personal contact across international boundaries between police which simultaneously can provide more globalised enforcement than that perhaps formally condoned by governments (see Andreas and Nadelmann, 2006) but equally can frustrate global investigations when the personal connection is not there. Overall, the speed and sheer number of criminal actors often with crude technologies can create asymmetrical clashes against and between high-tech systems which are under pressure from funding issues and personnel skill flaws. However, on balance, the growth of biometric information and surveillance technology and extension of powers to combat organised crime means that if a criminal network is targeted it will be more invasively policed than ever before.

If globalisation has brought growing inequalities between rich and poor nations as well as wealth disparities within nation states (Hallsworth and Lea, 2011), then globalisation theorists should not be drawn to the sheer enormity of global money flows generated by the illegal economy either in the virtual or real world but rather to the lack of criminal mobility within the criminal economy itself. Rather than being a utopian place where Mertonian dreams of fulfilment can be achieved without prejudice, the informal economy is full of the barricades which pertain within the legitimate economy and, as in the legitimate economy reward and risk are not evenly distributed. So for example, for those involved in the UK riots, most telling is their economic background rather than their criminal organisation. It has now been revealed that of those brought before the courts only 20 per cent belonged to gangs, however this was defined, whereas 64 per cent of those young people (for whom matched data was available) lived in one of the 20 most deprived areas in the country – only 3 per cent lived in one of the 20 least deprived areas (Home Office, 2010: 20, cited in Hallsworth and Brotherton, 2011)[8].

The exact socio-economic background of the organised criminal remains something of a mystery but the riots provide a clue. Away from the relatively affluent areas of Clapham Junction and Ealing, areas to which it is now thought rioters travelled in order to loot (Stenson, 2012), the majority of the rioting occurred in areas where social deprivation has been apparent since the 1980s. These parts of London boroughs – Peckham, Hackney, Tottenham, Brixton and relatively deprived areas in major cities such as Salford, Manchester and Handsworth in Birmingham – have been areas where organised criminality has long been apparent, despite efforts in social intervention. All of these areas were mentioned in a recent Home Office report as areas where illegal firearms were obtainable and were being sold and they also are consistently mentioned in popular but often accurate descriptions of where organised criminals come from (Hales *et al.*, 2006; London Street Gangs, 2012). Yet to label these areas as criminogenic in relation to producing organised criminals would also be mistaken as closer inspection reveals that there are often particular estates which stay of interest to the police service and as such criminality is intensely local rather than global. As Stanko and Hales (2009) note, in London 10 per cent of murders and grievous bodily harm occurred in only 13, or 2 per cent, of the wards in the city. Furthermore, one quarter of all serious violence in London occurred in just 49 wards (below 10 per cent). Instead of looking at fluidity and conspicuous consumption, criminologists ought to be drawn to the narrow and repetitive embeddings of organised criminals within the narrow locales of deprived backgrounds.

This narrow background of those involved in the criminal economy is also apparent when reviewing criminal groups from diaspora communities. Terms such as Chinese, Eastern European or Nigerian frequently obscure the evidence of criminality emanating from only small areas in these states and often from specific families. So for example, in recent work on Chinese illegal migration it is apparent first that the same area of illegal migration is still through chain migration providing migrants to the UK and, second, that those involved are from a narrow strip of coastal villages and provinces which share a particular outward-looking mentality rather than particular material conditions (Pieke *et al.*, 2004; Silverstone, 2011).

The second aspect of exploitation which is obscured by the huge estimates of profits generated by organised crime in the UK is the way in which criminal markets are structured. It has long been observed that within the drug economy and the gang/organised crime social world there are internal levels of exploitation and rapine behaviour (Ruggerio and South, 1997; Green, 1998). When the drugs market exploded in the late eighties, the business opened up and became accessible to anyone who had an appetite for risk regardless of their skill set. In the drugs market profit is often inversely related to risk, at both the importation stage where couriers or mules are paid proportionately little but risk significant sentences. Meanwhile, at the street drug market those selling small amounts of class A drugs[9] or offering protection make relatively little but run the risk of serious and frequent violence (Hales *et al.,* 2006).

One might imagine that the cyber economy is qualitatively different. However, it seems from evidence (admittedly not in the UK) that this pattern is replicated in the cyber economy. The cyber economy has now matured and there are also a number of criminal roles which will attract criminals with different skill sets. As has been observed by Symantec (2008), novice attackers can install their own attack toolkits by simply renting a botnet[10] or buying one. The openness of the underground economy is reflected in the price of these tactics which can cost thousands of dollars or ten of dollars dependent on their quality. Then there is also a secondary economy, whereby kit developers and others provide a range of additional, post-purchase services to enhance their effectiveness. As in the drug economy where there are mules who carry drugs into countries, here there are mules to cash cheques and to set up bank accounts to launder the proceeds of crime. There are websites that advertise recipes and tips for drug cultivation and manufacture. There are advice forums as well as websites which directly sell stolen credit cards. However, there are also numerous possibilities for systemic criminality; there are developers selling discounted or free versions of web-attack toolkits which they then could use against their purchases.[11] The main problem experienced by those buying illegal cards or services online is that they get ripped off, hence the preponderance of closed chat rooms where cyber criminals try to establish who is a trustworthy illicit business partner in a similar way to the way in which a prison offers non-virtual criminals an opportunity to establish criminal links. Again, like the drug economy, criminals offer test purchases to try and weed out those who are selling poor or fake goods. Can we also expect the background of those involved in cyber crime to have shared economic characteristics like their 'real' criminal counterparts?

Currently, as argued above, there are no data to support this but as the economy becomes more insecure and graduates slip into the 'precariat' consisting of people experiencing temporary jobs and doing short-time labour (Standing, 2011), could they be the ones going online buying botnets and attempting to skim-off bank accounts? We do not know but it is possible that as unemployment mounts the offenders caught will be graduates who are overeducated but underemployed from one of the most networked countries in Europe. Again, rather than situating the growth of cyber crime as the growth of organised crime groups exigent to us, it would be interesting to profile them in their socio-economic background and within the current economic climate. It might at first seem outlandish but in the light of cyber attacks on the British retail consortium on their members, the local rather than the global is still critical. Their data has been

remarkably consistent and reveals that most of their attacks within the UK origi-
nate from South East London and within this, from only two key postcodes.[12]

The future research agenda

In summary, evidence from the UK favours the hypothesis that an exaggerated
threat from organised crime is still rife and is a constituent in the governance of
the UK through the fear of crime. It is interesting, although disappointing for
those who see global crime groups as *über* examples of globalisation, that in the
UK, the evidence (such as it is) suggests that organised criminal networks have
stayed relatively small and impermanent, with different types of criminal groups
staying in their discrete markets despite the changes in the global economy.
Therefore, criminologists need to remain vigilant in challenging the narratives
which repeat the exaggerated picture and brave in seeking out further empirical
evidence. To do this (despite the narrative of globalisation) we need to remain
aware that the prohibitionist and punitive spectre of American law enforcement
is still a driver behind innovations within UK law enforcement[13] (Andreas and
Nadelmann, 2006; Stenson and Edwards, 2004).

There are numerous examples of this in relation to both cyber crime and
gangs. As Andreas and Nadelmann argue, 'The United States had played a key
role in both defining cybercrimes and in promoting laws and law enforcement
initiatives targeting such crimes' (p. 57). At the time of writing this is continuing
with the proposed Cyber-security Act of 2012. The bill would encourage
information-sharing about cyber threats between US government agencies and
the private sector and consolidate Homeland Security cyber-security programs.
In the UK American influence manifests itself, with the Virtual Global Task
Force, a collaboration between the USA, UK and Europe, including the influence
of the United States' secret service and its vast resource. It is also evident regarding the policing of organised crime most obviously in the advent and mutation
of SOCA, which was Britain's answer to the FBI (BBC, 2006). SOCA, composed of an amalgam of law enforcement agencies, with a national brief of
reducing harm caused by serious and organised crime, replaced the National
Criminal Intelligence Service and the National Crime Squad. However, under
the latest government it is not seen to be sufficiently national and is now recruit-
ing its own 'agents' with a graduate recruitment scheme, and it will have an even
more encompassing role when it changes into the National Crime Agency. This
will involve subsuming the Metropolitan's police central e-crime unit (and its
regional hubs) and the Child Exploitation Online Protection Centre within it. In
relation to law enforcement response to the 'gang' the summer riots illustrated
the sway of the American law enforcement paradigm nicely, as in quick succession the government requested an American Commissioner, American-type Zero
Tolerance Policing and, latterly 'gang call ins' intervention strategies based on
the so-called Boston Model.[14]

To make future research more compelling and to challenge exaggerated political claims, criminologists need to interrogate the claims of law enforcement more

closely to distinguish between the exception and the norm and, for this to happen, access to law enforcement data needs to be improved. There are real problems with intelligence-sharing between law enforcement agencies but these problems are even worse when it comes to sharing information on organised crime with criminologist (Sheptycki, 2007). There is a wealth of academic literature on policing and a growing literature on the security services written by academics from outside the discipline, but little research drawing on the files or problem profiles that law enforcement have built up on organised crime (Andrew, 2010; Ormand, 2010). Future research on organised crime should try to investigate how a particular networks' internal culture, broadly defined as codes of violence, views of masculinity/honour, family structure and political history, informs its criminal activities, its ability to travel and its proclivity for certain types of crime so that a group is enabled to maintain its criminal position despite the flux of globalisation. To do this criminologists need to employ time-consuming and often dangerous methodologies as, overall, the British literature is less detailed and less definitive than the work of European academics who have access to case files, phone taps and the police in ways that are superior to their British counterparts (Levi, 2009; Campana, 2011; Sapens, 2011). Beirne and Nelken (cited in Pakes, 2010: 18) define comparative criminology as 'the systematic and theoretically informed comparison of crime in two or more cultures', and this method could either usefully be applied in isolation to indigenous British crime groups or as stated, to map groups which have links both within the UK and internationally.

Without changing methodologies such as conducting police ethnographies and improving access to currently restricted data, it is hard to challenge the stock narratives. This means, as Levi (2009) rather forlornly observes, fraudsters are not subject to moral panics despite the amount of money they make and the taxpayer loses, and, despite globalisation theorists' preference for emphasising the hybrid, the iconography of the organised criminal has in general stayed the same. The emphasis on the organised and efficient groups in the exotic world of drugs, trafficking, violence and cyber crime still preoccupies law enforcement agencies and the public imagination regardless of the far more mundane reality. It would seem that the interesting question for researchers of British organised crime in the globalised world is to examine why the nation state has managed to maintain social order in both the real and virtual worlds, not to focus on the power of the new threats but to interrogate the evidential base for them in greater detail, to ask: why are the same sorts of people staying involved in organised crime in the same area in the same criminal market? And why is the UK so different from its European and North American counterparts? My guess is that, as more evidence is uncovered, more of the modernist structures of class, ethnicity and age will reappear to reassert themselves against the global dreams of cosmopolitanism and change. For me, even in a globalised world of 'gangs' and 'cyber criminals', Hobbs and Dunnighan's observation remains prescient: 'a serious shortcoming of global transnational international studies of organised crime is that they ignore or substantially underestimate the importance of the local context as an environment within which criminal networks function' (1998: 289).

Notes

1 There are European and International variations on the definition of organised crime but they all incorporate the core elements of generating profit in a structured way.
2 The most useful exploration of what is meant by a network is from Dorn *et al.* (2005) and amended in Levi and Edwards (2008). The most apt use of the term for the UK is as a

> way of describing the structure and or everyday workings of the market as a whole in the sense that the market can be regarded as complex social network (singular noun), within which different participants have to network (verb) to carefully seek out and interact with traffickers who may be like or unlike them-selves, etc. (see for example Pearson and Hobbs, 2001). In other words, through networking, traffickers [and other offenders] construct the market.
> (Levi and Edwards, 2008: 364)

3 See the arrest of 19-year-old hacker Ryan Cleary and Jake Davis, allegedly part of Lulzsec.
4 Intelligence-led law enforcement operations, such as Operation Connect, use network charts and risk matrices to focus on the key individuals in drug or gang groups which will hopefully disrupt the whole network.
5 As the UK still contains a relatively wealthy economy compared with the developing world and much of Eastern Europe.
6 After the shooting of Mark Duggan by the Police Service and a failure of the Police or the Independent Police Complaints Commission to disclose accurate and timely infor-mation concerning his death, riots began in Tottenham (IPCC, 2012). During the next four days in August 2011, Britain's inner cities experienced violent public unrest and looting as thousands of young people took to the streets.
7 It is revealing that one of the mundane examples of organised criminals effectively frustrating law enforcement highlighted by SOCA (2009–10) as effective is the use of 'pay as you go' phones.
8 For a more sustained analysis of what is wrong with the gang-centred account of the British riots see Hallsworth and Brotherton (2011).
9 Such as heroin or crack cocaine.
10 A botnet is a number of internet computers that, although their owners are unaware of it, have been set up to forward transmissions including spam or viruses to other com-puters on the Internet.
11 IcePack is only one of several click-to-attack malware tool kits in circulation. Malware is short for malicious software that is designed to disrupt or deny operation, gather information or gain unauthorized access to system resources.
12 Speech delivered by Mike Marshall and Mike Wyeth on e-crime in the retail sector at the ACPO cyber crime conference 2012.
13 Although scholars of the policing of organised crime are correct in outlining the European links as the paramount law enforcement connections for British police (Hartfield, 2008).
14 The ideas originating from Boston and the 'Operation Ceasefire a city-wide strategy aimed at deterring youth and gang firearm violence' (Shukor, 2007: 1).

References

Aas, K.F. (2007) *Globalization and Crime*. London: Sage.
Andreas, P. and Nadelmann, E. (2006) *Policing the Globe: Criminalization and Crime Control in International Relations*. Oxford: Oxford University Press.

Andrew, C. (2010) *The Defence of the Realm: The Authorized History of MI5*. London: Penguin Books.

Balasunderam, A. (2009) Gang-related violence among young people of the Tamil refugee diaspora. *London Safer Communities*, *8*, 34–41.

BBC News (2006) Agency 'to target brutal crime'. Available on line: http://news.bbc.co. uk/1/hi/uk/4870988.stm.

Berman, M. (1983) *All that is Solid Melts into Air: The Experience of Modernity*. New York: Penguin Books.

Cameron, D. (2011) *Riots:* David Cameron's Commons statement in full (11 August 2011). Available on line: http://www.bbc.co.uk/news/uk-politics-14492789.

Campana, P. (2011) Assessing the movement of criminal groups: Some analytical remarks. *Global Crime*, *12*, 207–217.

Castells, M. (1997) *The Information Age: Economy, Society and Culture Vol. II: The Power of Identity*. Oxford: Blackwell.

Christie, N. (2000) *Crime Control as Industry*. London: Routledge.

Chu, Y.K. (1998) *The Triads as Business*. London: Routledge.

Cisco Visual Networking Index (2011) *Global Mobile Data Traffic Forecast Update, 2010–2015*. Available on line: http://newsroom.cisco.com/ekits/Cisco_VNI_Global_ Mobile_Data_Traffic_Forecast_2010_2015.pdf.

Cluely, G. (2011) Will the UK Cyber Security Strategy make a difference? *Naked Security*. Available on line: http://nakedsecurity.sophos.com/2011/11/25/uk-cyber-security-strategy-difference.

Detica (2012) *Organised Crime in the Digital Age*. Available on line: http://www.bae systemsdetica.com/resources/organised-crime-in-the-digital-age/.

Detica, Cabinet Office (2011) *The Cost of Cyber Crime*. Available on line: http://www. baesystems.com/cs/groups/public/documents/document/mdaw/mdm5/~edisp/baes_020885. pdf.

Dorn, N., Levi, M., and King, L. (2005) *Literature Review on Upper Level Drug Trafficking*. London: Home Office.

Erhun, C. (2011) Presentation on the policing of social networking sites, 10/09/2012.

Garland, D. (2002) *The Culture of Control: Crime and Social Order in Contemporary Society*. Oxford: Oxford University Press.

Green, P. (1998) *Drugs, Trafficking and Criminal Policy: The Scapegoat Solution*. Winchester: Waterside Press.

Guardian (2012) Police target gangs in raids across London, 8 February. Available on line: http://www.guardian.co.uk/uk/2012/feb/08/police-target-gangs-raids-london.

Gunter, A. (2008) Growing up bad: Black youth, road culture and badness in an East London neighbourhood. *Crime Media Culture*, *4*, 349–365.

Gunter, A. (2010) *Growing up Bad? Road Culture, Badness and Black Youth Transitions in an East London Neighbourhood*. London: Tufnell Press.

Hales, G., Lewis, C. and Silverstone, D. (2006) *Gun Crime: The Market in and Use of Illegal Firearms*. London: Home Office.

Hallsworth, S. (2011) Gangland Britain? Realities, fantasies and industry. In B. Goldson (ed.) *Youth in Crisis: Gangs, Territoriality and Violence*. Oxford: Routledge.

Hallsworth, S. and Young, T. (2008) Gang talk and gang talkers: A critique. *Crime, Media, Culture*, *4*, 175–195.

Hallsworth, S. and Silverstone, D. (2009) 'That's life innit': A British perspective on guns, crime and social order. *Criminology and Criminal Justice*, *9*, 359–377.

Hallsworth, S. and Brotherton, D. (2011) *Urban Disorder and Gangs: A Critique and a Warning*. London: Runnymede Trust. Available on line: http://www.runnymedetrust. org/uploads/publications/pdfs/UrbanDisorderandGangs-2011.pdfrust.

Hallsworth, S. and Lea, J. (2011) Reconstructing Leviathan: Emerging contours of the security state. *Theoretical Criminology, 15*, 141–157.

Hartfield, C. (2008) The organization of 'organized crime policing' and its international context. *Criminology and Criminal Justice, 8*, 483–507.

Held, D., McGrew, A., Goldblatt, D. and Perraton, J. (1999) *Global Transformations: Politics, Economics and Culture*. Polity Press: Cambridge.

Hobbs, D. (1998) Going down the glocal: The local context of organised crime. *The Howard Journal, 37*, 407–422.

Hobbs, D. and Dunnighan, C. (1998) Global organised crime. In V. Ruggiero, N. South and I. Taylor (eds) *The New European Criminology*. London: Routledge.

Home Office (2010) *Cyber Crime Strategy*. Available on line: http://www.official-documents.gov.uk/document/cm78/7842/7842.pdf.

Hornsby, R. and Hobbs, D. (2007) A zone of ambiguity: The political economy of cigarette bootlegging. *British Journal of Criminology, 47*, 551–571.

IPCC (2012) Report of the investigation into a complaint made by the family of Mark Duggan about contact with them immediately after his death. Available on line: http:// www.ipcc.gov.uk/en/Pages/investigation_reports.aspx.

Kintrea, K., Bannister, J. and Pickering, J. (2011) It's just an area – everybody represents it. In: B. Goldson (ed.) *Youth in Crisis: Gangs Territoriality and Violence*. Oxford: Routledge.

Levi, M. (2007) Organised and terrorist crimes. In M. Maguire, R. Morgan and R. Reiner (eds) *The Oxford Handbook of Criminology* (4th edition). Oxford: Oxford University Press.

Levi, M. (2009) Suite revenge? The shaping of folk devils and moral panics about white-collar crimes. *British Journal of Criminology, 49*, 48–67.

Levi, M. and Edwards, A. (2008) The organisation of serious crimes: Developments in research and theory. *Criminology and Criminal Justice, 8*, 359–362.

Lewis, N. (2005) Expanding surveillance: Connecting biometric information systems to international police cooperation. In E. Zureik and M. Salter (eds) *Global Surveillance and Policing*. Cullumpton: Willan.

London Street Gangs (2012) *London Street Gangs*. Available on line: www.londonstreet-gangs.com.

Longo, F. (2010) *Transnational Organised Crime: In Search of a Definition*. Available on line: www.psa.ac.uk/journals/pdf/5/2010/1521_1415.pdf.

McIntosh, C. and Lawrence, A. (2011) Spatial mobility and organised crime. *Global Crime, 12*, 161–164.

Makarenko, T. (2004) The crime–terror continuum: Tracing the interplay between transnational organised crime and terrorism. *Global Crime, 6*, 129–145.

Matrix Knowledge Consultancy (2007) *The Illicit Drug Trade in the United Kingdom*. London: Home Office. http://www.homeoffice.gov.uk/rds/pdfs07/rdsolr2007.pdf.

Morselli, C. Turcotte, M. Tenti, V. (2011) The mobility of criminal groups. *Global Crime, 12*, 165–188.

Norton-Taylor, R., and Borger, J. (2011) Chinese cyber-spies penetrate Foreign Office computers. *The Guardian*, 4 February. Available on line: http://www.guardian.co.uk/ world/2011/feb/04/chinese-super-spies-foreign-office-computers.

Onay, K. (2008) *Policy Watch: PKK Criminal Networks and Fronts in Europe*. Washington: The Washington Institute for Near East Policy.

Ormand, D. (2010) *Securing the State*. London: Hurst.

Pakes, F. (2010) The comparative method in globalised criminology. *The Australian and New Zealand Journal of Criminology, 43,* 17–30.

Pearson, G. and D. Hobbs (2001) *Middle Market Drug Distribution*. Home Office Research Study 227. London: Home Office.

Pieke, F., Nyiri, P., Mette, T. and Ceccagno, A. (2004) *Transnational Chinese: Fujianese Migrants in Europe*. Stanford, CA: Stanford University Press.

Ruggerio, V. and South, N. (1997) The late-modern city as a bazaar: Drug markets, illegal enterprise and the 'barricades'. *British Journal of Sociology, 48,* 54–70.

Ruggerio, V. and Khan, K. (2006) British South Asian communities and drug supply networks in the UK: A qualitative study. *International Journal of Drug Policy, 17,* 473–483.

Sanders, B. (2005) *Youth Crime and Youth Culture in the Inner City*. London: Routledge.

Sapens, T. (2011) Interaction between criminal groups and law enforcement: The case of ecstasy in the Netherlands. *Global Crime, 12,* 19–40.

Seddon, T. (2008) Drugs, the informal economy and globalization. *International Journal of Social Economic, 35,* 717–728.

Sheptycki, J. (2007) High policing in the security control society. *Policing: A Journal of Policy and Practice, 1,* 70–80.

Sheptycki, J. (2008) Transnationalisation, orientalism and crime. *Asian Journal of Criminology, 3,* 13–35.

Shover, N., Coffey, G. and Hobbs, D. (2003) Crime on the line: Telemarketing fraud and professional crime. *British Journal of Criminology, 43,* 489–505.

Shukor, S. (2007) *Boston Miracle inspires UK's gang fight Friday*. BBC News, 16 November 2007. Available on line: http://news.bbc.co.uk/1/hi/england/london/7099049.stm.

Silverstone, D. (2011) From Triads to Snakeheads: The evolution of Chinese organized crime within the UK. *Global Crime, 12,* 93–111.

Silverstone, D. and Savage, S. (2010) Farmers, factories and funds: *Organised Crime and Illicit Drugs Cultivation within the British Vietnamese Community*. *Global Crime, 11,* 16–33.

SOCA (2009–10) *The United Kingdom Threat Assessment of Organised Crime 2009/2010*. Available on line: http://www.soca.gov.uk/about-soca/library?start=10.

Standing, G. (2011) *The Precariat: The New Dangerous Class*. London: Bloomsbury Academic.

Stanko, B. and Hales C. (2009) *Policing Violent Places: A Strategic Approach to Reducing the Harm of Violence in Communities*. London: MPS.

Stenson, K. (2012) Ealing calling: Riot in the Queen of London's suburbs. *Criminal Justice Matters, 87*(1), 12–13.

Stenson, K. and Edwards, A. (2004) *Policy transfer in local crime control: Beyond naive emulation*. In: T. Newburn and R. Sparks (eds) *Criminal Justice and Political Cultures, national and international dimensions of crime control*. Cullompton: Willan.

Sullivan, J. (2012) Lecture on online sex offenders by serving forensic psychologist at Child Exploitation Online Centre.

Symantec (2008) *Symantec Report on the Underground Economy July 07–June 08*. Available on line: http://eval.symantec.com/mktginfo/enterprise/white_papers/bwhitepaper_underground_economy_report_11-2008-14525717.en-us.pdf.

Symantec (2011) *The Norton Cybercrime Report: The Human Impact*. Available on line: http://www.symantec.com/content/en/uk/home_homeoffice/html/cybercrimereport.

Treadwell, J. (2012) From the car boot to booting it up? eBay, online counterfeit crime and the transformation of the criminal marketplace. *Criminology and Criminal Justice*, *12*, 175–191.

Verizon (2011) *Data Breach Investigations Report*. Available on line: http://www.verizon-business.com/resources/reports/rp_data-breach-investigations-report-2011_en_xg.pdf.

Voas, J. (2011) *IEEE Experts Predict Smartphone Hacking Will Soar in 2012*. Available on line: http://www.ieee.org/about/news/2011/17oct_2_2011.html.

Waddington. P. (2010) Are we really serious about organized crime? *Policing: A Journal of Policy and Practice*, *4*, 4–6.

Wall, D.S. (2007/10) Policing cybercrimes: Situating the public police in networks of security within cyberspace (revised May 2010). *Police Practice and Research: An International Journal*, *8*, 183–205.

Webb, S. and Burrows, J. (2009) *Organised Immigration Crime: A Post-Conviction Study*. London: Home Office.

Woodiwiss, M., and Hobbs, R. (2009) Organized evil and the Atlantic alliance: Moral panics and the rhetoric of organized crime policing in America and Britain. *British Journal of Criminology*, *49*, 106–128.

Wright, A. (2006) *Organised Crime*. Cullompton: Willan.

Zhang, S. (2008) *Chinese Human Smuggling Organizations. Families, Social Networks and Cultural Imperatives*. Stanford, CA: Stanford University Press.

4 Crimes of globalization as a criminological project

The case of international financial institutions

David O. Friedrichs and Dawn L. Rothe

Preface: an alleged attempted rape and metaphorical rape

In May 2011 the Managing Director of the International Monetary Fund (IMF), Dominique Strauss-Kahn, was arrested at JFK Airport in New York City and charged with attempted rape of a maid in the $3,000-a-night luxury hotel room he had just vacated (Erlanger and Bennhold, 2011). This was a dramatic major headline story, especially in the United States and France, and generated a huge volume of commentary. Strauss-Kahn was not only the head of a powerful international financial institution, but was also regarded as the most likely French presidential candidate of the Socialist Party in the next election, and a good prospect to be the next president of France. He was a key figure in high-stakes negotiations on European and international financial policies, and was a quintessential and long-established part of the global elite class. His accuser was a refugee from a poor developing-world country in Africa – Guinea – and a single mother of modest means. Accordingly, commentators could not help but be struck by the immense contrast between the status and circumstances of the accused and the accuser.

Both parties were also emblematic in certain respects of some dimensions of an increasingly globalized world. On the one hand, the accused was a central player in international policy-making in an increasingly financially interconnected world; on the other hand, the accuser had sought asylum in the United States within the context of increasing global recognition of basic human rights to which all human beings are entitled. But at least some of the commentators could not help noticing parallels between the specific criminal allegation in this case, involving individuals representative of the dramatic divide between the privileged of developed countries and the underprivileged of developing countries, but also that in more general terms the IMF, directed by developed-country interests, has been accused of 'metaphorical rape' of developing countries where its policies are implemented. An economic columnist observed that

> There's a certain grotesque echo in the fact that Strauss-Kahn has been accused of attempting to rape a maid from a developing nation. The IMF has been under fire for years for offering at best hypocritical and at worst

dangerous advice to developing countries about how to manage their economies.

(Foroohar, 2011)

An American anthropologist writing a book on Guinea noted that this case

has the aura of a parable. Many Africans feel that the International Monetary Fund, which Mr. Strauss-Kahn led, and the World Bank have been more committed to the free flow of money and commodities like bauxite than to the free flow of people and the fulfillment of their aspirations.

(McGovern, 2011)

Other commentators addressed various other issues brought into sharp relief by this case – including on-going forms of sexual harassment of women both within France and within the IMF itself, and the contradiction of a leader of the Socialist party enjoying a life of such privilege and lavish living – but for our purposes here the parallels between the familiar crime of sexual assault and the far less familiar 'crime' of imposing harmful policies on poor countries is the principal focus of concern.

By July 2011, the case against Strauss-Kahn had taken a new turn. Serious questions about the credibility of the accuser had arisen, and the prosecution of the sexual assault case was in jeopardy (Dwyer *et al.*, 2011). On August 23 2011, the Manhattan District Attorney's office announced that it was dropping the case against Strauss-Kahn (Eligon, 2011). The accuser had apparently made untrue statements to the prosecutors about having been gang-raped in Guinea and about her possible involvement in criminal activities, and in a phone conversation appeared to be focused on taking advantage of the wealth of the accused. But here too one could see some parallels with on-going claims that accusations against the IMF of implementing harmful policies are misguided and unwarranted, and harmful circumstances in the developing countries with which it is involved can be attributed to corruption and poor governance practices within these countries. Accordingly, this high-profile case usefully provides a point of departure for considering broader issues in a complex, globalized world.

The visibility of crime – and relatively invisible crime

What is the proper domain for a scholarly enterprise that calls itself criminology? This question has been a focus of contested dialogue for some time now, and is hardly resolved. Indeed, in 2011 we have the publication of a major anthology entitled *What is Criminology?* (Bosworth and Hoyle, 2011) wherein prominent criminologists explore this and related questions about the optimal character and form of criminology. But one can safely assert that certain forms of crime have been wholly visible to criminologists from the outset, with conventional crimes (including homicide, assault, robbery, theft, and burglary as prominent examples) being the most visible. Juvenile delinquency, encompassing both the commission of conventional crimes by juveniles as well as status offenses by juveniles, has long been a major realm of criminological inquiry. Victimless crimes – or public order crimes – have also long preoccupied criminologists, with drug-related offenses especially high on this list. All of these crimes and delinquent acts are clearly defined as such by the state, and have long been the primary focus of the criminal justice system. Organized crime and professional crime – and especially since 9/11 terrorism – have also been the focus of much criminological attention. Early in the twenty-first century it remains the case that the great majority of criminologists are engaged with the study of such crime and delinquency and the control of such crime and delinquency. This claim can be easily substantiated by anyone perusing recent issues of leading journals in the field, such as *Criminology*, the *British Journal of Criminology*, *Justice Quarterly* and *Criminology & Public Policy*, or the programs of recent meetings of the American Society of Criminology, the British Society of Criminology and the Academy of Criminal Justice Sciences. That such crime and delinquency is a significant source of social harm and a legitimate area of criminological inquiry is hardly denied here. But some prominent criminologists and their disciples have long criticized a form of criminological parochialism that adopts a rather narrow conception of crime and that focuses quite exclusively on forms of crime and delinquency that are the source of less demonstrable social harm than forms of 'crime' that render immense social harm. An 'inverse hypothesis' suggests that the degree of criminological attention to different forms of crime has varied inversely with the demonstrable degree of social harm involved. What are the reasons for such parochialism? In part, as was long ago recognized by C. Wright Mills (1943), early criminologists (or social pathologists) saw crime and social problems in terms of patterns of behavior engaged in disproportionately by segments of the population different from themselves: i.e., not small-town, middle-class WASPs but rather inner-city, lower-class minorities. Conventional forms of crime are highlighted in the media – especially in their most sensationalistic forms – and become a focus of much public anxiety and panic, in turn making them a priority for politicians and public officials. Ultimately, conventional crimes and delinquencies tend not to be the most complex forms of crime, and criminal justice institutions have long been organized to respond to these less complex forms of crime. There are other reasons for the conventional crime and crime control bias that we won't explore here, but the conventional crime and criminal justice focus has long been reinforced by the self-perpetuating dynamics of criminology and criminal justice graduate education.

Francis Bacon (1963), in his *Novum Organum*, first published in 1620, famously observed that one of the 'idols' that interferes with the production of a scientific understanding of the world is 'Idols of the Tribe'. What Bacon meant by this is that we perceive the world through our senses and overlook that the universe is not necessarily congruent with human perceptions. Another way of putting this is that we create categories and then forget that these categories are human constructs, and not necessarily a reproduction of the world as it is. The production of categories or 'types' is absolutely necessary if we are to make sense of our world and address it coherently. Accordingly, the production of 'ideal types' – as set forth by Max Weber (Parkin, 1982) – is a key attribute of social science. Criminology has very fully embraced the use of typologies (e.g., Clinard and Quinney, 1973). But once a typology has been produced and adopted it strongly influences criminological inquiry going forward.

Since we invoked the crime of rape in our opening preface, some observations of the relative visibility of rape are called for here. Rape is a classic form of conventional crime, one that is widely recognized as a serious type of crime, and a crime that gets considerable attention from the media (both in news and in entertainment formats) and from criminologists themselves. Even young teenagers are surely quite uniformly conscious of rape as a crime. But it is arguably worth noting that the visibility of rape as a crime has not always had the status it presently has, at least in developed Western nations such as the United States and the United Kingdom. In a contemporary classic, Susan Brownmiller (1975) argued that, historically, rape of women by men was often tolerated if not encouraged (for example, in the context of war), and was rendered more difficult to successfully prosecute than equivalent serious crimes. Since the 1970s, feminists have had some measurable success in bringing about reforms of rape laws and promoting broader public awareness of rape; there is also now a large criminological literature on rape (e.g., see Caringella, 2009). Rape, then, is a form of crime that has been rendered increasingly visible in a number of important respects. It is incorporated into any comprehensive typology of crime.

This chapter addresses 'crimes of globalization'. Without a widely recognized category of 'Crimes of Globalization: International Financial Institutions' the harms of these entities have been quite largely invisible to criminologists. Obviously international financial institutions and their activities are not encompassed by traditional criminological typologies. But they also do not readily fit into categories or types created in expanded criminological typologies, including corporate crime, crimes of states, or state-corporate crimes. International financial institutions are not corporations – i.e., private, profit-oriented enterprises. But they are also not states or state-based entities. Rather, they are organizational entities with multiple and important ties to both corporations and states, but also both different from and relatively independent of them. In at least one interpretation, states in the recent era have increasingly transferred rule-making powers to international institutions, broadly defined (Zweifel, 2006). The growth of such institutions has been one of the noteworthy developments of the past century. This trend raises many important questions, going forward: To what extent are international institutions over-shadowing states in the global arena? To whom are such institutions truly accountable, if they are not direct products of a democratic process, and what is the source of their legitimacy? Whose interests are primarily served by international institutions, and are they on balance a force promoting or subverting social justice globally?

Crimes of globalization defined

Conventional crime and its control is principally a local phenomenon, and somewhat less so a state and national (or federal) phenomenon. Accordingly, most criminologists are not especially receptive to adopting a global framework for defining crime or for the study of crime and its control. In the conventional view, crime as defined by law on the state level – or locally or nationally – is the proper domain of criminology, along with its control, and it is through the study of such crime and its control that criminology is most likely to make its contribution to the advancement of human knowledge and to produce knowledge specifically useful for identifying optimal public policies in response to crime. But an accelerating process of globalization has generated new and expanded opportunities for crimes carried out within the 'global village' (Grabosky, 2009). The framework within which crime must be studied and understood is being transformed.

Crimes of globalization are those demonstrably harmful policies and practices of institutions and entities that are specifically a product of the forces of globalization, and that by their very nature operate within a global context. Although these crimes can involve violations of criminal laws on the state or international level, they may also incorporate harms not specifically addressed by statutory law. The vastly disproportionate influence of elite interests over the formal criminal law is accordingly taken into account in a definition that transcends the boundaries of such law. It is not typically the specific intent of those who engage in crimes of globalization to cause harm. Rather, the devastating harm to vulnerable people in developing countries is a consequence of the skewed priorities of institutions and entities which favor the interests of the powerful and the privileged.

The concept of crimes of globalization is not synonymous with two formulations that have received significant recent attention: The 'globalization of crime' and 'globalization and crime' (e.g., Aas, 2007; Friman, 2009; Larsen and Smandych, 2008). The first of these terms refers broadly to long-standing forms of crime now carried out in an increasingly global context, and the second term refers broadly to the influence of globalization on crime, conventionally defined. Simon Mackenzie (2006) has introduced the term 'systematic crime' in his discussion of the broad forms of global harm emanating from the practices of international financial institutions, and their complicity in denying the link between supporting interests of advanced economies and harm in developing countries.

The concept of crimes of globalization, as originally formulated, was limited to the demonstrably harmful activities of international financial institutions, with a special focus on one of these institutions, the World Bank. However, these crimes intersect with a range of other forms of crime engaged in by powerful entities, including crimes of states, political white-collar crime, and state-corporate crime (Friedrichs, 2010). Multiple complex interconnections exist between these different types of globalized harm.

Some refinement of the definition of crimes of globalization seems warranted. In the interest of greater clarity, the notion of crimes of international financial institutions specifically is best classified as a subtype of the broader category of crimes of globalization. The two principal international financial institutions are the IMF, which seeks to maximize financial stability, and the World Bank, primarily focused on promoting development (Woods, 2006). The World Trade Organization (WTO) is often aligned with these international financial institutions, and has many parallel attributes and issues, but strictly speaking is an international regulatory entity, with its primary formal mission being to foster trade. In a rapidly changing global economy, the roles of the international financial institutions have been increasingly questioned. These institutions have many ties with each other, and the lines of demarcation between their activities can become quite blurred.

Globalization in relation to crimes of globalization

Globalization clearly has many different dimensions. Those most pertinent within the realm of white-collar crime generally, and crimes of globalization specifically, include the following: (1) the growing global dominance and reach of neo-liberalism and a free market, capitalist system that disproportionately benefits wealthy and powerful organizations and individuals; (2) the increasing vulnerability of indigenous people with a traditional way of life to the forces of globalized capitalism; (3) the growing influence and impact of international financial institutions and the related, relative decline of power of local or state-based institutions; and (4) the non-democratic operation of international financial institutions, taking the form of globalization from above instead of globalization from below. We will not engage with the huge, on-going dialogue here on whether globalization has on balance promoted improvements in the quality of human life or has been a destructive force (Gillespie, 2006; Held *et al.*, 2005; Stiglitz, 2007). We do not contest that by some measures, in at least some developing countries, the quality of life has improved during the era of expanding globalization (Kenny, 2011). But our focus here – as criminologists – is necessarily on the dark side of globalization.

Crimes of globalization, transnational crimes, and international crimes

The relationship of crimes of globalization to familiar but sometimes unclear terms such as transnational crimes and international crimes requires some attention here. *Transnational crimes* are essentially forms of crime that are increasingly carried out across borders and via international or global networks. The forces of globalization are transforming and amplifying structures of opportunity for a wide range of different forms of criminal activity (Aas, 2007). Some of these forms of crime (e.g., human, arms and drug trafficking) are hardly new, but the transnational dimension of them has expanded (Albanese, 2011). Some of these forms of crime are quite new (e.g., cybercrime) and their transnational dimension greatly enhances the challenges of controlling them.

Organized crime has long had transnational dimensions. The processes of globalization have been transforming some dimensions of such crime, with these transnational dimensions increasingly central to the operation of emerging forms of organized crime. But Hazel Croall (2005) is surely correct in arguing that there has been a disproportionate amount of criminological attention to the globalization of organized crime, when the global activities of multinational corporations and financial institutions cause far greater harm. Certainly the threat of transnational or global terrorism is substantial, but the argument can be made that it also has received disproportionate attention relative to other forms of transnational or global harm. Especially since 9/11, there has been a huge amount of attention to transnational or global terrorism.

International crimes are best conceived of as violations of international law, which in their generic form (e.g., genocide, war crimes, crimes against humanity, and massive violations of human rights) have a long history. Such crimes have often been committed within national boundaries, but are increasingly carried out globally. International crimes are most typically thought of as crimes of states, but may also be committed by insurgencies, militias, and other parties. Corporations – and increasingly multinational corporations – are also complicit in international crimes. Some of the corporations operating in Nazi Germany and its occupied territories, playing a role in the Holocaust, are classic cases of such crimes. In the more recent era such corporations as Blackwater, Sandline, and Halliburton have been accused of violations of international law (Rothe, 2009). The conditions of globalization produce expanding opportunities for such crime.

The lines of demarcation between crimes of globalization, transnational crimes, and international crimes are sometimes fluid and complex. But the key actors typically involved, and the bodies of law violated, tend to be different.

Any coherent discussion of 'crimes of globalization' must also address this phenomenon historically and cross-culturally. Some activities carried out in ancient times can be described as early forms of globalized white-collar crime. Monumental historical crimes were committed in the name of imperialism and colonial expansion globally, over a period of many centuries. Obviously the global slave trade in conjunction with this, continuing into the nineteenth century, was a crime of epic proportions. Furthermore, imperialistic enterprises continued through the twentieth century into the twenty-first, and slavery and a thriving slave market have hardly become extinct in the contemporary world, despite the collapse of traditional colonial regimes and forms of slave trade.

More broadly, 'crimes of empire' are a feature of our world today.

Crimes of globalization, state-corporate crime, and crimes of states

The crimes of international financial institutions (IFIs) have a generic relationship to state-corporate crimes insofar as they are cooperative ventures involving public sector and private sector entities, and in some respects are hybrid public/ private sector entities. The literature on state-corporate crime (e.g., Michalowski and Kramer, 2006) has focused on crimes arising out of cooperative ventures involving states and corporations. In one sense, crimes of globalization could be characterized as a neglected, cognate form of such crime: i.e., state-international financial institution crime.

While the above categories may appear to be separate phenomena, we suggest the connections between them are not so easily separated. The intersection of business and government has led to increased cases of a 'globalized criminality.' In the recent era, Western states as well as corporations have promoted neo-liberalism or a supposed 'free market' model for the global political economy. Within such an environment the crimes of globalization of international financial institutions are intertwined with crimes of states. The policies and practices of the international financial institutions are largely driven by the global agenda of powerful developed states such as the United States.

In many of the developing countries, corrupt political oligarchs facilitate the promotion of this agenda, despite it being largely at odds with the interests of their citizens. Cases of such corrupt practices have been especially pronounced and well-documented in the case of sub-Saharan countries of Africa, such as the Democratic Republic of Congo, East Timor, Rwanda, and Senegal (Rothe, 2010b). But altogether these corrupt practices are a global phenomenon.

Origins of the concept of crimes of globalization

The concept of 'crimes of globalization' was first put forth in a paper for the American Society of Criminology Annual Meeting in 2000 (subsequently published as an article in *Social Justice* in 2002) with the specific title 'The World Bank and Crimes of Globalization: A Case Study' by David O. Friedrichs and Jessica Friedrichs. The specific inspiration for this concept was the experience of the junior author, Jessica Friedrichs, living among poor fishing people in Northeast Thailand whose way of life was being destroyed by a dam at least partially financed by the World Bank. Jessica Friedrichs returned to the United States in April 2000, from her junior year experience in Thailand, two months earlier than anticipated, to make a presentation on the Pak Mun Dam situation at an anti-globalization (or global justice) demonstration in Washington, D.C., that month. The senior author of the article, David Friedrichs, with a long-standing interest in crimes of the powerful, realized that while at least some of the policies and practices of international financial institutions such as the World Bank had demonstrably harmful consequences, this form of harm had been quite wholly neglected by criminologists.

The World Bank as an international financial institution

The World Bank is here addressed in some detail, to exemplify the fundamental nature of an international financial institution (Goldman, 2005; Marshall, 2008; Weaver, 2008). The *World Bank*, formally the International Bank for Reconstruction and Development (IBRD), was established at the Bretton Woods Conference in 1944 to help stabilize and rebuild economies ravaged by World War II. Eventually it shifted its focus to an emphasis on aiding developing nations. The Bank makes low-interest loans to governments of its member nations and to private development projects backed by those governments with the stated aim to benefit the citizens of those countries. The World Bank claims to contribute to the reduction of poverty and to the improvement of living standards in developing countries. Today the Bank is a large, international operation with more than 10,000 employees, 180 member states, and annual loans of $170 billion (Strom, 2011). Although it continued to be an important source of loans for developing countries, these countries were increasingly turning to regional development banks, Wall Street, and national governments for such economic support.

The World Bank was established, along with the IMF, at the behest of dominant Western nations, with little input from developing countries. It is disproportionately influenced by or manipulated by elite economic institutions and entities – e.g., transnational mining companies – and has been characterized as an agent of global capital. In developing countries, it deals primarily with the political and economic elites of those countries with little direct attention to the perspectives and needs of indigenous peoples (Babb, 2009; Goldman, 2005; Weaver, 2008). It has loaned money to ruthless military dictatorships engaged in murder and torture, and denied loans to democratic governments subsequently overthrown by the military. It has favored strong dictatorships over struggling democracies because it believes that the former are more able to introduce and see through the unpopular reforms its loans require. World Bank borrowers typically are political elites of developing countries and their cronies, although repaying the debt becomes the responsibility of these countries' citizens, most of whom do not benefit from the loans. Ultimately, more money flows out of the borrowing countries, to the World Bank and the IMF, than the reverse (Goldman, 2005). The Bank has lost $100 billion due to fraud and corruption, in one estimate, over a period of several decades. The privileged in developing countries have been the principal beneficiaries of World Bank loans, not poor people in those countries. An outside observer witnesses the on-the-ground harm from a World Bank-financed irrigation project in a developing country; meanwhile, the project engineers and government officials are building palatial homes nearby (Goldman, 2005). World Bank officials have little if any direct contact with the indigenous peoples in developing countries most affected by its projects.

The World Bank has been the target of much criticism, especially in the recent era. It has been characterized as paternalistic, secretive, and counterproductive in terms of its claimed goals of improving people's lives. It has been called fundamentally hypocritical due to the gap between the professed objectives for the projects it supports and the actual outcomes (Weaver, 2008). It has been charged with complicity in policies with genocidal consequences, with exacerbating ethnic conflict, with increasing the gap between rich and poor, with fostering immense ecological and environmental damage, with neglecting agriculture crucial to survival in developing countries, and with the callous displacement of vast numbers of indigenous people in these countries from their original homes and communities (see Caulfield, 1996; Goldman, 2005; and Rich, 1994, as some of the sources documenting these effects of World Bank policies). By any measure, there has been a wide range of suffering arising out of World Bank policies.

In the wake of the widespread criticism of the ineffectiveness and harmful consequences of the structural adjustment programs imposed on developing countries by the World Bank (and the IMF) a shift to poverty reduction was announced as a new goal in the more recent period (Abouharb and Cingranelli, 2006; Brady, 2010). Although the Bank has continued to identify the reduction of poverty in developing countries as a primary goal, a former official of the bank questions its capacity to do so (Shaman, 2009). Since 9/11 in particular foreign aid overall has been directed principally toward fighting terrorism, not toward alleviating poverty, and the World Bank's anti-poverty campaign has become increasingly marginalized. The sad irony in all of this is the perception of many observers that developing country poverty is one of the primary forces driving international terrorism. Since the global economic crisis of 2008 it has been estimated that an additional fifty million people will be locked into poverty at least through 2015 (Chan, 2010). If the World Bank is not directly responsible for this circumstance, it has also not been a clearly effective counter-force.

Critics claim that many less developed countries that received World Bank (and IMF) loans are worse off today in terms of poverty and that the severe austerity measures imposed on borrowing countries, deemed necessary to maximize the chances of loans being repaid, impact most heavily on the poorest and most vulnerable citizens. Its 'structural adjustment agreements' in developing countries have been shown to also impact negatively on human rights in those countries. The building of dams has been the single most favored World Bank project, but even its own experts concede that millions of people have been displaced as a result of these dams. In many of these dam projects, resettlement plans have either been nonexistent – in violation of the Bank's own guidelines – or have been inadequately implemented. In one notorious case in the 1970s, anti-dam protesters in Guatemala were massacred by the military.

Over a long period of time, critics have characterized the World Bank as engaged in crimes (Friedrichs, 2010). A union organizer in Haiti, after observing the effects of World Bank activities in his country, calls for putting the bank on trial for crimes against humanity (Goldman, 2005: 284). In a recent documentary, 'Bamako' (2007), many ordinary Africans testify about the range of cruel consequences they regard as linked to the practices of the World Bank, and call for some accountability. We can find other such calls in recent decades, but of course to date no trials of the World Bank have occurred.

The study of crimes of globalization: to date

The Pak Mun dam case

In the Pak Mun dam case, the World Bank helped finance the building of the dam in eastern Thailand in the early 1990s. The process of planning, constructing, and operating this dam was undertaken without obtaining input from the fishermen and villagers who lived along the river. The construction of the dam had a detrimental effect on the environment, flooding the adjacent forests. This effect violated the World Bank's own policies on cultural property destruction. Many edible plants upon which locals were dependent for their sustenance and for income were lost. Villagers who used the river waters for drinking, bathing, and laundry developed skin rashes. Most importantly, a severe decline in the fish population occurred. As a consequence, the way of life of indigenous fishermen dependent upon abundant fish for food and income was annihilated. The resettlement of the fishermen and compensation for their losses were wholly inadequate. Traditional communities began to disintegrate. Many of those affected by these developments organized protest villages (encampments established adjacent to the dam projects by indigenous community members engaged in the protest movement) and engaged in other actions calling for the Thai government and the World Bank to take responsibility for the devastation they caused by building the dam, which cost far more than expected and generated far less electricity than had been anticipated.

Subsequent studies

In the wake of the original article focusing upon the World Bank and the case of the Pak Mun dam, a number of criminologists have applied the concept of crimes of globalization to other circumstances. For example, Rothe *et al.* (2006) conducted research that explored the interrelations between the IMF and the World Bank, and legacies of colonialism along with foreign policies that set the stage for large-scale atrocities and crimes of states. Exploring the circumstances leading to the sinking of the ferry *Le Joola*, the authors demonstrated that the state of Senegal itself had core liability for this maritime tragedy, with its dramatic loss of lives. The ferry capsized with only one of its two engines functioning, resulting in the deaths of 1,863 passengers. This was the second largest maritime disaster in history. The ferry was clearly unsafe and was allowed to depart for Dakar in violation of minimal safety standards. The government readily admitted its errors and several ministers either stepped down or were removed from their positions. However, despite unequivocal governmental responsibility, Rothe *et al.* (2006) advance the case that the sinking could not be characterized simply as a case of state crime. Rather, a thorough investigation and analysis of the reasons and forces behind the *Le Joola* sinking suggested that international financial institutions bore some clear culpability for the disaster. In response to Structural Adjustment Programs (SAPs) imposed by the IMF, the Senegalese government was forced to cut spending in many areas. These spending cuts extended to ferry programs central to transportation in Senegal, especially in relation to its geographic location. This had a direct impact on the upkeep and return of the *Le Joola* to open waters. Most crucially, the authors of this study demonstrated why scholars need to examine the criminogenic effects of policies and practices of international financial institutions in developing countries such as Senegal.

These policies and practices privilege capitalistic profit over human lives and a better quality of life for people in developing countries. Accordingly, this is crime against vulnerable human beings.

An article by Rothe *et al.* (2009) took a parallel approach, exploring the role of international financial institution policies in the conditions leading to the Rwandan genocide in 1994. While the World Bank and the IMF did not seek to instigate economic collapse or to promote genocide, their policies and their systematic inattention in Rwanda set the stage for political and economic disaster as well as the genocide itself. The authors suggested that these international financial institutions knowingly violated their own standards, as well as international human rights principles. Through the imposition of harsh conditions tied to their financial aid, they facilitated criminal activities on a massive scale.

In an article published in 2008, Ezeonu and Koku also adopted the crimes of globalization concept. They demonstrated the key contributing role played by the neo-liberal policies of international financial institutions in sub-Saharan Africa, in expanding the vulnerability of people in this region to HIV infection. They called for more systematic criminological attention to the victimization of people in developing countries as a consequence of the promotion of neo-liberal policies and practices in an increasingly globalized world (see also Ezeonu, 2008).

In a similar vein, Rothe (2010a, b, c) has provided an analysis of the complicity of international financial institutions in heightened levels of corruption and the suppression or violation of human rights in developing countries. Analyzing such complicity seems especially important given that these institutions claim to be engaged in combating corruption in developing countries, including those linked to transnational and multinational corporations. The anti-corruption initiatives include threatening to withhold much needed economic aid and loans in the absence of action taken against corrupt activities in these countries. Rothe has illustrated the specific role of the international financial institutions in the illegal expropriation of the rich natural resources of the Democratic Republic of Congo by the neighboring countries of Uganda and Rwanda. Beyond theft on a grand scale, Rwandan and Ugandan state forces and militias also engaged in especially atrocious human rights violations conducted against civilian populations, including forced labor, systematic rape, and widespread killing. Through their funding of African states engaged in crimes against both their own citizens and those of neighboring countries, the international financial institutions bear some responsibility for these crimes.

Parallel circumstances have arisen in other parts of the world. Stanley (2009) has analyzed the role of the international financial institutions in Indonesia. They directed some $30 billion to the Suharto regime, despite its known record of massive corruption, false accounting, and a militaristic appropriation of aid funds. As the World Bank's focus was on supporting Indonesia, the state was able to use funds supposedly intended to reduce poverty in its brutal campaign against civilians in the state of Timor-Leste. This campaign had as its purpose terrorizing people to deter them from voting for independence from Indonesia. One could identify many other cases in Asia and other parts of the world where the international financial institutions have been complicit in supporting corrupt, authoritarian regimes and facilitating their massive violations of human rights.

The concept of crimes of globalization has also been adopted in relation to forms of crime that occur in the context of globalization but do not specifically involve the international financial institutions. Wright and Muzzatti (2007) have addressed the global restructuring of agriculture and food systems – agri-food globalization – with some specific attention to the victimization of huge numbers of animals: e.g., 58,000 sheep stranded at sea for almost three months in 2003, in violation of animal welfare law. Altogether, policies and practices relating to the global restructuring of agriculture and food systems were driving up food prices, pushing tens of millions of people towards hunger and starvation, and developed country farm subsidies were driving large numbers of farmers in developing countries into desperate circumstances – to the advantage of corporate and high finance interests in the wealthy countries of the world. Giant American agribusiness corporations such as Cargill and Archer Daniels Midland (ADM), through their exploitative activities in developing countries, were contributing to the on-going suffering on many levels in those countries (North, 2011). This is a phenomenon under-studied by criminologists.

'Economic hit men' and crimes of globalization

The notion of crimes of globalization has also been implicitly adopted by some authors who are not criminologists, and who are addressing a broad public audience. A book by John Perkins (2005), entitled *Confessions of an Economic Hit Man*, became a best-seller following its publication in 2005. He defined economic hit men (EHM) as 'highly paid professionals who cheat countries around the globe out of trillions of dollars' (Perkins, 2005: ix). In his case, as an employee of an international consulting firm, Perkins claims to have participated in a range of activities involved in funneling funds from international financial institutions and international aid organizations into the hands of major transnational corporations and a small number of wealthy and influential families in developing countries. Economic hit men are engaged in persuading developing country leaders to become part of a vast global network that ultimately serves the interest of US-based corporations and US businesses generally, at the enormous expense of the people of the developing countries. In a subsequent book, *The Secret History of the American Empire*, Perkins (2007) further explores some of these themes. Although these two books have been criticized as self-dramatizing, they may have succeeded in raising the consciousness of new audiences about crimes of globalization.

In *A Game as Old as Empire: The Secret World of Economic Hit Men and the Web of Global Corruption* (Hiatt, 2007), a book inspired by the Perkins' bestseller, various authors address aspects of 'the corporatocracy' ('the powerful people who run the world's biggest corporations, the most powerful governments, and history's first truly global empire,' p. 20), These authors address such matters as the hundreds of billions of dollars that developing countries spend annually for servicing their debt, the world of offshore banking, the expropriation of Africa's oil wealth, the role of export credit agencies in boosting overseas sales for multinational corporations, and the mirage of debt relief.

The criminological study of crimes of globalization: an agenda

The criminological study of crimes of globalization could be said to be in its infancy at present, with only the handful of studies discussed earlier in this chapter currently constituting the basic literature on this topic. It is generally acknowledged that it took a long time after Edwin Sutherland (1940) introduced the concept of white-collar crime before a significant number of criminologists began to pursue the study of such crime. Until the 1970s, aside from Sutherland's own classic book in 1949 and a relative handful of other studies, there was little criminological work on white-collar crime, but for some time now it has been a significant (if still marginal, relative to conventional crime) area of criminological inquiry. Crimes of states were largely ignored by criminologists (with isolated exceptions) for most of the history of criminology. William J. Chambliss's (1989) 1988 American Society of Criminology Presidential Address on 'State-organized crime' was one important impetus for a growing number of criminologists to focus upon crimes of states. In recent years, in particular, we have the publication of overviews of the criminology of state crimes as well as some anthologies (e.g., Chambliss *et al.,* 2010; Green and Ward, 2004; Rothe 2009; Rothe and Mullins, 2011; and Smeulers and Haveman, 2008). While those who have addressed crimes of states have been disproportionately affiliated with critical criminology, some well-known mainstream criminologists have also begun to address such crime (e.g., Hagan and Rymond-Richmond, 2009; Savelsberg, 2010). As one more illustrative case of transcending criminological parochialism, the case of state-corporate crime can be mentioned. This concept was introduced by Kramer and Michalowski in 1990; by the middle of the first decade of the new century there was enough of a criminological literature on such crime to merit the publication of an anthology (Michalowski and Kramer, 2006). Our objective here is to encourage a significant growth of criminological attention to crimes of globalization. Accordingly, we offer a provisional agenda for this enterprise.

First, we invite further dialogue on the conceptual and definitional issues relating to crimes of globalization, on the premise that much is to be gained if a relatively high degree of consensus on these matters can be realized earlier rather than later. Have we set forth here the optimal approach of differentiating between crimes of globalization, international (supranational) crimes, and transnational crimes, or would an alternative approach be better? A fully developed typology of the principal forms of crimes of globalization would be helpful. Altogether, a comparative exploration of how crimes of globalization differ from (and have parallel features with) other types of crime, including conventional forms of crimes and corporate crimes – as well as crimes of states and transnational forms of crime – would also be useful. What has been learned by criminologists in their study of other forms of crime that can and cannot be usefully applied to crimes of globalization? And in relation to this project, we need further attention questions of how crimes of globalization intersect with, arise out of, and mote, other forms of crime.

It has been long noted that the study of white-collar crime and crimes of states presents criminologists with special methodological and research-related challenges beyond those confronting those who engage in research on conventional forms of crime. Which unique challenges arise specifically in relation to research on crimes of globalization, and which methodological strategies are optimal for such research? Ulrich Beck and Edgar Grande's (2010) 'methodological cosmopolitanism' — with its call for reconfiguring the key units of analysis, beyond the local and the national — would appear to provide one obvious point of departure for research in this realm. More narrowly, we need surveys of perceptions of and attitudes towards crimes of globalization as well as acceptance of and resistance to the application of the term 'crime' to the harmful practices and policies of international financial institutions. As part of survey initiatives the 'seriousness' ranking of crimes of globalization relative to other forms of crime should be undertaken. Content analysis studies of the treatment of what we have characterized as crimes of globalization, in diverse forms of media (including, in the present environment, Internet sources such as blogs), can be more easily carried out than many other types of research projects in this realm. Ethnographic studies (or participant observer studies) addressing both the internal workings of the international financial institutions and the experiences of people in developing countries with programs implemented or supported by these institutions are much needed. We have reported on the small number of case studies of specific cases of crimes of globalization carried out to date, but the deeper understanding of such crimes calls for many further case studies. More broadly, socio-historical and comparative studies of crimes of globalization are essential to provide a sophisticated framework for the understanding of contemporary cases of crimes of globalization. Obviously this brief review does not exhaust other possible methods that could be usefully applied to the study of crimes of globalization.

If we adopt a concept of 'crimes of globalization' we then also need fuller exploration of what some of the primary sources of resistance within the international legal community are to apply a conception of 'crime' to these policies and practices. Are there currently international tribunals that can and do exercise jurisdiction over alleged crimes of the international financial institutions? What form of international justice could hypothetically address such crimes most effectively?

The formulation and refinement of an integrated theory of crimes of globalization is obviously one core project, as is a systematic exploration of the existing and the still-needed forms of control in relation to such crimes. The authors drafted sections of the original manuscript of this chapter that address these matters, but had to exclude these sections for reasons of space. However, these issues will presumably be addressed in a future project on crimes of globalization.

The 'anti-globalization' or 'global justice' movement has to date not been much studied by criminologists. It would be useful to have fuller exploration of effectiveness and the limitations of this movement in responding to the crimes of international financial institutions. What does this movement have in common with, and how does it differ from, social movements (e.g., the feminist 'Take Back the Night' initiative) that have addressed conventional forms of crime?

If crimes of globalization come to be recognized as a significant criminological phenomenon, it is our view that there is much useful work that can be undertaken by criminologists to more fully understand such crime and the challenges involved in its control. We have here only provided some preliminary indicators of the relevant research agenda.

Concluding observations

In a world where citizens of developing countries increasingly have access through the Internet to specific information about the exploitative activities of Western governments, institutions, and transnational corporations in their own countries, direct demands for addressing these 'crimes' are highly likely to increase. Populist challenges to autocratic, corrupt regimes and the immense economic inequality that they sustain will surely be one of the defining themes of the twenty-first century. In developing countries, growing numbers of people, increasingly better informed and more easily mobilized via the Internet, are characterizing themselves as victims of monumental crimes carried out by these regimes, and Western governments and institutions are seen as complicit in fundamental ways in these crimes. Early in 2011 this situation was playing out in Egypt, Tunisia, Libya, Bahrain, Yemen, and other Middle Eastern countries (Friedrichs, forthcoming). The gross mal-distribution in terms of consumption of natural resources that exists between the developed and developing world is also highly likely to be subjected to increasing challenge. Going forward, it seems highly likely that Western entities, including international financial institutions, will increasingly be 'indicted' for their perceived crimes against the people of developing countries. It is our conviction that a criminology that aspires to be relevant in a rapidly changing world of the twenty-first century needs to address these crimes.

References

Aas, K.F. (2007) *Globalization and Crime*. Los Angeles, CA: Sage.

Abouharb, M.R. and Cingranelli, D.L. (2006) The human rights effects of World Bank structural adjustment, 1981–2000. *International Studies Quarterly*, 50, 233–262.

Albanese, J. (2011) *Transnational Crime and the 21st Century*. New York: Oxford University Press.

Babb, S. (2009) *Behind the Development Banks: Washington Politics, World Poverty, and the Wealth of Nations*. Chicago: University of Chicago Press.

Bacon, F. (1620; 1963) *Novum organum*. In: *The Complete Essays of Francis Bacon*. New York: Washington University Press.

Beck, U. and Grande, E. (2010) Varieties of second modernity: The cosmopolitan turn in social and political theory and research. *British Journal of Sociology*, 61, 409–443.

Bosworth, M. and Hoyle, C. (eds) (2011) *What is Criminology?* Oxford: Oxford University Press.

Brady, D. (2010) Common ground for sociology and the World Bank? *Contemporary Sociology, 39*, 530–532.

Brownmiller, S. (1975) *Against our Will: Men, Women and Rape.* New York: Simon & Schuster.

Caringella, S. (2009) *Addressing Rape Reform in Law and Practice.* New York: Columbia University Press.

Caufield, C. (1996) *Masters of Illusion: The World Bank and the Poverty of Nations.* New York: Henry Hold and Co.

Chambliss, W.J. (1989) State-organized crime. *Criminology, 27*, 183–208.

Chambliss, W.J., Michalowski, R. and Kramer, R.C. (eds) (2010) *State Crime in a Global Age.* Cullompton: Willan.

Chan, S. (2010) Poorer nations get larger role in World Bank. *New York Times* (April 26): B3.

Clinard, M.B. and Quinney, R. (1973) *Criminal Behavior Systems: A typology* (2nd edition). New York: Holt, Rinehart and Winston.

Croall, H. (2005) Transnational white-collar crime. In: J. Sheptycki and A. Wardak (eds) *Transnational and Comparative Criminology.* London: Glasshouse Press.

Dwyer, J., Rashbaum, W.K. and Eligon, J. (2011) Strauss-Kahn prosecution said to be near collapse. *New York Times* (July 1): A1.

Eligon, J. (2011) Strauss-Kahn drama ends with a short final act. *New York Times* (August 24); A1.

Erlanger, S. and Bennhold, K. (2011) IMF chief's arrest upends political landscape in a shocked France. *New York Times* (May 16): A1.

Ezeonu, I. (2008) Crimes of globalization: Health care, HIV and the poverty of neo-liberalism in Sub-Saharan Africa. *International Journal of Social Inquiry, 1*, 113–134.

Ezeonu, I. and Koku, E. (2008) Crimes of globalization: The feminization of HIV pandemic in Sub-Saharan Africa. *The Global South, 2*, 112–129.

Foroohar, R. (2011) No more gentleman's agreements. *Time* (June 6): 22.

Friedrichs, D.O. (2010) *Trusted Criminals: White collar crime in contemporary society* (4th edition). Belmont, CA: Cengage.

Friedrichs, D.O. (forthcoming) Resisting state crime as a criminological project: In the context of the Arab Spring'. In: E. Stanley and J. McCulloch (eds) *State Crime and Resistance.* London: Routledge.

Friedrichs, D.O. and Friedrichs, J. (2002) The World Bank and crimes of globalization: A case study. *Social Justice, 29*, 1–12.

Friman, R.H. (2009) *Crime and the Global Political Economy.* Boulder, CO: Lynne Rienner.

Gillespie, W. (2006) Capitalist world-economy, globalization, and violence: Implications for criminology and social justice. *International Criminal Justice Review, 16*, 24–44.

Goldman, M. (2005) *Imperial Nature: The World Bank and Struggles for Justice in the Age of Globalization.* New Haven, CT: Yale University Press.

Grabosky, P. (2009) Globalization and white-collar crime. In S.S. Simpson and D. Weisburd (eds) *The Criminology of White-Collar Crime.* New York: Springer.

Green, P. and Ward, T. (2004) *State Crime: Governments, Violence and Corruption.* London: Pluto Press.

Hagan, J. and Rymond-Richmond, W. (2009) *Darfur and the Crime of Genocide.* Cambridge: Cambridge: University Press.

Held, D. *et al.* (2005) *Debating Globalization.* Cambridge: Polity.

Hiatt, S. (ed.) (2007) *A Game as Old as Empire: The Secret World of Economic Hit Men and the Web of Global Corruption*. San Francisco: Berrett-Koehler Publishers.

Kenny, C. (2011) Attention doomsayers: Global quality of life is improving. *The Chronicle Review* (April 1): B10–11.

Kramer, R.C. and Michalowski, R.J. (1990) Toward an integrated theory of state-corporate crime. Paper presented at a *Meeting of the American Society of Criminology*. Baltimore, MD, November.

Larsen, N., and Smandych, R. (eds.) (2008) *Global Criminology and Criminal Justice*. Toronto: Broadview Press.

McGovern, M. (2011) Before you judge, stand in her shoes. *New York Times* (July 6); A21.

Mackenzie, S. (2006) Systematic crimes of the powerful: Criminal aspects of the global economy. *Social Justice, 33*, 162–182.

Marshall, K. (2008) *The World Bank: From Reconstruction to Development to Equity*. London: Routledge.

Michalowski, R.J. and Kramer, R.C. (eds) (2006) *State-Corporate Crime: Wrongdoing at the Intersection of Business and Government*. New Brunswick, NJ: Rutgers University Press.

Mills, C.W. (1943) The professional ideology of social pathologists. *American Journal of Sociology, 49*, 165–180.

North, J. (2011) The roots of the Cote d'Ivoire crisis. *The Nation* (April 25): 24–26.

Parkin, F. (1982) *Max Weber*. London: Tavistock.

Perkins, J. (2005) *Confessions of an Economic Hit Man*. London: Ebury Press.

Perkins, J. (2007) *The Secret History of the American Empire: The Truth about Economic Hit Men, Jackals, and How to Change the World*. London: Penguin.

Rich, B. (1994) *Mortgaging the Earth: The World Bank, Environmental Impoverishment and the Crisis of Development*. Boston: Beacon Press.

Rothe, D.L. (2009) *State Criminality: The Crime of all Crimes*. Lanham, MD: Lexington.

Rothe, D.L. (2010a) Facilitating corruption and human rights violations: The role of international financial institutions. *Crime, Law and Social Change, 53*, 457–476.

Rothe, D.L. (2010b) The dragon rising: International financial institutions and the emerging role of China. In: W. Chambliss, R. Michalowski and R.C. Kramer (eds) *State Crime in a Globalized Age*. Cullompton: Willan.

Rothe, D.L. (2010c) International financial institutions, corruption and human rights. In: M. Boersma and H. Nelen (eds) *Corruption and Human Rights*. Antwerp: Intersentia.

Rothe, D.L. and Mullins, C.W. (eds) (2011) *State Crime: Current Perspectives*. New Brunswick, NJ: Rutgers University Press.

Rothe, D.L., Muzzatti, S. and Mullins, C.W. (2006) Crime on the high seas: Crimes of globalization and the sinking of the Senegalese ferry Le Joola. *Critical Criminology, 14*, 159–180.

Rothe, D.L., Mullins, C.W. and Sandstrom, K. (2009) The Rwandan genocide: International finance policies and human rights. *Social Justice, 35*, 66–86.

Savelsberg, J. (2010) *Crime and Human Rights*. Los Angeles: Sage.

Shaman, D.I. (2009) *The World Bank Unveiled: Inside the Revolutionary Struggle for Transparency*. Little Rock, AR: Parkhurst Brothers.

Smeulers, A. and Haveman, R. (eds.) (2008) *Supranational Criminology: Towards a Criminology of International Crimes*. Antwerp: Intersentia.

Stanley, E. (2009) *Torture, Truth and Justice: The Case of Timor-Leste*. London: Routledge.

Stiglitz, J. (2007) *Making Globalization Work*. New York: W.W. Norton.

Strom, S. (2011) Cracking open the World Bank. *New York Times* (July 3): Business 1.

Sutherland, E. H. (1940) White-collar criminality. *American Sociological Review*, *5*, 1–12.

Sutherland, E. H. (1949) *White Collar Crime*. New York: Holt, Rinehart and Winston.

Weaver, C. (2008) *Hypocrisy Trap: The World Bank and the Poverty of Reform*. Princeton, NJ: Princeton University Press.

Woods, N. (2006) *The Globalizers: The IMF, the World Bank and Their Borrowers*. Ithaca, NY: Cornell University Press.

Wright, W., and Muzzatti, S. (2007) Not in my port: The 'death ship' of sheep and crimes of agri-food globalization. *Agriculture and Human Values*, *24*, 133–145.

Zweifel, T.D. (2006) *International Organizations and Democracy: Accountability, politics and power*. Boulder, CO: Lynne Rienner.

5 Policing international terrorism

Mathieu Deflem and Samantha Hauptman

Introduction

The field of international criminal justice and criminology has progressed exponentially over the past few decades for reasons that relate to both the development of relevant scholarship and the continual globalization of society. Among the most noteworthy developments have been issues related to terrorism and counterterrorism. Since the events of September 11, 2001, the criminological study of relevant structures and processes has also accelerated investigations of the policing of terrorism, especially at an international level. The most important aspects and dynamics of the international policing of terrorism form the centerpiece of this chapter.

Theoretically informed by the bureaucratization perspective of policing (Deflem, 2002, 2010), this review will bring out the central characteristics of the policing of international terrorism in selected nations and at the level of international police organizations. It will be shown, most critically, that the international activities and objectives of the policing of terrorism are not aimed at fighting a (military) war on terror but are instead focused on terrorism as a matter of crime and criminal justice. The crime-control functions of counterterrorism policing are thereby framed in terms of efficiency considerations rather than political concerns or related legal and military objectives defined in terms of national security. Police agencies are relatively autonomous in determining the technically most advanced methods of criminal investigation in counterterrorism, including cooperation efforts among police from different nations.

Examining the essential components of the policing of international terrorism within relevant legal and political contexts will reveal the extent to which the objectives of international cooperation of counterterrorism since 9/11 have been realized. Exploring the most important aspects of counterterrorism policing in the United States and selected nations across the globe as well as major international organizations involved in coordinating global policing efforts will elucidate the state and development of the international policing of terrorism in the context of other international counterterrorism efforts. Appropriate lessons can be drawn from this analysis both for our understanding of counterterrorism in the world today and in the near future and for criminological theorizing and research in these areas.

International counterterrorism by US law enforcement

It is not only in view of the centrality of 9/11 that this chapter begins with an analysis of international counterterrorism policing by agencies from the United States, for US law enforcement had long before taken a lead in international police activities (Nadelmann, 1993; Deflem, 2004). The events of September 11 accelerated this so-called 'Americanization' of international policing at various levels. Among the most central agencies, thereby, are the Federal Bureau of Investigation (FBI) in the Justice Department, selected enforcement agencies in the newly formed Department of Homeland Security, and the Bureau of Diplomatic Security in the Department of State (Deflem, 2010).

The FBI

Within the US Department of Justice, the FBI is the primary federal US law enforcement agency, responsible for a variety of criminal offenses, including terrorism. Among its chief international investigative mechanisms, the FBI has just over 1 percent of its 12,590 force (a total of 165 agents) permanently stationed overseas as legal attachés at US embassies across the world. An increasing number of federal regulations involving terrorism, most notably President Ronald Reagan's National Security Directive 30 of 1982, led the FBI to expand its counterterrorism operations which resulted in their lead-agency status in all matters of counterterrorism. With an increasing number of attacks on Americans abroad occurring during the 1980s, the FBI's Criminal Investigative Division established a Specialized Terrorism Section that focused on both domestic and international terrorism.

In the 1990s, terrorism incidents such as the 1993 bombing of the World Trade Center and the 1998 US embassy bombings in Tanzania and Kenya further stepped up the FBI's counterterrorism efforts. An FBI Counterterrorism Division was newly established, while foreign counterintelligence responsibilities were assigned to the National Security Division, a detachment of the US Department of Justice. In 1995, then President Bill Clinton reaffirmed the FBI's counterterrorism role with Presidential Directive 39 which affirmed the lead investigative agency role of the FBI in acts of terrorism both in the United States and overseas. Counterterrorism had become one of the FBI's principal missions by the late 1990s and shortly after the events on 9/11, the counterterrorism enforcement role, as stated by then Attorney General John Ashcroft, had become the 'FBI's central mission of preventing the commission of terrorist acts against the United States and its people' (IGnet, 2002).

Within this framework the Joint Terrorism Task Forces (JTTFs) are arguably the most significant counterterrorism tool at the police level in the United States. Overseen by the FBI, these task forces are composed of emergency personnel and law enforcement agents from multiple levels of government. Thus, acting as force-multipliers, the JTTFs act as the chief counterterrorism mechanism for specific terrorism-related investigations. At present, more than 100 such JTTFs are coordinated through a National Joint Terrorism Task Force that is headquartered in Washington, DC.

With more attention devoted to terrorism in the post-9/11 era, the FBI diverted agents from other investigative branches into counterterrorism as the number of both intelligence analysts and linguists have doubled and tripled, respectively. The increase in surveillance and the use of National Security Letters have both resulted in enhanced intelligence capabilities. In addition to the Counterterrorism Division, a new Foreign Terrorist Tracking Task Force was established to promote cooperation between other federal agencies, such as the Central Intelligence Agency (CIA), Immigration and Customs Enforcement (ICE), and the Department of Defense, as a new specialized FBI program dealing with terrorism intelligence.

Homeland Security

Following the events of September 11, the newly created Department of Homeland Security (DHS) was conceived to specify and coordinate counterterrorism efforts and to clearly stipulate dedicated agencies for each counterterrorism task. As a result, the former Immigration and Naturalization Service (INS) was divided into separate agencies serving both administrative and enforcement functions. US Citizenship and Immigration Services now handle all the administrative facets of immigration while the enforcement aspect is handled by two new agencies. The two new agencies divide their immigration responsibilities among Immigration and Customs Enforcement (ICE), specializing in investigation and enforcement and customs, and Customs and Border Protection (CBP), taking on all security responsibilities related to the US borders.

Given that all 19 hijackers involved in the 9/11 attacks entered the country legally (Shutt and Deflem, 2005), the concern over the security of the US immigration system after September 11 was palpable. Yet, continuing to allow the large numbers of legitimate immigrants and visitors entry into the US required immediate and expanded efforts to ferret out potential terrorists. As the primary investigative branch of DHS and the federal immigration enforcement branch, ICE is therefore responsible for the enforcement of immigration and customs laws in the United States.

With the center of operations in Washington, DC and as the largest DHS investigative force, ICE consists of several specialized branches, including intelligence, investigations, detention and removal, and international affairs. In addition to the 27 domestic offices, ICE also maintains 50 international field offices in 39 countries around the world. Each external detachment serves as an attaché, developing partnerships and assisting with the training of foreign affiliates. Since its inception in 2003, ICE has been involved in a very wide variety of international enforcement operations, including cases involving smuggling and illegal immigration. Also established in 2003 as a direct result of the Enhanced Border Security and Visa Reform Act of 2002 (Salter, 2004), the Student and Exchange Visitor Information System (SEVIS) is monitored by ICE. The system is used to supervise and approve foreign students in partnership with educational institutions.

Given its border-related objectives, ICE created Border Enforcement Security Task Forces in cooperation with several other law enforcement agencies. ICE also oversees the Law Enforcement Support Center, a cooperative operations facility that serves as the DHS's national point of contact for law enforcement agencies seeking immigration status and identification information on crimes of suspected, arrested, or convicted aliens. Finally, Project Shield America is an organization designed to 'prevent the export of sensitive US munitions and strategic technology to terrorists, criminal organizations, and foreign adversaries' (Deflem, 2010: 50).

With the principal assignment of border protection, Customs and Border Protection (CBP) comprises the US Customs Service, US Border Patrol, the INS, and the enforcement divisions of the Department of Agriculture. The agency's main focus is therefore on the protection from terrorists and on safeguarding lawful trade with and travel to the United States. With more than 500 million people visiting the United States each year, managing immigration and protecting the US borders is a formidable task. Consequently, the responsibility of CBP is divided into three functionally distinct divisions, including field operations, border patrol, and alien smuggling, and several specialized programs designed to accomplish its law numerous enforcement duties. With federal programs such as the Secure Borders Initiative and the Secure Fence Act of 2006, CBP strives to not only control the US border but also to promote temporary worker programs, strengthen interior enforcement and infrastructure while changing their traditional practice of 'catch and release' of non-Mexican illegal aliens, to redirecting the their efforts to temporary detention. There is also a heightened focus on controlling the cross-border trafficking of goods and humans by prospective terrorist and criminal organizations. With respect to interior enforcement, the investigation of illegal alien workers and consequent reprimanding for hiring, along with promoting legal temporary worker programs to reduce and gain control over illegal employment is targeted.

Shortly after the September 11 attacks, the Container Security Initiative (CSI) was implemented to detect potential risks of terrorism at foreign ports through the investigation and inspection of containers before cargo arrives in the United States (Shutt and Deflem, 2005). CBP and ICE officers in a partnership with 58 overseas port officials therefore monitor approximately 86 percent of all containers traveling to the United States from foreign ports. In addition, Canadian and Mexican border forces have partnered with CBP to create initiatives such as the Customs-Trade Partnership Against Terrorism (with 6,500 businesses involved) and a Canadian/US venture that targets cross-border terrorist activities the Integrated Border Enforcement Teams. CBP also serves as the executive agency for the Export Control and Related Border Security program in the prevention of the international distribution of nuclear, chemical, biological, and other weapons.

The Bureau of Diplomatic Security

Housed under the Department of the State, the Bureau of Diplomatic Security (DS) is the chief security and law enforcement arm that conducts investigations of immigration document fraud, technology security, protection of US interests abroad (including citizens, property and information) and international terrorism (Bayer, 2005; Deflem, 2010). DS also aids in the protection of US embassies, personnel stationed abroad, and a several other operations involving security and counterterrorism.

Beginning in the 1970s, the State Department's Office of Security reacted to the increasing terrorist threats against US citizens abroad by initiating an assessment of the threat level against US interests abroad and subsequently, advised US personnel who were based overseas. Since the inception of the Diplomatic Security Service branch in November of 1984, DS has continued to expand its security missions, especially abroad, making it the largest law enforcement force for the rendition of US fugitives from foreign countries. First acquiring its antiterrorism directive on the basis of the 1986 Omnibus Diplomatic Security and Antiterrorism Act and since 1992, DS has supervised the Rewards for Justice Program which offers monetary rewards to individuals that provide information deemed useful in solving acts of terrorism against the US and its assets.

In counterterrorism efforts, DS oversees the Antiterrorism Assistance Program, which trains foreign nationals in security affairs, and the Office of Investigations and Counterintelligence, which counters foreign intelligence acts against the Department of the State's operations abroad. Recent DS counterterrorism investigations have resulted in some high-profile successes, such as the capture of World Trade Center mastermind Ramzi Yousef through the Rewards for Justice Program. However, the success of the DS was tarnished with the resignation of agency head Richard Griffin in 2007, due to the then Secretary of State Condoleezza Rice's newly imposed measures in the management of private security contractors in Iraq. Rice's ruling came after the DS investigation into the killings of 17 Iraqi civilians was taken over by the FBI due to DS granting immunity waivers to Blackwater guards that were under criminal investigation. Since 2007, stricter rules require that all convoys and security activities of Blackwater be overseen by DS agents.

Counterterrorism policing across the globe

Like the United States, many other nations have also accelerated counterterrorism capacities among their respective police forces. However, not all nations respond to terrorism in like manner, as political and legal conditions differ, with all due consequences for the role of counterterrorism policing (Beckman, 2007; Deflem, 2008, 2010; Zimmerman and Wenger, 2007).

Global counterterrorism policy and law

At the political level, the governments of national states rely on a wide assortment of tools to counter the threat of terrorism as a matter of national security. These efforts range from a domestically organized coordination of counterterrorism activities and the organization of intelligence operations to diplomatic initiatives and military interventions. National governments have implemented various measures and established specialized institutions that seek to organize and streamline various counterterrorism functions. In order to ensure a proper coordination of counterterrorism and related security policies, several nations have since 9/11 developed new specialized branches of government. Mirroring the Department of Homeland Security in the United States, for instance, is Public Safety Canada. Other nations seek to streamline their various counterterrorism activities through existing departments, such as the Counterterrorism Strategy in the British Home Office.

Intelligence activities against terrorism are enacted by national governments both at home as well as abroad. In some nations (such as in the United Kingdom and France), domestic intelligence services exist next to foreign intelligence agencies, whereas in other nations (such as in the United States) domestic intelligence functions are not assigned to a specialized agency but part of broader law enforcement or intelligence functions.

At the military level, states also engage in armed interventions against terrorist targets, either by direct strikes against certain terrorist groups and their facilities or by subversive activities, such as by means of espionage and sabotage, to undermine the potential or reality of terrorism taking hold in certain areas or among certain groups. The US-led invasion of Afghanistan in 2001 is the most critical example of such a military strategy based on considerations of counterterrorism.

Through international diplomacy, governments seek to attain counterterrorism objectives by the peaceful means of negotiation. These efforts are coordinated through various government representatives of national states (ambassadors, ministers of foreign affairs) and through meetings and conventions organized by international governing bodies, such as the European Union and the United Nations.

From a legal viewpoint, it can be noted that many nations have developed laws that seek to specifically prevent and respond to terrorism. Many of the implications of such laws extend their reach across the boundaries of the jurisdictions in which they are passed to also control extra-national developments. Among the examples are laws concerning migration, asylum, border control, and international terrorism. Some countries have a long history of specialized counterterrorism laws (i.e., Syria, Egypt, Spain, and Turkey), while others, such as Canada and the Netherlands have a much shorter record that has only recently been modified. The Netherlands, by example, was among the European nations that historically had virtually no experience with terrorism and therefore had not established any significant counterterrorism strategies. It was not until the 9/11 attacks that the Dutch government implemented the 'Action Plan on Counterterrorism and Security' which provoked a strengthening of border-control activities by the Dutch Royal Military Constabulary. In contrast to the Dutch experience, other nations, such as Spain and Israel, have a long history with terrorism. In Israel, counterterrorism is dominated by the conflicts with the country's surrounding Arab nations and are controlled by a strongly interconnected system of police, intelligence, and military. In Spain, the central terrorism concern is locally dominated by the Basque separatist group ETA, which from 1959 until at least 2003 has engaged in violent protests that caused hundreds of fatalities. Interestingly, the 9/11 attacks led Spain to further enhance its terrorism legislation, while the railway bombings in Madrid on March 11, 2004 did not lead to any additional legislative measures.

Global counterterrorism policing

Historically, the policing of international terrorism across the world can be traced back to developments in nineteenth-century Europe whereby the governments of autocratic states directed police institutions to track down the international movement of political opponents, including social democrats and anarchists (Deflem, 2002). From these early political efforts gradually developed cooperative efforts to focus on non-political criminal violations, which have remained in existence, albeit in refashioned and considerably expanded form, until this day. Although vast political differences between countries practicing liberal democratic, mixed, or autocratic rule exist, certain aspects of counterterrorism do not differ greatly among many customarily dissimilar countries. This isomorphism can be attributed to the fact that in the implementation of counterterrorism policies and laws, similar law enforcement and security strategies are manifested. Despite the existence of global trends in counterterrorism policing, there are also variations in the application of national counterterrorism policies by each of the individual country's police agencies (Deflem, 2010).

In most Western democracies, concerns over civil liberties and personal freedoms influence the appropriate framework for counterterrorism police practices. These counterterrorism practices, as they exist in countries such as the United States, France, Spain, and the United Kingdom, are in stark contrast with the oppressive and uncompromising counterterrorism principles of non-democratic governments, such as Russia, Turkey, and many of the Arab states. Therefore, in battling the war on terror, the method of implementation that each individual police and security agency utilizes, functions differently and is accordingly shaped by each country's unique political and legal objectives.

Depending on the nature of a nation's political system, the level of bureaucratization of its police agencies will influence counterterrorism policing practices, ranging from highly politicized and militaristic to more autonomously driven by a criminal-justice orientation. Western democratic counterterrorism policing approaches and goals are generally in line with bureaucratized institutions. Typical for continental Europe, by example, Spain's National Police Force (*Grupos Especiales de Operaciones*) and Guardia Civil (*Undades Antiterroristas Rurales*) serve as the primary special counterterrorism forces. But other countries are greatly influenced and regulated by political mandates (i.e., in Russia, Turkey, and some Arab countries), where the head of state dictates counterterrorism practices which are often used as a tool of political repression. In highly centralized and autocratic regimes, counterterrorism is much more integrated throughout the military, intelligence, and police agencies. In Russia, most notably, counterterrorism practices are extremely repressive, and policing and security operations are controlled top-down in a highly politicized and centralized structure.

As to the organization of policing, an additional difference exists in the relation between intelligence and law enforcement, where a divergence exists in both function and organization. Variance in intelligence and law enforcement function takes place both amid democratic states as well as between different types of regimes, i.e., between democratic and autocratic governments. Some nations even place counterterrorism functions under the supervision of military intelligence, due to its national security implications. Irrespective of a country's designated configuration, separating domestic intelligence entirely allows intelligence and law enforcement duties to have much more well-defined boundaries. However, due to the methods needed to combat terrorism, both components must also work in concert whether or not they are housed in separate agencies.

International police organizations

At least since the early twentieth century, police agencies across the world have collaborated with one another in the form of international organizations. While *ad hoc* cooperation efforts occur in the case of specific investigations on a need basis, such organizations provide a permanent structure to foster cooperation in police matters. Again the events of September 11 are to be noted for having accelerated these collaboration efforts. At least two organizations deserve special attention: the International Criminal Police Organization (Interpol), which seeks to provide police cooperation on a global scale; and the European Police Office (Europol), which has been established in the European Union.

Interpol

Rather than being an international police force with investigative responsibilities, Interpol has continually, since its formation in 1923 as the International Criminal Police Commission, been conceived as a collaborative organization that supports international assistance in law enforcement functions amongst police agencies (Anderson, 1997; Deflem, 2002). Through its central headquarters in Lyon, France, Interpol's participating agencies are linked together through specialized units in each country, called National Central Bureaus (NCBs).

The primary method of communication between the NCBs and the central office is via a color-coded notification system, using six colors that represent specific requests. There are two frequent requests: Red Notices, signifying the request of a wanted person's arrest with a view towards extradition, and Blue Notices, which are requests to seek information about a person's identity or illegal activities related to a crime. In 2005, the addition of an Interpol–United Nations Special Notice was implemented to handle requests concerning groups or individuals that were subject to United Nations sanctions against both al-Qaeda and the Taliban. A 1996 agreement also granted Interpol and the United Nations observer status in sessions of their corresponding assemblies, thus allowing the organizations to collaborate on the Special Notice program. Similarly, Interpol has formed cooperative arrangements with other agencies, such as Europol and the International Criminal Court.

Interpol has passed several counterterrorism resolutions in order to effectively combat terrorism and terrorism related issues. In 1985, a resolution was designed to both enhance and coordinate the fight against international terrorism, the initiative led to the creation of the sub-directorate Public Safety and Terrorism. In the 1990s, the rise of terrorism resulted in the 1998 'Declaration Against Terrorism' that was reached at the General Assembly meeting in Egypt, which further solidified Interpol's pledge to combating international terrorism.

The 9/11 attacks influenced Interpol to make significant changes to its existing counterterrorism operations, both as a matter of policy and with respect to the organization's structure. Shortly after September 11, the Interpol General Assembly in Budapest, Hungary, drafted Resolution AG-2001-RES-05 which condemned the attacks as 'murderous attacks against the world's citizens' and 'an abhorrent violation of law and of the standards of human decency . . . a crime against humanity' (Interpol, 2001). As a result, it was decided that in order for Interpol and its affiliates to more effectively deal with terrorism and organized crime, priority would be given to Red Notices for terrorists connected to the attacks.

To enhance Interpol's counterterrorism efforts, specialized programs have been established, specifically an Incident Response Team, providing member agencies with investigative and analytical support, and a Fusion Task Force, established in 2002 to assist in identifying members, gathering intelligence, and providing analytical support on terrorists. Given that the finances and funds available to terrorist organizations often dictates the rate and magnitude of terrorist attacks, special attention is given to the financing of terrorist activities. Since 2005, Interpol also began to direct more attention to internet usage by terrorist groups and individuals, encouraging more cooperation in international police investigations on terrorism-related websites and by 2006, encouraging a similar emphasis on increased police cooperation on al-Qaeda groups and individuals motivated by Al-Qaeda at the international level.

After the September 11 attacks, many of Interpol's members were involved in the global investigations that ensued. Interpol and member agencies responded to the strikes through its international communication networks and by posting Red Notices on the organization's website, which would ensure the widest possible distribution. Immediately after the September 11 attacks, 55 Red Notices for suspects thought to be involved in the strikes were disseminated by Interpol. Blue Notices were also circulated, concerning the 19 hijackers that executed the attacks. Following the creation of a '11 September Task Force' at Interpol's headquarters, several other post-9/11 organizational changes have been made, including the creation of a permanent General Secretariat Command and Coordination Center and the establishment of an encrypted internet-based communications system called I-24/7.

Europol

The nations of Europe have long been involved in the organization of international police efforts to control terrorism (Bures, 2008; Deflem, 2010). As early as 1975, Terrorism, Radicalism, Extremism, and International Violence group (or the TREVI group) was formed as a partnership of several European police agencies, promoting the exchange of information and support in terrorism and associated international crimes. Other European police agency partnerships that provided assistance in terrorism investigations included the Police Working Group on Terrorism and the Counter Terrorist Group (or 'Club of Berne').

Europol is an international association of police organizations, mandated and regulated by the European Union, to coordinate existing EU member-state police and security agencies in matters of serious international crime, including terrorism. Although initiated as part of the political union of the EU, Europol employs a criminal-justice model with efficiency in policing and counterterrorism as the central objective. Europol's primary task in crime fighting, therefore, is to facilitate the rapid communication and information exchange among participating agencies. Despite the diversity among member states' legal systems, Europol and its cooperatives are able to come to a consensus on the scope of terrorism-related activities (Tak, 2000). Especially since 9/11, Europol and its participating agencies have thus been able to establish cooperation on the basis of a shared understanding of terrorism across European and other international police.

The attacks on September 11 aided in prompting Europol into creating new counterterrorism programs. The Counterterrorism Task Force (also briefly known as the Task Force Terrorism), a specialized counterterrorism unit, was set up at Europol's headquarters shortly after the 9/11 strikes. A year later, Europol incorporated the Task Force into the Serious Crimes Department. However, after the Madrid terrorist bombings on March 11, 2004, the unit regained its status as an independent entity. More recently, it has yet again been reassigned as the Counter Terrorism Unit, housed under Europol's Serious Crime Department.

The 9/11 attacks had a profound effect on the EU's formal counterterrorism policy. Some of the most important policy changes include the framework decisions on terrorism, confirmed in June 2002 by the Council of the European Union, and involving such issues as joint investigation teams and mutual legal assistance. In its framework decisions, the Council defines offenses by terrorists as 'criminal activities, or the threat to commit them, aimed at seriously intimidating a population, unduly compelling a government or international organization from performing or abstaining from any act, and/or seriously destabilizing or destroying the fundamental structures of a country or of an international organization' (Deflem, 2010: 131). Further, the EU framework decisions require member states to improve cooperative counterterrorism unit's efforts in police matters. As a result, two or more member states can organize security forces as a joint investigation team for a specific purpose and limited time, providing that the leader of the team is native to one of the EU countries and that the team abides by the prevailing law of the member state concerned. To this end, the direct handing over of wanted persons under judicial authority between EU member states can be accomplished through the new European Arrest Warrant initiative. Another one of the EU's 2002 framework decisions was to expand the counterterrorism mandates of Europol and the related cooperative activities.

Thus, Europol was granted approval to formally maintain relationships with agencies (especially Interpol) and police and security forces in non-EU countries, such as Canada, the United States, and Russia.

The criminological relevance of counterterrorism policing

Reviewing the most important patterns of the policing of international terrorism in the post-9/11 era, certain trends emerge that raise important questions for the criminological study of relevant developments related to globalization and terrorism. At least two issues are of note: first, the bureaucratization of policing is unevenly accomplished across the globe and has, even in democratic regimes, been confronted with renewed attempts of politicization; and, second, there are distinct trends to be noted of a globalization of counterterrorism policing because of the impact of the momentous events of September 11, 2001.

The possibility of a renewed politicization of law enforcement is more than real during times of social upheaval, such as the terrorist attacks of September 11. In the United States, in particular, the creation of the Department of Homeland Security and the passage of the USA PATRIOT Act were distinct politically directed attempts to manage the policing of counterterrorism and to lead the law enforcement community to accept and comply with the political goals associated with the fight against terrorism. Yet, the PATRIOT Act and related policies can also be observed to have reaffirmed the role of law enforcement in counterterrorism activities, rather than transfer those functions to the military or intelligence communities. The FBI has retained and expanded its lead-agency status in counterterrorism activities, while law enforcement roles have also increased for other federal agencies, such as ICE, CBP, and DS. Counterterrorism police agencies have also added a distinct intelligence component to their mission and they rely heavily on technology and advanced communication systems to achieve its intelligence and investigative tasks. The objectives of counterterrorism are thereby defined in distinctly criminal terms (terrorism as crime) rather than as matters of national security (counterterrorism as war).

Related to the emphasis on efficiency, interagency partnerships and cooperation through an efficient system of information exchange are essential components of counterterrorism. Given the extra-jurisdictional demands of international counterterrorism policing, US federal law enforcement agencies are better able to fulfill organizational tasks by operating unilaterally, thus leading to those agencies in a better position, in terms of technology, personnel, and budget, to carry out counterterrorism efforts independently. The prevalence of federal agencies operating unilaterally is accomplished through foreign field offices, the so-called legal attaché (legat) offices, which have permanent agents from federal US law enforcement stationed abroad. Besides such unilaterally enacted international mechanisms, collaborative counterterrorism initiatives are typically limited in scope, restricted to organizations in close proximity (in both location and function), employed only for the duration of an investigation, and limited in the number or participating agencies. Therefore, close functional proximity as opposed to remote operations are preferred, as are bilateral as opposed to multilateral operations. These operational norms aid in explaining US federal agencies' cooperation and need for permanent foreign attachés, functioning as locales and typically forming bilateral partnerships. Counterterrorism activities abroad are similarly conducted, with proximity as a chief consideration among police organizations. Generally, US federal law enforcement cooperatives operate directly with international police agencies, through personal contacts or local attachés. It is crucial that international partnerships operate irrespective of the political, legal, and ideological outlooks of the participating organizations. As participating police agencies are motivated to appreciate the nature of crime and crime control, national boundaries are therefore transcended in favor of operational efficiency.

Due to their comparative strength, both the course and agenda of international counterterrorism operations are greatly influenced by US federal law enforcement agencies, though formally all partners in cooperation are considered to be equal. For example, in border and migration issues, the responsibilities of US agencies ICE and CBP vastly exceed the contributions from Canadian and, even more so, Mexican counterparts. Further contributing to the dissemination of American counterterrorism policing ideas and techniques on an international scale, are the training programs that are organized by US federal agencies. In addition, an 'Americanization' of law enforcement and counterterrorism will occur when and that to the extent that more attention is devoted to terrorism issues that concern the US law enforcement community (Nadelmann, 1993). Generally, with a preference for unilateral and bilateral cooperatives in counterterrorism and other international police functions, US federal law enforcement agencies are less willing to take advantage of multilateral cooperation efforts such as Interpol.

As in the United States, many nations across the world have stepped up their counterterrorism efforts, including those initiated by police agencies, albeit it in sometimes different ways. Yet, even with the considerable differences that exist in the configuration of different countries' approaches to counterterrorism, it is also to be noted that the September 11 attacks induced a near-global increase in international cooperation as well as an upgrade in political, legislative, and police efforts in the global fight against terrorism. In fact, most nations of the world have approved new counterterrorism policies and statutes or, at a minimum, adjusted existing laws following the events of 9/11. Countries also reorganized counterterrorism police practices by expanding their police agencies' investigative powers in terrorism-related cases and making counterterrorism a priority in their law enforcement and security organizations. Also uniting many countries in the war on terrorism is the shift in focus toward jihadist extremism, including several largely Muslim countries in the Middle East. Consequently, there exists a global counterterrorism network that comprises many nations as an international constellation.

Changes that have been made to counterterrorism legislation can be observed to be dependent upon each individual country's historical experiences with terrorism, which in turn determines the degree to which counterterrorism measures are implemented. However, even as countries such as Spain and the United Kingdom have had their own high-profile terrorist attacks (in 2004 and 2005, respectively), it was nonetheless September 11 that had global ramifications and served as the most influential factor in shaping many nations' counterterrorism responses.

In counterterrorism policing activities, collaboration and information exchange are vital, both intra-nationally and internationally. Within nations, cooperation includes efforts between intelligence and police organizations and associated policy and legal institutions. With coordinating institutions existing at both the governmental and inter-agency levels, synchronizing cooperative counterterrorism activities are again dependent on the degree of centrality various national governments maintain as well as the extent to which they are democratically organized.

Although several levels of cooperation are enacted to foster international counterterrorism, any attempts to create a truly global and unified administration of counterterrorism have not been successful. Even with the drafting of international counterterrorism policies by the United Nations, a shift towards standardizing international counterterrorism laws and regulating counterterrorism police activities has also not materialized. As international counterterrorism policing efforts are based upon the establishment of relevant strategies that are drafted independently by law enforcement, any formal international regulations will remain inconsequential to the global police community.

Conclusion

There is no doubt that the September 11 terrorist attacks have greatly altered counterterrorism measures throughout the world. Regardless of political, legal, cultural, and other societal characteristics that mark the world's nations, terrorism has thereby served as a powerful catalyst to strengthen and expand counterterrorist strategies in many nations. International plans and operations in matters of counterterrorism can be observed to take place at multiple institutional levels and in a variety of forms. Among the primary institutions engaged in counterterrorism are political bodies, legal instruments, and police agencies. The forms of counterterrorism cooperation range from unilaterally enacted international initiatives to bilateral and broader multilateral collaborative efforts. It is a sign of our present era of globalization that all forms of international counterterrorism cooperation have expanded at all institutional levels.

Yet, while recent events concerning the global and local terrorism threat have implied that counterterrorism efforts have stepped up at all levels, it should not be concluded that such developments are undertaken effortlessly and without discord. In fact, counterterrorism measures consist of a multitude of practices and institutions that are often not in tune with one another. There is presently no harmonization or standardization of structures and practices across the various institutional domains and the forms that are involved. At the political level, cooperation may exist only as an expression of goodwill while ideological divisive sentiments over the causes and patterns of terrorism preclude effective cooperation. Yet, the police agencies of countries across the world, even when these countries are politically hostile to one another, can often cooperate more smoothly on the basis of a common professional understanding of terrorism as a crime. This professional police understanding of terrorism enables international activities by police agencies from across a variety of nations and additionally affects international organizations of police, such as Interpol and Europol.

The organization of counterterrorism by police institutions does not harmonize well with other counterterrorism efforts, especially those that are tightly related, politically, legally and military, to the war on terror. Contradictions in counterterrorism are thereby most distinctly revealed in the duality of terrorism at the military and policing levels. For whereas military operations target terrorists and terrorist groups as enemies, police activities center on the targets of their investigations as criminal suspects. Factually co-existing in the world of counterterrorism cooperation, then, are the disparate structures and processes of multiple counterterrorism models in the worlds of politics, law, and policing. It is the distinct province of criminological research to analyze the unique contribution of police agencies in counterterrorism relative to the efforts undertaken by other institutions, both at the national and international level.

References

Anderson, M. (1997) Interpol and the developing system of international police cooperation. In: W.F. McDonald (ed.) *Crime and Law Enforcement in the Global Village.* Cincinnati, OH: Anderson.

Bayer, M. (2005) Operation global pursuit: In pursuit of the world's most dangerous fugitives and terrorists. *The Police Chief, 72,* 32–37.

Beckman, J. (2007) *Comparative Legal Approaches to Homeland Security and Antiterrorism.* Aldershot: Ashgate.

Bures, O. (2008) Europol's fledgling counterterrorism role. *Terrorism and Political Violence, 20,* 498–517.

Deflem, M. (2002) *Policing World Society: Historical Foundations of International Police Cooperation.* Oxford: Oxford University Press.

Deflem, M. (2004) The boundaries of international cooperation: Problems and prospects of US–Mexican police relations. In: M. Amir and S. Einstein (eds) *Police Corruption: Challenges for Developed Countries.* Huntsville, TX: Office of International Criminal Justice.

Deflem, M. (2008) Terrorism: Counterterrorism approaches. In: V.N. Parrillo (ed.) *Encyclopedia of Social Problems.* Thousand Oaks, CA: Sage.

Deflem, M. (2010) *The Policing of Terrorism: Organizational and Global Perspectives.* New York: Routledge.

IGnet (2002) *The Attorney General's Guidelines for Domestic FBI Operations.* Available on line: http://www.ignet.gov/pande/standards/prgexhibitg1.pdf.

Interpol (2001) *September 11, 2001: Attack on America* (26 September 2001.) Available on line: http://www.interpol.int/Public/ICPO/GeneralAssembly/AGN70/Resolutions/ AGN70RES5.asp.

Nadelmann, E. A. (1993) *Cops across Borders: The Internationalization of US Criminal Law Enforcement.* University Park, PA: Pennsylvania State University Press.

Salter, M. B. (2004) Passports, mobility, and security: How smart can the border be? *International Studies Perspectives, 5,* 71–91.

Shutt, J.E. and Deflem, M. (2005) Whose face at the border? Homeland security and border policing since 9/11. *Journal of Social and Ecological Boundaries*, *1*, 81–105.

Tak, P.J.P. (2000) Bottlenecks in international police and judicial cooperation in the EU. *European Journal of Crime Criminal Law and Criminal Justice*, *8*, 343–360.

Zimmermann, D. and A. Wenger (eds) (2007) *How States Fight Terrorism: Policy Dynamics in the West*. Boulder, CO: Lynne Rienner.

6 Policing in peace operations

Change and challenge

B.K. Greener

Policing has become an integral part of contemporary peace operations. This is due, in no small part, to the various consequences of globalisation. The rise of the global human rights agenda, the growth of the Cable Network News (CNN) effect, the consolidation of hegemonic liberal peacebuilding norms, changing conceptions of international security and the demand that governments 'do something' in the face of post-Cold War famines, wars and disasters are all consequences of a more globalised world. These developments have in turn impacted upon demands for the increased use of police as well as military personnel in international roles.

This chapter outlines recent developments with respect to the increasing use of police in the particular practices of peacekeeping and peacebuilding before focusing on critiques and analysis of both the underlying philosophy and the practical implications of these changes. This involves an investigation of the concern that international policing is a form of imperial policing, an assessment of the rise of police as part of the broader liberal peacebuilding project, as well as a consideration of the salience of the practices that have been pursued in post-conflict settings. This chapter asserts that international policing is in a dynamic phase at the present time, presenting a number of significant opportunities and risks for the international community. Important choices are currently being made as to sites of ownership and control, the suitability of models used, the personnel recruited, and the desirable shape of relations between police and other agencies – choices that will have significant impact upon the international policing agenda for years to come.

Policing peace in contemporary times

Since the end of the Cold War, policing has become an integral part of peace operations (Ban Ki-Moon in United Nations Department of Peacekeeping Operations (UNDPKO), 2011) in contributing to internal security and the rule of law that are deemed to be 'the cement which holds the bricks of peace operations together' (McNamara cited in Fullilove, 2006: 2). UN, regional and bilateral policing initiatives have become increasingly complex arrangements as the need for the restoration of law and order has come to be seen as vitally important for post-conflict peacekeeping, peace enforcement and peacebuilding (Greener, 2009a). Cold War models of policing in peacekeeping operations focused on the elements of Support, Monitoring, Advising, Reporting and Training; reflecting the traditional norms of neutrality and consent-based operations undertaken in situations where peace had already been achieved The development of the possibilities of peace enforcement in the early 1990s, which as the moniker suggests requires more forceful intervention, and a more recent focus on peacebuilding (which seeks to prevent post-conflict populations from returning to conflict) have pushed contemporary policing efforts into a wider range of roles.

The range of policing roles in peace operations can be divided up into stability-type tasks versus capacity building-type tasks. Under the first category, police personnel deployed to peace missions may potentially undertake more 'active' roles in the earlier phases of an operation when an executive policing mandate allows external police the power of arrest in circumstances where local law and order has broken down. Such roles can be sited within a robust peacekeeping or peace enforcement frame. With regards to the second category, alternative and less obviously interventionist roles can occur either in later or more permissive stages in a mission. These may involve external police in roles such as monitoring, training, mentoring, capacity building or programmes to 'reform, rebuild, and restructure' existing police capabilities (Greener, 2009b) and relate to longer-term peacebuilding efforts.

Recent peace operations have therefore witnessed police undertaking a wide range of roles. To use Timor Leste as an example, UN police have been involved in a variety of tasks under different mandates as the missions to Timor evolved. Under the United Nations Mission in East Timor (UNAMET) in 1999, UN Civilian Police (known as CIVPOL) were sent to Timor to advise the Indonesian police and supervise the movements of ballot boxes and papers during the referendum for independence, whilst responsibility for security remained with the Indonesian Government. Under the United Nations Security Council (UNSC) Resolution 1272, however, the policing aspect of the UN mandate expanded UN Civilian Police (later known as UNPOL or UN Police) tasks significantly. Those CIVPOL deployed to the United Nations Transitional Administration in East Timor (UNTAET) in late 1999 were therefore tasked with helping to provide security and maintain law and order through the provision of executive policing, where they were explicitly provided with powers of arrest, as well as being tasked with helping in the development of the nascent Policia National Timor Leste (PNTL). The civilian police component was significant in size at around 1,500-strong, and this notion of facilitating and supporting indigenous 'police development' was intended to be a major part both of UNTAET and its follow-on mission UNMISET (United Nations Mission of Support in East Timor).

However, both of these missions were criticised for being ineffective – especially in the area of 'police development'. This was in part due to a lack of engagement with local agencies and local priorities, but was arguably also due to a lack of specificity in the UN mandate as to what this task actually entailed and a lack of preparation for this task. As Martin and Mayer-Rieckh (2005) argue, the security aspect of UNTAET in particular has been described as a peacekeeping-rather than peacebuilding-driven model. This was evident in the fact that, despite 'police development' being intended to be a major part of UNTAET and UNMISET, in the former none of the 1,270 officers was recruited to be trainers or institution-building experts, whilst in UNMISET too, none of the 150 police advisors had development or capacity building expertise (Hood, 2006: 146, 149). It wasn't until the establishment of the United Nations Mission in Timor (UNMIT) in mid-2006 following a major breakdown in law and order and fighting between and within different parts of the security sector in Timor Leste that a more explicit focus on police reform as part of broader peacebuilding efforts came into being. Yet, as a number of commentators have suggested, by this point in time relations between local police and the UN policing contingent had become somewhat soured, and since 2006 the international policing effort has still been categorised by a number of commentators as being somewhat patchy in terms of positive effects and the type of interaction ongoing with local actors (Wilson, 2008; ICG, 2009; Lemay-Hebert, 2009). Relations between UNPOL and PNTL (with the exception of some individual working relationships) typically remain cool today, despite more focused attempts to implement various joint development plans.

As the Timor case intimates there have been a number of concerns raised about the rise of the international policing agenda. The Timor case demonstrates the salience of concerns about how police personnel from outside a jurisdiction could possibly hope to successfully 'police' or 'reform' a local police service in an area that they are not connected to nor necessarily very familiar with. The success of international efforts both depend on whether or not there is any local appetite for such policing and reform efforts (Baker, 2009: 329). And it also depends on whether or not there is any global appetite or ability to press on with broader reforms that may impact significantly on the political and social situation at hand. After all, the 2006 crisis in Timor Leste may have been, at least in part, caused by the initiation of a process that did not go far enough in depoliticising the security sector as a whole. Similar problems arose out of the fact that the broader relationship between the policing and justice sectors was not prioritised. For example, in the early missions, even if CIVPOL successfully arrested suspects, there were often too many delays or problems with the court and corrections systems to be able to capitalise on good police work as not enough planning and preparation had gone into considering the critical relationship between these co-dependent sectors.

In addition to difficulties met in matching external and local interests and demands, other problems with such policing efforts so far relate to the quantity and quality of the policing provided. There are never enough civilian police available to deploy on international operations in a timely fashion. Numbers of UNPOL personnel have increased exponentially since UN missions during the Cold War peaked at around 1,500 for the Namibia deployment in 1989. The UN now typically requires at least 14,000 police personnel to be deployed annually. A number of national governments and regional institutions have created specialised policing deployment pools or groups in response to the demand for international policing capabilities, but there are still difficulties in deploying enough civilian police to post-conflict settings. In Africa, in 2009, for example, the UNSC had authorised the use of 6,400 police for the UN Assistance Mission in Darfur (UNAMID) but were only able to deploy 3000 whilst only 600 of the 1,400 were deployed for the UN Mission in the Congo (MONUC) (Williams, 2009). The issue of getting enough police on the ground, particularly within short time frames, continues to bedevil the planners of peace missions as such police are typically already being utilised in a domestic setting.

However, concerns over quantity are almost overshadowed by concerns over the quality of police deployed. Problems with a lack of cultural sensitivity and language barriers are significant and add to fundamental issues caused by some personnel lacking basic policing skill sets (Peake, 2009; Linden *et al.,* 2007). Police operating overseas may also both be getting paid very well whilst at the same time feeling less ethical constraints and being less accountable to oversight mechanisms as they are not 'securely grounded in "local" and/or "national" accountability structures' (Sheptycki, 2007: 41). There have been a number of problems with charges of abuse of office, unwillingness to carry out policing tasks or corrupt, immoral or illegal behaviour being reported. For example, in Kosovo a number of UN police were arrested for taking part in a human trafficking ring in 2005, and an Amnesty International report demonstrated that international personnel made up about 20 per cent of sex-trafficking customers, although its members comprised only 2 per cent of Kosovo's population (Amnesty International cited in Krasniqi, 2005). In light of these concerns over quality control, efforts are underway to try to standardise training and improve policing standards through the UN system (Rotmann, 2009), or to create and 'craft' transnational and international policing efforts (Goldsmith and Sheptycki, 2007) in addition to strengthening accountability controls over personnel in country to help offset such critique. However, there are broader concerns at play over the international policing project itself as internal and external security agendas merge (Hardt and Negri, 2000).

The politics of the policing of peace operations: risk, imperial policing and consent

A number of authors have recently questioned the relevance, utility and agenda of contemporary international peacekeeping and peacebuilding efforts. At the level of the governance of peace operations, Cunliffe (2009), for example, has recently expressed serious concern about the politics of UN peacekeeping as a whole, stressing that it leaves the weakest members of the international community dealing with the most risk whilst wealthier developed countries retain power over decision-making processes. Cunliffe's work has salience for the study of international policing given the changing profiles of those providing boots on the ground for peace operations in both military and policing terms. Police Contributing Countries (PCCs) are predominantly from the south. UNPOL figures show that the top ten PCCs for 2010 were, in respective order: Bangladesh, Jordan, Pakistan, India, Nepal, Nigeria, Senegal, Ghana, Egypt and the Philippines (UN Police Division, 2011). Significantly, this constitutes a major change from the list of top PCCs for 2000 which included a number of Western countries such as: United States (1), Germany (4), United Kingdom (7), Portugal (9) and Spain (10) (Carpenter, 2010). There are no official reasons to explain why this development has occurred. However, we could speculate on the desire for international status or perhaps consider the rise of the importance of UN missions for remittances in poorer countries as potential reasons for why these figures appear. Importantly, such figures also lend some credence to charges as to risks being borne more by certain members of the international community and not others. Such changes may also be due to the reticence of wealthier countries to contribute to UN operations.

On a different note, and perhaps in slight contradiction to the figures that demonstrate where such police personnel come from, Rubenstein (2010) has asserted that UN peacekeeping writ large has become a form of imperial policing, moving away from the centrality of consent and placing concerns of international actors ahead of those of local communities. However, the apparent contradiction here might also be explained by an agenda that is set by the powerful but that is carried out by others who bear the risk of maintaining that agenda. This term 'imperial policing' may be a somewhat confusing use of the term in the context of this particular chapter which focuses on police personnel carrying out typical policing tasks, but it serves to highlight a relevant concern that actual international *policing* efforts, as significant and increasingly fundamental parts of wider efforts to try to achieve peace and stability through peacekeeping, may lack a level of legitimacy and consent that is normally required for policing in democratic states. This is because there are disconnects between the local context (where consent is typically embedded for police) and the international (where international police may potentially lack some levels of accountability themselves or where their *tasks* in the pursuit of political and social change may lack local support).

For example, policing in the Anglo-Peelian tradition is very much based on the notion of consent. As noted by Mather, the idea in the development of policing in England was that 'modern police principles recognize that the power of police depends upon public approval of their existence, actions and behaviour, and their ability to win respect' (1959: 123–4). Reith further asserted that the English police were based on 'principles, methods, and constitution make it impossible for them to oppose the will of the people, and to enforce laws in the face of sustained public refusal to observe them' (1943: 10). Populations have to accept the role of state representatives in the policing of their community, or at least a certain critical mass must do so in order for this to constitute policing rather than more oppressive forms of control. Policing in the continental tradition has admittedly typically been concerned more with policing from above, with *gendarmerie* and the like being used more like colonial enforcers, flying the flag for the state and with a more military-like approach (Emsley, 1993: 84, 87), but the growth of democratic principles over time has tempered this colonising role, and contemporary policing guidelines in developed democratic states emphasise the importance of democratic policing models.

Police in democratic societies ideally must give top priority to individual citizens and private groups; are accountable to the law rather than the government; protect human rights; and are transparent in their activities (Bayley, 2001: 13–15). The OSCE's *Guidebook on Democratic Policing* further emphasises that the objectives of democratic policing define police duties as: maintaining 'public tranquillity and law and order'; protecting and respecting 'the individual's rights and freedoms'; the prevention and combating of crime and the provision of 'assistance and services to the public' and where police are 'responsive to public needs and expectations' and 'use the authority of the State in the people's interest' (2008: 12). The overall goal of democratic policing is to build a web of relationships between police and the local community to help the police control crime and to incline citizens to trust and cooperate with their local police force (Wiatrowski and Goldstone, 2010: 80).

The ability of international policing agendas to spread democratic policing ideals has been questioned due to problems with: police corruption and the adverse consequences of folding in prior security agents into the new police forces being created; the overwhelming drive to get enough numbers; a lack of a sufficient division of labour between security agencies; and, importantly, the lack of international police that are able to 'follow and teach the principles of democracy-friendly policing' (Wiatrowski and Goldstone, 2010: 82).

Perhaps even more fundamentally, the achievement of key values such as 'responsiveness' and 'participation' in policing is difficult in an international policing context where foreigners are given policing powers, and those international policing efforts will be perceived as having different levels of consent depending upon the local situation. In Timor Leste, for example, it is difficult to assert that UNPOL personnel still have the strong support of the PNTL and the local population. There is a real concern too that despite the democratic policing agenda, external actors can (often inadvertently) act to impose a process that lacks resonance for the local population. International policing efforts that involve actually policing a country by way of executive action are particularly problematic when it comes to understanding whether or not enough levels of consent remain. In addition to the alienating effects of the policing of another's territory with police who may not be sensitive to context, another reason for a loss of consent typically relates to the fact that there has been a lack of institutional 'fit' in terms of the longer-term efforts made in the peacebuilding rather than peacekeeping field.

Models of policing in peace operations: international agendas and local realities

Related to the above concerns about the quality of policing and the governance of policing efforts, a recurring criticism of recent international policing efforts have centred on the lack of cultural 'fit' of policing models advocated. For example, the Regional Assistance Mission to Solomon Islands (RAMSI) was and is a wide-ranging mission predominantly established to restore law and order. As per the legal arrangement made with the Solomon Islands government, Participating Police Force (PPF) officers were legally empowered with executive authority, able to arrest and detain people within the jurisdiction of the Solomon Islands. Formal efforts to undertake more centralised policing and to reinstate law and order therefore were, and are, key to the RAMSI effort. Less than 100 minutes after the first RAMSI contingents arrived in country on 24 July 2003 joint Royal Solomon Islands Police (RSIP) and RAMSI PPF foot patrols were on the street, and by day 100 of the operation there were 16 police posts operational across all nine provinces of Solomon Islands (McDevitt, 2006: 8–10). In the first year 3,390 arrests were made, 4,900 criminal charges were laid, and over 400 police officers removed from the RSIP (McDevitt, 2006: 15–16). A number of evaluations of the mission, then, have argued that the first phase of the mission to restore law and order in the country was successful (Glenn, 2007; Fullilove, 2006).

However, a number of other writers have commented on the shortfalls of these formal policing endeavours in this particular context. Here, for instance, Matthew Allen (2006: 197) argues that relationships are vital to building levels of trust in the Solomon Islands and that the PPF's deliberate isolation from the community was inimical to the process of interaction. Later critiques focused on the PPF's emphasis on 'professional practice', whereby the placement of outsiders in leadership positions and the management approach used risked undermining the institutions the PPF wanted to build (Dinnen *et al.*, 2006: 98).

In addition to these criticisms of the PPF's formal policing efforts, it was clear that 'non-official' sites of policing authority existed alongside the PPF and the newly reformed RSIP. For example, previous experiences of policing in Solomon Islands demonstrated that, as almost 85 per cent of the population is based in rural areas where community-based approaches are typically the main option for addressing problems, 'formal police did not conduct much of the 'policing' or conflict resolution that was of relevance to citizens', and that in many areas, chiefs, elders and other community-based mechanisms with no formal connection to the state often played a more significant role than the police in the settlement of disputes and maintenance of order (Dinnen *et al.*, 2006: 100–101). The suitability of expensive, formal and centralised models of policing promoted by the international community has therefore come into question in this and other cases.

Interestingly, in the RAMSI case, there is evidence that these criticisms are being taken on board. Evidence can be found in new initiatives such as the Community Officers Project, a project that was set up in late 2010 to help formal policing structures better engage with isolated areas and such sites of informal policing. Individuals nominated by their communities are trained to act as mediators between the formal police services and the wider community at large (Braithwaite *et al.*, 2010). Related concerns over the suitability of externally generated models of justice have similarly been addressed to some extent in recent times. The use of local forms of restorative justice and reconciliation was highlighted by the case of the fatal shooting of Harry Lolongo by two Tongan RAMSI soldiers in August 2010. The shooting resulted in the Solomon Island government and RAMSI both taking part in reconciliation meetings both with local villagers and Lolongo's family over 2010 and 2011 where monetary and other compensation was given to try to help reconcile the various parties (RAMSI, 2011).

The Solomon Islands case therefore helps to demonstrate that questions of local versus international ownership are at least being discussed in more detail (Hansen, 2008) and to some extent being put into action. Efforts to address questions of ownership, consultation and input may help mitigate some of the concerns about the particular operational aspects and details of international policing (remembering here one of the major critiques of UNTAET in Timor Leste was the lack of local engagement and participation). There is a dynamism at play in the field of international policing which is bringing both change and challenge.

The future of policing peace operations

The policing of peace operations has altered dramatically over the last two decades. The UN Police Division has grown significantly over the last few years and has had to grapple with these contentious issues. As such it is considered here as a concrete example of just how much has changed in this field and as an indicator of where some trends may be heading into the future.

The UN Police Division has grown in terms of numbers employed at the headquarter level (for example, in 2008 there were 33 staff, but in 2009 another 19 had been approved) and in terms of the type of work such staff may be involved in – with a move away from simple firefighting tasks and towards strategic planning. The Division now has a Standing Police Capacity to travel to potential sites for UN deployments to assess the situation on the ground and to proffer advice about the likely policing needs in country. The Division has also been developing standardised training modules to buttress and support its pre-deployment training for police deploying to missions – in part a response to the concerns noted above whereby the ability of some police to implement democratic policing has been tenuous at times. This material was sent out to member states in mid-2009 and special 'Train the Trainer' courses were conducted throughout the year in Sweden, Ghana, Argentina and Australia (UNDPKO, 2010: 17). In late 2009 the UN Police Division also began work on an overarching strategic doctrinal framework to understand both the core business of UNPOL in the field (the outer limits of what should be taken on in a UN context) and also the types of values that needed to be inculcated – with particular focus here again being on the protection of civilians and the respect for human rights. Over the course of 2009–10 the Division has been working to consolidate a 'new UN police identity', issuing new badges and a documented 'vision' for *Professionalising United Nations Police in Peacekeeping* (Orler, 2010). This document briefly summarises how the UN 'has to be far more professional about how we design the police components and mission mandates, how we recruit, train and deploy, and how we implement police assignments'; discussing the need for clear policy, strategy, operational support and oversight to ensure more effective delivery (UNDPKO, 2010: 1). Such moves will ideally help to improve operational effectiveness and to create a more professional police ethos in UN missions in the first instance, helping to rebut scepticism that 'the changes of developing a transnational police ethic are minimal' (Hills, 2009: 302). More fundamentally, what is deemed to be 'effective' or 'professional' will also arguably have to be measured against the yardstick of those types of democratic policing values noted earlier – values that include responsiveness, accountability and participation.

An additional issue that these types of developments raises is the possibility of transnational or international policing becoming a specialist job that police personnel from various countries seek out – either through this UN system or through their own national deployment pools. With respect to the latter, the Australian Federal Police have a standing deployment group around 1,200 strong. When not on international deployments in the Pacific or elsewhere, they are typically at present rotated into airport policing roles or specialist roles. Deployment lengths have increased, with a number of two-year term deployments available. Should domestic police become permanent international policing personnel this may compound existing concerns like that expressed by Cunliffe above about South–North issues and the question of who provides boots on the ground. The locus of control of possible permanent international policing personnel might either raise concerns if such police are part of the still as yet under regulated private security sector, or mitigate them if they are held accountable to international or national legal frameworks. Permanent international policing roles might also provide some positive developments in that such change could encourage capacity and norm transfer across and between contributing countries as personnel strive to meet global professional standards.

Lastly, the use of international police personnel has an additional normative value. In Iraq and Afghanistan military personnel have been used to perform certain policing duties and to mentor fledgling police forces (Keller, 2011). This blurring of the police-military divide is, however, inimical both to general liberal democratic values in the political sense and to democratic policing values in the operational sense (Greener and Fish, 2011; Friesendorf, 2010). The use of international police personnel has had its critics and, admittedly, there are a number of areas for improvement, but the rise of police as international actors also allows for an alternative, less militarised approach to responding to security problems in peace operations.

Conclusions

The policing of peace operations is in a dynamic phase. Recent operational changes have seen: increases in police numbers in peace operations; increases in police tasks in peace operations; lesser developed countries increasingly carrying the burden of provision of personnel; norm development within the UN Police Division to encourage human rights centred policing; and reorientation of policing programmes when resistance or problems have been met. Significantly, what might appear to be fairly neutral or technical activities involved in upholding the rule of law are highly political. The policing of peace brings in questions of power, of inequality, of quality controls, of underpinning policing norms and norm transfer. These tie the international policing agenda strongly to processes of globalisation. Politically these policing roles relate strongly to: the role of hegemonic norms; the rolling out of the liberal peacebuilding agenda; more critical concerns over the unequal impacts of globalisation processes as witnessed by the agenda setters and those who provide boots on the ground (as well as by the disconnect between local and international priorities); and the politics of risk in a globalised world. All of these issues highlight the centrality of changes in policing practice to more fundamental political and social changes at the international level – with policing practices stemming from and in turn shaping some of these broader processes. Policing peace operations has therefore been full of change and challenge, both at the operational level and at the level of international politics. The future of such policing, moreover, offers up the possibility of even greater change should, for example, a transnational policing class of sorts emerge, a possibility that could see a more 'globalised' approach to policing evolve.

References

Allen, M. (2006) Dissenting voices: Local perspectives on the Regional Assistance Mission to the Solomon Islands. *Pacific Economic Bulletin*, *21*(2), 194–201.

Baker, B. (2009) Policing post conflict societies: Helping out the state. *Policing and Society*, *19*, 329–332.

Bayley, D. (2001) *Democratizing the Police Abroad: What to Do and How to Do It.* Washington, DC: US Department of Justice.

Braithwaite, J., Dinnen, S., Allen, M., Braithwaite, V. and Charlesworth, H. (2010) *Pillars and Shadows: Statebuilding as Peacebuilding in Solomon Islands*. Canberra: ANU.

Carpenter, A. (2010) *UN Police Peacekeeping: It's Different from the Day Job.* Powerpoint Presentation. Retrieved from www.docstoc.com/docs/49053445/UN-Police-Presentation.

Cunliffe, P. (2009) Politics of global governance in UN peacekeeping. *International Peacekeeping*, *16*, 323–336.

Dinnen, S., McLeod, A. and Goldsmith, A. (2006) Police-building in weak states: Australian approaches in Papua New Guinea and Solomon Islands. *Civil Wars*, *8*, 87–108.

Emsley, C. (1993) Peasants, gendarmes and state formation. In: M. Fulbrook (ed.) *National Histories and European History*. London: UCL Press.

Friesendorf, C. (2010) *The Military and Law Enforcement in Peace Operations: Lessons from Bosnia Herzegovina and Kosovo*. Geneva: Geneva Centre for the Democratic Control of the Armed Forces.

Fullilove, M. (2006) *The Testament of Solomons: RAMSI and International State-Building. Lowy Institute Analysis*, March. Sydney: Lowy Institute.

Glenn R. (2007) *Counterinsurgency in a Test Tube: Analyzing the Success of the Regional Assistance Mission to Solomon Islands (RAMSI)*. Santa Monica: RAND.

Goldsmith, A. and Scheptycki, J. (2007). *Crafting Transnational Policing: Police Capacity-Building and Global Policing Reform.* Oxford: Hart.

Greener, B.K. (2009a) *The New International Policing.* Houndsmills: Palgrave.

Greener, B.K. (2009b) UNPOL: Police as peacekeepers. *Policing and Society, 19,* 106–118.

Greener, B.K. and Fish W.J. (2011) *Situating Police and Military in Contemporary Peace Operations.* Asia Pacific Civil Military Centre of Excellence Civil Military Occasional Papers, 3/2011. Canberra: APCMCoE.

Hansen, A. (2008) Local ownership in peace operations. In: T. Donais (ed.) *Local Ownership and Security Sector Reform.* Geneva: Geneva Centre for the Democratic Control of the Armed Forces.

Hardt, M. and Negri, A. (2000) *Empire.* Cambridge, MA: Harvard University Press.

Hills, A. (2009) The possibility of transnational policing. *Policing and Society, 19,* 300–317.

Hood, L. (2006) Security sector reform in East Timor, 1999–2004. *International Peacekeeping, 13,* 60–77.

Keller, D.E. (2011) *US Military Forces and Police Assistance in Stability Operations: The Least Worst Option to Fill the US Capability Gap.* Carlisle, SA: Strategic Studies Institute US Army War College.

Krasniqi, E. (2005) UN Kosovo police arrested for sex trafficking. *International Relations and Security Network,* 01/09/2005. Available on line: http://www.isn.ethz.ch/news/sw/details.cfm?ID = 12681.

Lemay-Hebert, N. (2009) UNPOL and police reform in Timor-Leste: Accomplishments and setbacks. *International Peacekeeping, 16,* 393–406.

Linden, R., Last, D. and Murphy, C. (2007) Obstacles on the road to peace and justice: The role of civilian police in peacekeeping. In: A. Goldsmith and J. Sheptycki (eds) *Crafting Transnational Policing: Police Capacity-Building and Global Policing Reform.* Oxford: Hart.

McDevitt, B. (2006) Operation Helpem Fren: A personal perspective. *Australian Army Journal, 3,* 1–18.

Martin, I. and Mayer-Rieckh, A. (2005) The United Nations and East Timor: From self-determination to state-building. *International Peacekeeping, 12,* 104–120.

Mather, F. (1959) *Public Order in the Age of Chartists.* Manchester: Manchester University Press.

Orler, A.M. (2010) *Professionalising United Nations Police in Peacekeeping: Vision for the Police Division and United Nations Police in Peace Operations, September 2010.* Retrieved from http://www.un.org/en/peacekeeping/sites/police/documents/unpol_vision.pdf.

OSCE (2008) *Guidebook on Democratic Policing.* Paris: OSCE.

Peake, G. (2009) Police reform in Timor-Leste. In: M.S. Hinton and T. Newburn (eds) *Policing Developing Democracies.* Milton Park: Routledge.

RAMSI (2011) RAMSI and government reconcile over Titinge incident. Press Release 30 March 2011.

Reith, C. (1943) *British Police and the Democratic Ideal.* London: Oxford University Press.

Rotmann, P. (2009) *First Steps towards a UN Police Doctrine for Peace Operations 2001–2006.* Geneva: Geneva Centre for the Democratic Control of the Armed Forces.

Rubenstein, R.A. (2010) Peacekeeping and the return of imperial policing. *International Peacekeeping, 17,* 457–70.

Sheptycki, J. (2007) The constabulary ethic and the transnational condition. In: A. Goldsmith and J. Sheptycki (eds) *Crafting Transnational Policing: Police Capacity-Building and Global Policing Reform*. Oxford: Hart.

UN Police Division (2011) *The New UN Police Identity*. United Nations. Available on line: http://www.un.org/en/peacekeeping/sites/police/new_identity.shtml.

UNDPKO (2010) *UN Police Magazine*, 4th edition, January. New York: United Nations Department of Peacekeeping Operations.

UNDPKO (2011) *UN Police Magazine*, 6th edition, January. New York: United Nations Department of Peacekeeping Operations.

Wiatrowski, M.D. and Goldstone, J.A. (2010) The ballot and the badge democratic policing. *The Journal of Democracy*, *21*, 79–92.

Williams, P. (2009) Peace operations in Africa: Seven challenges, any solutions? *Conflict Trends*. Available on line: kms1.isn.ethz.ch/serviceengine/Files/ISN/109805/.../2009347f.../1.pdf.

Wilson, B.V.E. (2008) Smoke and mirrors: Institutionalising fragility in the Policia Nacional Timor Leste. Paper delivered to the *Democratic Governance in Timor-Leste: Reconciling the National and Local Conference*, Charles Darwin University, Darwin 7–8 February.

7 Two profiles of crimmigration law
Criminal deportation and illegal migration

Juliet P. Stumpf

Introduction

Jose Padilla, a native of Honduras, came to the United States in the 1960s. Over the next several decades, he served in the US military in the Vietnam War and became a lawful permanent resident of the United States. He started a family, settled in California, and took a job as a truck driver. Forty years after entering the United States, Padilla was arrested and charged with transporting in his tractor-trailer truck about a half-ton of marijuana. Faced with a plea bargain that would impose a five-year sentence and five years probation in exchange for his guilty plea, he conferred with his attorney about the immigration consequences of accepting the deal. Padilla's attorney assured him that taking the plea deal would not lead to deportation.[1]

While the offered plea may have been a great deal for any criminal defendant with US citizenship, Padilla's defense counsel was wrong about the immigration consequence of the conviction. Conviction of the crime Padilla was accused of paved a clear pathway to deportation and the specter of a lifetime bar to re-entering the United States.[2] The deportation system provided Padilla no chance to present evidence to a judge of mitigating circumstances, such as the length of his residence in the United States or the impact on his US family members, that could avert his exile.[3]

Nine years later, the Supreme Court decided that Padilla's criminal defense counsel had had a constitutional duty to advise Padilla that his conviction would lead to deportation, and that the attorney had fallen short of that duty.[4] The Court determined that 'deportation is an integral part – indeed, sometimes the most important part – of the penalty' imposed after a guilty plea.[5] When that penalty is foreseeable, criminal defense attorneys have an obligation to advise their clients about it. The Court sent the case back to the lower court to decide whether the attorney's failure to meet that obligation justified overturning the negotiated conviction.[6]

In 2008, the US government expanded a program evocatively dubbed 'Operation Streamline', which criminally prosecuted virtually every noncitizen caught unlawfully crossing a certain stretch of the US–Mexico border.[7] Prior to Operation Streamline, the government had relied on the immigration system to respond to unlawful border-crossing, excluding or deporting those entering without authorization. With Operation Streamline, immigration enforcement turned to the criminal justice system. In addition to removing the arrested migrants from the country, the government also charged them criminally with a petty offense, mainly entry without inspection.[8] The zero-tolerance approach almost completely removed the discretion that government officials had exercised over whether to deploy the immigration enforcement apparatus.

Together, *Padilla v. Kentucky* and Operation Streamline illustrate the challenges that US courts and policymakers face when grappling with the shifting geography of 'crimmigration law', which describes the interaction between criminal and immigration law. Crimmigration law has altered the landscape of both immigration and criminal law.[9] Criminal law has taken on a new role as a promisor of safety and security for a society captivated by risk-avoidance. Immigration law too holds out a similar promise of protecting society against the perceived risks that incoming outsiders pose. As a result, crimmigration law has become a major feature of the modern relationship between government and noncitizen.

The development of crimmigration law in the United States comes at a critical moment internationally. In pursuit of a common European immigration policy, the European Commission is investigating new approaches to regulating migration.[10] The example of crimmigration law in the United States is only an ocean away. Still closer is Canada, which has experienced a rise in criminalization generally. It remains to be seen whether the crimmigration trend will seep into immigration law beyond the US experience.

Why are we seeing such a strong trend toward merging the immigration and criminal justice systems, toward unfettered borrowing of enforcement tools and intermeshing of statutes, regulations, and concepts across these two areas of law? One answer is that immigration law, like criminal law, lends itself to government efforts to exert social control over classes and communities that are perceived as outsiders. To the extent that our social systems construct noncitizens and criminal defendants as groups that exist on the margins of society or outside of it, heightened sensitivity to the presence of those groups will trigger social insecurities which are then salved through political crackdowns on crime and migration.[11]

Sorting out how social control plays a role in shaping crimmigration law and driving its expansion requires an understanding of the divided nature of crimmigration law. Crimmigration law describes two distinct trends. First, it has caused a remarkable increase in deportation of lawfully present noncitizens through the expansion of criminal deportability grounds combined with the repeal of all but a few forms of relief from deportation.[12] Second, crimmigration law has become a major tool for regulating the migration of noncitizens across borders. Crimmigration regulates migration by criminalizing migration-related conduct through crimes such as unlawful entry, unlawful re-entry and smuggling, as well as by increasing discretionary enforcement of these migration crimes and reducing the procedural protections that traditionally restrain government power in criminal proceedings in the United States.[13]

Although these two trends are often lumped together as crimmigration law, in fact they are distinct phenomena with disparate effects. First, the harms tend to fall on two different classes of migrant. Expansion of criminal deportability grounds tends to impact lawful permanent residents and other admitted migrants. In contrast, prosecutions for unlawful entry and re-entry are almost always brought against migrants outside of the law who have recently crossed the border or are caught in the act of crossing.[14]

Second, when the legal system expands the grounds for deportation based on crimes, the critical question becomes whether there are pathways either in the immigration or the criminal justice proceeding to avoid deportation if a noncitizen's circumstances seem to warrant mitigation. In contrast, because criminalizing migration-related conduct usually targets recent migrants, deportation is almost unavoidable. The question here is whether criminalization will pile on other consequences, like criminal punishment, social stigma, and bars to re-entering the country when a basis for lawful entry becomes possible later.[15]

The difference between these two trends has created a political battleground in the United States over the impact that crimmigration law has on the people – both citizens and noncitizens – who feel its effects. When crimmigration law has the effect of deporting noncitizens whose crimes occurred well in the past, especially long-term residents who are integrated into US communities and have US citizen or lawful permanent resident spouses and children, the public response tends to be negative and there are calls for more a compassionate immigration policy.[16] In contrast, statistics about criminal acts by migrants or reports of high levels of unlawful migration have fueled policymakers' efforts to magnify border exclusion, deportation, and continued criminalization of migration.[17]

This chapter will describe these two trends, map their effects, and assess the differing and sometimes conflicting approaches that those who make and carry out the law have taken in response. It will begin with the story of the rise of crimmigration law in the United States, assessing its possible causes and its impacts. The chapter will then sketch the two profiles of crimmigration law: the expansion of deportation based on criminal conduct and the criminalization of acts of migration. Finally, it will explore the differences and similarities between these two trends and evaluate how they might affect the trajectory of crimmigration law.

The rise of crimmigration law

Prior to the mid-1980s, the immigration and criminal justice systems operated relatively autonomously. Immigration law operated primarily as a civil scheme with admission of noncitizens connected administratively and philosophically to enforcement of immigration restrictions. Deportation based on criminal convictions was generally reserved for 'crimes involving moral turpitude' or the specific crimes of murder, drug trafficking, and weapons trafficking.[18]

Similarly, while a noncitizen's entry without inspection or unlawful re-entry had the potential to carry criminal consequences, these acts were generally handled through the administrative deportation system rather than through the criminal justice system. Using criminal enforcement resources to pursue individuals for border-crossing may have seemed outside of the mainstream of federal prosecutors' work. Unauthorized migration was an ingrained part of the cyclical nature of the seasonal agricultural economy, and it supplied labor to other industries. It also resulted from ordinary activity within long-established Mexican-American communities that were cross-sectioned by the border when it was drawn through them.

Immigration law in the United States has always ridden a pendulum between expansion and restriction of immigration, often depending on the magnetism of factors such as economic demand for labor or US involvement in international affairs. Beginning in the 1980s, the nature of immigration law began to change in a way that altered the course of that pendulum. Following the movement in criminal law away from rehabilitation and integration into society, immigration law took a turn towards a more retributive approach to immigration law violations, one that highlighted the outsider status of noncitizens. Criminal penology in the 1970s grew more punitive, lengthening sentences, emphasizing incarceration over social re-entry, and inventing civil consequences for criminal convictions such as loss of voting rights that stripped the earmarks of citizenship of those convicted of crimes.[19] This sharper edge to criminal law may have been a means of asserting social control over elements of society considered to be outsiders because of their social status, class, or race.[20]

In the 1980s and continuing through the turn of the century, immigration law began to parallel the punitive trajectory of criminal penology in ways that tightened the interlacing of criminal and immigration law. The federal legislature passed laws targeting noncitizens that uniquely blended criminal law with deportation and immigration control.[21] Enforcement of criminal laws affecting noncitizens became a high priority and the United States began to invest in higher detention and deportation levels. Law enforcement policies and practices brought to bear on migrants the apparatus of criminal enforcement, such as arrest, detention, and incarceration. Expanded discretion for law enforcement officials increased the level of contact between noncitizens and enforcers of criminal and immigration laws.[22]

At the same time, the constitutional procedural protections that have traditionally shielded criminal defendants from some of the excesses of government power failed to cross the boundary between immigration and criminal law.[23] The right to counsel at government expense or to a jury trial, to protection from self-incrimination or to being tried twice for the same offense, or to the retroactive application of the law, among other procedural protections, are absent from the US deportation proceeding.[24]

These changes had dual consequences. First, the establishment of a crimmigration regime led inevitably to higher numbers of immigration-related prosecutions. Immigration crimes became the largest category of US federal prosecutions, surpassing crimes related to weapons and drugs.[25]

Second, crimmigration contributed to a meteoric rise in the numbers of noncitizens deported. In 1985, at the threshold of the crimmigration era, the United States formally deported about 23,000 noncitizens.[26] In 2010, a decade into the new century, deportations from the United States had risen to nearly 400,000 annually.[27]

Shifting political administrations have not slowed this momentum. The emphasis on deportation has been consistent throughout the Bush, Clinton and Obama administrations. President Barack Obama deported more than a million noncitizens well before the end of his first term, far outpacing his predecessor, George W. Bush.[28] Under Obama, the percentage of deportations that were based on criminal convictions rather than on civil unlawful presence or other administrative immigration violations rose to 46 percent of the total, or 196,000.[29]

Crimmigration law has also revived an ancient debate over whether the federal government or the states have primary control over migration. With criminal law as the traditional bailiwick of the states, criminalizing migration became an entrée for states to try to control the entry of noncitizens into their territories. The state of Arizona has begun to explore the outer reaches of the power of the states to regulate noncitizens. In 2010, the Arizona legislature passed a law that permitted non-federal police officers to stop a person based on a suspicion that the individual was in the United States without authorization.[30] Copycat legislation in other states has similarly sought to use the criminal enforcement resources of state and local law enforcement to restrict migration.[31] The legislation brought to a head the debate over whether the federal government has primacy in matters of immigration enforcement, and the US courts continue to grapple with that issue.

Crimmigration law, then, is the legal space where immigration law and criminal law overlap. It channels the relationship between government officials and migrant communities toward restrictionism rather than integration. The backbone of crimmigration law comprises a latticework of federal immigration laws that rely on criminal statutes as well as federal and state criminal laws that regulate migration through criminal prohibitions. High levels of enforcement suffuse it with immediacy and political and social salience.

Why are we seeing this powerful trend toward the intermeshing of immigration and criminal law? If there is truth to the theory that the harshening of criminal law and penology is a form of social control of those considered at the margins of society, there is at least as strong a case that social control underlies the rise of crimmigration law. There is a strong parallel between the rise of harsher criminal punishment and the increasing centrality of deportation in immigration law. The turn away from rehabilitation in criminal law and toward deportation in immigration law represents a rejection of the ideal of integration in both areas. The point of incarceration is to separate the convicted individual from society. When deportation is used as a consequence of a criminal offense, deportation becomes functionally identical to criminal punishment.

These means of excluding those convicted of crimes translate directly to their exclusion from social membership and to the stripping of functional citizenship. Civil consequences of a criminal conviction may include prohibitions on voting, holding public office, or serving as a juror,[32] all of which are privileges of citizenship denied to aliens. Other collateral consequences of convictions, such as ineligibility for public housing, welfare, job opportunities, or education, deny access to society's entitlements and benefits, functionally excluding the individual.

Combining incarceration with these civil consequences of conviction exacts a more complete severance from society, one that extends the loss of full citizenship beyond the period of incarceration.

Deportation exacts almost all of these civil consequences, directly or *de facto*. It differs from incarceration in that it returns or removes the deportee to another society rather than imposing physical confinement. Deportation and incarceration, however, are similar in that they physically separate the individual from US society. Likewise, deportation has the effect of cutting off deported noncitizens from access to public housing, education, jobs or other benefits for which they may have been eligible.[33]

Finally, the fact that the government's deportation power is used only for noncitizens, along with the substantial increase in the use of that power, channels a broad line between citizen and noncitizen in the delineations of membership in US society. Deportation has become a means of expressing, defining, and performing acts of exclusion from US civil society. When combined with the modern bars to re-entry exacting lifetime exclusion of many noncitizens convicted of crimes,[34] deportation renders that social exclusion permanent. The exercise of government power here is unidirectional: the absolute and permanent nature of the deportation stands opposed to the potential for return to US civil society, inclusion into its membership, or integration. In this, immigration enforcement tracks criminal law's trajectory toward retributive forms of punishment and the turn away from rehabilitation, emphasizing the sovereign power to penalize and to express moral condemnation. The common root is the exercise of sovereign power toward the ends of social control.

This emphasis on membership gains salience when viewed in light of the effect that both criminal and immigration enforcement have on groups already challenged to establish full membership in US society. These tend to be stigmatized racial and ethnic groups, and those that have low socioeconomic status. The disproportion of African-American and Latino men in US jails and prisons is well documented.[35] Immigration enforcement results in a demographic of deportation that is heavily Latino and Asian.[36] The reasons for this are complex. It is, in part, a reflection of the relatively heavy migration to the United States of Latin American and Asian citizens. It also results from US legislation that restricted migration to numbers far below historical levels of migration from Mexico as well as from increased enforcement that discouraged the cyclical flow of return migration.[37]

US immigration law, more than criminal law, overtly makes distinctions based on race, ethnicity, or national origin.[38] As examples, the US Constitution permits immigration officials to rely on national origin or ethnicity as one factor among others in making an immigration stop.[39] The federal government has imposed special registration requirements on noncitizens from predominantly Arab or Muslim countries, and targeted those same populations for immigration enforcement actions.[40]

In this light, both criminal law and immigration law serve the function of exerting social control over people seen as inside US territory but who are nevertheless outsiders: those convicted of crimes and those who lack citizenship. In combination, noncitizens convicted of crimes find themselves on the outer perimeter of outsider status, subject to the penology of the criminal justice system and the penalties of the deportation system. Both express social condemnation; both are devoid of a pathway to redemption.

Scholars studying European immigration regulation have documented trends similar to those occurring in the United States. There are signs that crimmigration law is gaining some toeholds in Europe. The 'securitization' measures taken in Europe both before and after the events of September 11, 2001 have expanded the role of police and other security forces and shifted the balance between law enforcement and civil liberties to emphasize enforcement.[41] There is evidence that some European law enforcement measures, such as those in the Netherlands and Italy, single out marginalized immigrant ethnic groups.[42] Recent legislation has applied criminal sanctions to immigration-related conduct, such as fines and detention for unlawful presence in Italy.[43] When criminal law seems to lie within easy reach, it becomes easy to use it expansively.

The two faces of crimmigration law

The rise of crimmigration law can be parsed into two major elements: the expansion of deportation and the criminalization of migration. While the terms 'crimmigration law' and 'criminal alien' conflate these, they are distinct parts of the merging of immigration and criminal law, targeting different immigrants and having disparate consequences.

The expansion of deportation

One of crimmigration law's innovations was the expansion of deportation based on criminal offenses. Traditionally, deportation of noncitizens who had settled in the United States was reserved for those who had committed crimes before entering the United States or crimes involving moral turpitude such as fraud or prostitution.[44] Crimmigration law has expanded deportation in several ways. In the 1990s, the US Congress passed harsher laws that mandated deportation for a wide variety of criminal convictions under the deportation ground for 'aggravated felonies'.[45] Many were major offenses such as murder or rape, but the statutory expansions swept in an array of crimes, including gambling offenses or tax evasion, that were more minor or were classified as misdemeanors rather than felonies. The law mandated deportation regardless of how old the criminal conviction was.

Suddenly, as a result of this legislation, a noncitizen could be convicted for a crime in the normal course of the criminal justice system, serve a sentence – even a suspended sentence - and then be subject to a civil removal proceeding to determine deportability. Because the aggravated felony ground was a creature of immigration law and not criminal law, the conviction for the offense was often enough to trigger deportation even in the face of a light sentence or alternative to incarceration.

At the same time that Congress expanded the criminal grounds for deportation, it abolished almost completely the circumstances under which a noncitizen could obtain relief from deportation. Mitigating circumstances such as family ties or ill-ness that immigration officials and judges traditionally used to exercise discretion to avert deportation became irrelevant for many noncitizens with criminal con-victions. The law mandated that the deportation order issue.[46]

These laws raised the public profile of deportation based on crime. The 'crimi-nal alien' –threatening, unmanageable, an intruder who embodies the 'other' – became the face of the unlawful alien. Deportation became a matter of national self-defense and self-definition. Yet the greatest impact of the new laws was to a group well-known to US society and formally welcomed by it: lawful permanent residents. The expansion of deportability grounds to include more traditional criminal offenses, along with the lack of a statute of limitations on deportation and the scarcity of relief from it, meant that many lawful permanent residents became eligible for deportation.

One such noncitizen was Jose Padilla, whose story introduces this chapter. Prior to his crime and later deportation proceeding, he had lived in the United States for decades and had established a life and family in the country. His crime, involving a large quantity of marijuana, was either an aggravated felony or a drug trafficking crime under crimmigration law, triggering a near-certain likelihood of being deported.[47] Similarly, long-term permanent residents who had committed crimes in the distant past found themselves deported to countries they never knew or had left a lifetime ago.[48]

The vulnerability of lawful permanent residents to removal from the United States on criminal grounds was exacerbated by the expansion of inadmissibility grounds, which govern when a noncitizen may be denied admission to the United States even when they meet the basic admissions criteria.[49] The 1996 laws expanded the inadmissibility grounds to apply to lawful permanent residents returning to the United States who had been convicted of certain crimes.[50] As a result, lawful perma-nent residents attempting to return to homes to the US could be excluded on the same grounds as a noncitizen seeking admission for the first time.

These crime-based inadmissibility grounds also affected noncitizens seeking lawful permanent residence in the United States who were otherwise eligible for that status based on family relationships, employment, or other reasons. While some applied from abroad, many sought to adjust their immigration status from within the United States where they had family or work ties or had otherwise established themselves in US communities. In these circumstances, the removal from the United States of a lawful permanent resident or a noncitizen eligible for that status, while technically an exclusion from admission, acts as a *de facto* depor-tation in that it expels these noncitizens from the US community in which they have settled.

This profile of crimmigration law, the expansion of deportation, may best be envisioned as the face of the lawful permanent resident. While the affected popu-lation includes noncitizens who do not have permanent status in the United States, the expansion of deportation has its greatest impact on lawful permanent residents. Moreover, the permanent residents deported under the expanded depor-tation system represent the full gamut of individuals convicted of crimes, from the recidivist to redeemed residents whose crimes occurred long ago and whose deportation impacts US citizens and others in the community.

The criminalization of migration

The expansion of deportation relies on traditional crimes as defined by federal or state law as the criteria for expulsion. In contrast, the second profile of crimmigration law is the criminalization of migration. In place of expulsion based on traditional crimes, this form of crimmigration law criminalizes acts of migration by noncitizens and others involved in the migration of noncitizens across borders.

The most common form that this crimmigration profile takes is prosecution for the crimes of entry without inspection and unlawful re-entry.[51] These acts of migration were criminalized many years ago, but under US law the government had discretion whether to press criminal charges or pursue deportation instead. Enforcement officials tended to view most unlawful entry and re-entry cases as immigration matters suitable for civil immigration proceedings. The rise of crimmigration law initiated a strong shift toward using the criminal justice system to address this migration-related conduct. Noncitizens caught crossing the border without authorization are significantly more likely to find themselves first convicted for the unlawful crossing and then deported.[52]

While unlawfully entering or re-entering the United States has constituted criminal conduct for nearly a century, many migration-related acts have only recently come to carry criminal consequences. It was not until 1986 that the government could prosecute employers for a pattern or practice of knowingly hiring employees who were not authorized to work in the United States, or charge spouses with the new crime of marrying to evade the immigration laws.[53] After that, legislation criminalizing migration-related conduct proliferated. Some of the new crimes included falsely claiming US citizenship to obtain a government benefit or unlawful employment, speeding while fleeing an immigration checkpoint, or concealing the preparation of a fraudulent immigration document.[54]

The trend toward using criminal law to regulate acts of migration is not limited to this flurry of criminalizing legislation. As with the expansion of deportation, enforcement priorities have shifted toward the combined use of the criminal justice system and deportation to govern migration. Operation Streamline represents a prominent edge of this enforcement approach, epitomizing the blending of immigration and criminal enforcement in this arena.

Operation Streamline's zero-tolerance policy, which charges almost every noncitizen caught unlawfully crossing the border with the crime of entry without inspection, is a big step toward standardizing criminal prosecution on top of the deportation sanction.[55] On its face, this may seem unremarkable. The program prosecutes conduct that has been classified as criminal for decades, as a formal matter shifting from a civil approach to one utilizing criminal justice tools. It seems directed toward some of the traditional goals of criminal punishment: retribution for violating the law, deterring future violations, and incapacitating the violator from unauthorized border-crossing at least for the term of imprisonment.

Some might view the Operation as merely an intensified effort to ensure that migrants follow the law on the books.

On closer examination, however, Operation Streamline departs radically from the traditional criminal justice system model. Noncitizens channeled into Operation Streamline find themselves ushered through a truncated proceeding that bears little resemblance to the procedural norms followed in the criminal case in the courtroom next door. Because the volume of Operation Streamline arrests places a heavy burden on the federal courts and attorneys, the cases have proceeded *en masse* with sometimes 60 to 80 defendants in the courtroom. Judges shepherd the defendants as a group through the case from the initial appearance to the waiver of criminal constitutional rights to the taking of guilty pleas and on through sentencing, usually in less than a day. Because the government usually charges the noncitizens with a misdemeanor for unlawful entry rather than a felony for unlawful re-entry, US law permits a magistrate judge rather than a district court judge to administer them, and there is no right to a jury trial.[56]

Operation Streamline defendants found themselves sentenced as a crowd in the courtrooms of magistrate judges, without the check on prosecutorial overreaching that a grand jury provides. As a group, they were asked to waive most criminal constitutional rights and then sentenced pursuant to a plea bargain in a proceeding that often lasted mere minutes.[57] In 2009, a US appellate court declared that the *en masse* nature of the criminal proceeding violated federal criminal procedural rules because it was impossible for a judge taking criminal pleas in bulk to evaluate whether the noncitizen defendant's consent was knowing and voluntary.[58]

Because the plea bargain that the prosecutor offers is usually shorter than the time it would take to go to trial, there is little incentive for a defendant to reject it. The conviction rate is close to 100 percent.[59] And, until the US Supreme Court's decision in *Padilla v. Kentucky,* defense counsel and courts had no constitutional duty to inform the defendant about the immigration consequences of the proceeding.

Comparing the two profiles

Although the expansion of deportation and the criminalization of migration fall under the rubric of crimmigration law, they have very different features. This section will sketch some of the distinctions between them and why they are important.

First, the consequences of crimmigration law fall on different groups of noncitizens. Prosecution for entry without inspection and unlawful re-entry impacts noncitizens migrating outside of the law, those who have recently crossed the border or are caught in the act of crossing. In contrast, the expansion of criminal deportability grounds and enforcement most heavily affects lawful permanent residents and other long-term residents.

Second, the nature of the crime is different. With the expansion of deportation, the reason for deportation tends to be a crime of general applicability, that is, a crime for which anyone, regardless of immigration or citizenship status, could be prosecuted. A permanent resident deported for committing burglary has committed a crime of general applicability because burglary is illegal regardless of whether the burglar is a citizen or a foreign tourist. But criminalizing acts of migration creates 'status' crimes, crimes that punish conduct only if the acts are performed by noncitizens who are unlawfully present. The same act committed by an individual with a different status – a US citizen or lawful permanent resident – would not be a crime. A US citizen who crosses the US border is undertaking a lawful act. A noncitizen taking the same step across the same border is acting criminally unless the US government has authorized that step.

Third, the relevant legal questions shift. With the expansion of deportation, once a conviction has occurred the proceeding in the criminal justice system becomes the foundation for the immigration proceeding. The critical question becomes whether deportation will occur, that is, whether the crime triggers a deportability ground and, often more importantly, whether there is some exception or other form of relief from deportation.

In contrast, with the criminal regulation of migration, deportation is usually a foregone conclusion because of the unlawful presence of most of the noncitizens. The question here is whether there will be an additional criminal prosecution. Operation Streamline answers that question in the affirmative for almost all those who cross certain stretches of the US–Mexico border without authorization.

The result of these differences is that different legal arguments come to the fore depending on which crimmigration profile is at issue. Legal arguments and policy discussions often draw on analogies between an individual party and a group. With respect to the expansion of deportation, arguments often center on whether lawful permanent residents threatened with removal are like US citizens, who are in no danger of expulsion from the United States regardless of the severity of their crime. Arguments against deportation emphasize the long-term nature of lawful permanent residence and the explicit commitment to joining the national community. Arguments justifying deportation, on the other hand, tend to distinguish lawful permanent residents from citizens or emphasize that committing a crime equates to rejecting the norms of the national community. These arguments exclude convicted permanent residents from membership in that community.[60]

In the context of the criminalization of migration, legal and policy arguments center around whether unauthorized migrants are like criminals. Arguments for prosecuting acts of migration emphasize trespass – the breaching of the sovereign nation's property line – and national security concerns. Arguments against prosecuting unauthorized entrants distinguish them from traditional criminal defendants, framing the act of migration as driven by economic or humanitarian need or family unification. The arguments change, however, when it comes to the level of procedural protections for noncitizens in the criminal proceeding. Here, the arguments shift to analogize the noncitizen defendants to traditional criminal defendants requiring the same level of procedural protection that criminal defendants prosecuted for traditional crimes receive.

These differences, and the different arguments they generate, matter. They impact the kind of solutions offered and the compulsion that courts and policymakers may feel to resolve the challenges that the rise of crimmigration law presents. These differences lead, for example, to disparate approaches to the level of procedural protection that courts and policymakers provide.[61] With expansion of deportation based on crimes, arguments that emphasize the near-citizenship of noncitizens, successfully framing them as embedded in US families and integrated into US communities, evoke a more generous response in the form of greater procedural protections. In contrast, when arguments frame unauthorized immigrants as criminal trespassers into US society, the criminalization of migration results in decreased procedural protections such as expedited removal processes in the immigration system or mass processing and plea-taking in the criminal justice system.

The two vignettes that lead this chapter are good examples. Jose Padilla's status as a lawful permanent resident and the characteristics of permanent residence that resound in citizenship strongly influenced the Supreme Court's decision to establish procedural protection for criminal defendants at risk of removal, requiring defense counsel to warn noncitizens of certain deportation consequences of a conviction. Characterizing deportation under these circumstances as equivalent to banishment or exile, the Court conjured the image of long-term residents settled firmly in their adopted home, with families that would be severely impacted by the deportation. The Court stated 'When [criminal defense] attorneys know that their clients face possible exile from this country and separation from their families, they should not be encouraged to say nothing at all'.[62]

With the criminalization of migration, the policy arguments supporting Operation Streamline have constructed parallels between the targeted migrants and terrorists and criminals. A government spokesperson introducing the expanded program stated that '[s]ecuring our nation's borders from a potential terrorist threat and from the illegal entry of people, weapons and drugs is absolutely paramount'.[63] On the other hand, arguments to expand procedural protections seek to close the gap between traditional criminal cases and those involving migration and noncitizens. When a US appeals court invalidated aspects of the *en masse* nature of the Operation Streamline proceedings, the court applied the criminal rules of procedure without mentioning the immigration status of the defendants at all, treating the case like any other criminal case and quoting a section of the rules that emphasized 'according equal justice to all'[64] in the criminal courts.

These arguments carry pitfalls as well. When policymakers and courts rely on arguments that compare one group to another, there is a danger that they may bargain away the rights of one group to benefit a more favored group. We see this in the rise of crimmigration law itself, with the willingness to bargain away the rights of 'criminal immigrants' in exchange for protections for the rest of the immigrant population. Similarly, when courts and advocates make arguments about why long-term lawful permanent residents deserve special consideration under the law, that argument implicitly distinguishes the lesser status of the undocumented migrant or the newly arrived lawful migrant.

Conclusion

Crimmigration law has taken a powerful hold in the United States that has gone far in entrenching the restrictive nature of modern immigration law. As Europe, Canada, and other international regions craft their own approaches to the global phenomenon of increasing migration, crimmigration is likely to emerge as a potential pathway pursued when immigrants appear to threaten established social orders, economic stability, or cultural norms. The two profiles of crimmigration law, however, assail noncitizens in two different forms: established residents invested in and engaged with a national community who experience deportation as an adjunct to criminal punishment; and migrants at the border, perceived as trespassers but also as potential newcomers. Crimmigration puts a heavy thumb on the side of exile and exclusion for both groups, erasing the potential for discretion in deportation and exacting heavy penalties for migration outside of the law.[65]

Notes

1 Padilla v. Kentucky, 130 S. Ct. 1473, 1483 (2010).
2 See Stumpf (2011) 1736–1738 (discussing the immigration consequences of an aggravated felony conviction).
3 See ibid.; *Padilla,* 130 S. Ct. at 1480 (stating that removal of a noncitizen convicted of a deportable crime is 'practically inevitable but for the possible exercise of limited remnants of equitable discretion vested in the Attorney General to cancel removal').
4 *Padilla,* 130 S. Ct. at 1483.
5 Ibid. at 1480.
6 Ibid. at 1487.
7 See Transactional Records Access Clearinghouse, Immigration, Surge in Immigration Prosecutions Continues (2008), *available at* http://trac.syr.edu/immigration/reports/188.
8 Eagly (2010) 1327–29.
9 See Stumpf (2011) n. 2, at 1726–1730 (discussing how the intermeshing of criminal and immigration law magnifies the government's exclusionary power).
10 Communication from the Commission to the European Parliament, the Council, the Economic and Social Committee and the Committee of the Regions (2011).
11 See Garland (2001) 184–90 (describing the 'criminology of the dangerous other' and the politicization of crime control).
12 The number of noncitizens removed for criminal convictions rose from below 15,000 in 1991 to more than 40,000 in 2005. Office of Immigration Statistics, U.S. Department of Homeland Security, *2005 Yearbook of Immigration Statistics,* Table 40 (2005). Beginning in 2006, published statistics reflect the numbers of deportees who had criminal convictions, however, they do not indicate whether the convictions led to the deportations. See, e.g., Office of Immigration Statistics, US Department of Homeland Security (2006), Table 39.
13 See *infra,* notes 51–59 and accompanying text.
14 See *infra,* notes 51–52, 55 and accompanying text.
15 See *infra,* 'Comparing the two profiles'.
16 See e.g., Hakim and Bernstein (2010).
17 See e.g. Lamar Smith (2011); Gabriel (2011) (reporting that Representative Michele Bachmann 'called for a fence "on every mile, on every yard, on every foot" of the border.').

18 Stumpf (2006) ('Only the most serious crimes or crimes involving "moral turpitude" that presumably revealed an inherent moral flaw in the individual resulted in the ultimate sanction of deportation'); Anti-Drug Abuse Act of 1988, Pub. L. No. 100-690, § 7342, 102 Stat. 4181, 4469–70 (defining conviction of an "aggravated felony" as a deportability ground).

19 See Garland (2001) note 11, at 34–35, 46, 54 (tracking the rise and fall of the rehabilitative model and describing the trajectory of criminal penology toward a more punitive social control model).

20 Ibid.

21 See Stumpf (2006) note 18, at 382–384 (discussing the expansion of deportable offenses and the transformation of certain immigration offenses from civil to criminal).

22 Stumpf (2011) note 2, at 1729 (discussing the use of criminal law approaches in the enforcement of immigration law, and noting that '[i]n place of the formalized discretion traditionally held by institutional actors such as immigration authorities and criminal sentencing judges, decisions whether to exclude noncitizens from belonging in U.S. society are increasingly made by … prosecutors, police officers, or Border Patrol agents').

23 Legomsky (2007) 515–16 ('[C]ertain constitutional rights operate only in criminal proceedings; the courts have explicitly invoked the civil regulatory model of deportation to hold those rights inapplicable to deportation').

24 Ibid. See also Brown (2011) 1394; Kanstroom (2011) 1465–1466; Stumpf (2011) note 2, at 1710.

25 Stumpf (2006) note 18, at 388 (citing statistics).

26 Office of Immigration Statistics, U.S. Department of Homeland Security (2011), Table 36. This figure would increase considerably if it included "returns" of noncitizens without a formal removal order that occur primarily at the U.S.-Mexico border. Ibid. at Table 36, n.2.

27 Ibid. at Table 36.

28 *Obama set to outpace Bush on deportations*, Reuters, September 20, 2011.

29 Ibid. (noting that in 2010, 'convicted criminals numbered about 196,000 of those removed, an increase of 71 percent from Bush' in 2008.)

30 Support Our Law Enforcement and Safe Neighborhoods Act, S. 1070 (S.B. 1070), 49th Leg., 2d Reg. Sess. (Ariz. 2010), *amended by* H.R. 2162, 49th Leg., 2d Reg. Sess. (Ariz. 2010); see also Arizona v. United States, 132 S. Ct. 2492 (2012) (enjoining portions of Arizona's statute and upholding another).

31 E.g., Illegal Immigration Reform and Enforcement Act of 2011, 2011 Ga. Laws, Act 252 (H.B. 87); Beason-Hammon Alabama Taxpayer and Citizen Protection Act, 2011 Ala. Laws Act 2011–535 (H.B. 56).

32 Roberts (2009) ('Courts have labeled many consequences 'collateral,' including deportation …, the loss of voting rights, and the loss of housing and employment opportunities.'); Olivares *et al.* (1996) 14–15 (documenting an increase 'in the number of states restricting … voting, holding office, parenting, divorce, firearm ownership, and criminal registration'); Chin and Holmes (2002) (explaining that a convicted individual may be 'ineligible to serve on a federal jury and in some states will lose her right to vote').

33 Many noncitizens, whether or not lawfully present, are ineligible for social programs due to federal and state restrictions based on citizenship status. See Stumpf (2008) 1585 (describing federal legislation permitting states to deny various public benefits to noncitizens, including lawful permanent residents).

34 See Immigration and Nationality Act (INA) § 212(a)(9)(A)(i) (barring from admission to the United States 'at any time' a noncitizen convicted of an 'aggravated felony' who was ordered removed from the country or who departed under a removal order).

35 See The Pew Charitable Trusts (2010) 6–8 (providing statistics of high incarceration rates among African-American and Hispanic men). See also Moore (forthcoming) (citing studies).

36 The US Department of Homeland Security reports that a total of 476,405 noncitizens were 'returned' in 2010 (Office of Immigration Statistics, US Department of Homeland Security, 2011, Table 37). Of the noncitizens removed, 57,949 were from Asia (ibid). The total number of noncitizens removed from Mexico, Central America and South America, combined, exceeded 363,000 (ibid).

37 See Massey (2009) ('Between 1980 and 2005 the likelihood of returning to Mexico within 12 months of an undocumented entry fell by more than half').

38 See Stumpf (2006) note 18, at 415–417.

39 See United States v. Brignoni-Ponce, 422 U.S. 873, 886–87 (1975).

40 See 8 C.F.R. § 264.1(f) (2006); Registration of Certain Nonimmigrant Aliens from Designated Countries, 67 Fed. Reg. 77, 642 (Dec. 18, 2002); US Department of Justice (2002).

41 Mitsilegas (2003) 164 (describing the turn toward greater security measures in the European Union and analyzing its effect on the protection of rights and liberties in Europe); see, generally, van der Leun (2010) (discussing three theories underlying the criminalization of immigration law, comparing the literature on securitization with that on crimmigration, and raising the question whether the Netherlands has taken steps toward crimmigration).

42 See van der Leun and van der Woude, *Crimmigration and the Role of the Police* (2011, manuscript on file with author) (discussing the ways in which police activity disproportionately affects marginalized ethnic groups and examining whether ethnic profiling is a possible consequence of expanded stop and search powers in the Netherlands) (citing van der Woude, 2009); Pakes (2004) 293 (describing a 'cultural security complex' in which minority groups are seen as endangering not just individual victims but also the permissive and tolerant nature of Dutch society). See also Morris (2009) (describing police singling out café patrons of African appearance for questioning about immigration status).

43 Gazz (2009) (providing for fines and detention for unlawful presence in Italy); see also Pacella (2011) (noting that the 2009 Italian law 'criminalize[d] irregular immigration').

44 Kanstroom (2000) 1889, 1906–14 (tracing the development of deportation from its origin as an 'immediate part of the exclusion process' to a means of post-entry social control divorced from entry determinations; Stumpf (2009) 1711–14 ('When deportation laws finally appeared in the late 1880s, their reach was very limited.... The first federal deportation laws confined deportation to conditions existing at or prior to entry into the country.... Deportation for causes arising after entry appeared only after the turn of the century').

45 Anti-Drug Abuse Act of 1988, Pub. L. No. 100–690, §7342, 102 Stat. 4181, 4469–70 (establishing the 'aggravated felony' deportation grounds and including only murder, drug trafficking, and firearm trafficking); Illegal Immigration Reform and Immigrant Responsibility Act of 1996, Pub. L. No. 104-208, §321, 110 Stat. 3009-546, 3009-627 to -628 (adding a substantial list of offenses to the definition of 'aggravated felony'); see also Stumpf (2009) note 44, at 1722–25 (describing the evolution of the aggravated felony ground).

46 Stumpf (2009) note 44, at 1727–1728 ('Federal judges now have authority to order deportation during sentencing, though they no longer have the power to prevent deportation.').

47 See Brown (2011) note 24, at 1400–01.

48 See US Immigration and Customs Enforcement (2011).

49 See INA § 212(a), 8 U.S.C §1182 (2006) (listing the inadmissibility grounds).

50 Camins v. Gonzales, 500 F. 3d 872, 875 (9th Cir. 2007) (explaining that prior to 'the Illegal Immigration Reform and Immigrant Responsibility Act of 1996 . . . , a lawful permanent resident . . . who pled guilty to an offense making him "inadmissible" retained the right under . . . the Immigration and Nationality Act . . . to make "innocent, casual, and brief" overseas trips without being classified as seeking "entry" upon return and thus being exposed to a charge of being inadmissible').

51 See 8 U.S.C. § 1325 (defining the crime of improper entry and providing for criminal fines and incarceration); § 1326 (defining the crime of illegal re-entry and providing for criminal fines and incarceration).

52 See Eagly (2010), note 8, at 1282, 1328.

53 Immigration Reform and Control Act of 1986, Pub. L. No. 99-603, 100 Stat. 3359, 3360 (codified at 8 U.S.C. § 1324a); Immigration Marriage Fraud Amendments of 1986, Pub. L. No. 99-639, 100 Stat. 3537, 3542 (codified at 8 U.S.C. § 1325).

54 18 U.S.C. § 1015(e) (2006) (criminalizing false citizenship claims); Illegal Immigration Reform and Immigrant Responsibility Act of 1996 (IIRIRA), Pub. L. No. 104-208, div. C., tit. I, § 108, 110 Stat. 3009-546, 3009-557 (codified at 18 U.S.C. § 758) (criminalizing fleeing a checkpoint while speeding); 8 U.S.C. § 1324c (criminalizing concealment of preparation of a fraudulent immigration document); see also 18 U.S.C. § 1546 (criminalizing knowingly presenting a baseless document).

55 Department of Homeland Security Fact Sheet (2006). See also Eagly (2010) note 8, at 1327-29.

56 Eagly (2010) note 8, at 1327–29.

57 Ibid.

58 See United States v. Roblero-Solis, 588 F.3d 692, 693–94 (9th Cir. 2009).

59 See Eagly (2010) note 8, at 1327–29; Transactional Records Access Clearinghouse Immigration (2008) note 7; Lydgate (2010).

60 See Motomura (2006) 195–196 (offering competing arguments about membership and deportation for lawful permanent residents).

61 See Legomsky (2007) note 23, at 472–473.

62 *Padilla,* 130 S. Ct. at 1848.

63 US Customs & Border Patrol (2005).

64 *United States v. Roblero-Solis,* 588 F.3d 692, 699 (9th Cir. 2009) (quoting Advisory Committee Notes on the 1966 Amendments to the Rules of Criminal Procedure).

65 See Motomura (2008), 2037.

References

8 C.F.R. § 264.1(f)

8 U.S.C. § 1324a

8 U.S.C. § 1324c

18 U.S.C. § 1015(e)

18 U.S.C. § 1325

18 U.S.C § 1326

18 U.S.C. § 1546

Anti-Drug Abuse Act of 1988 (1988) 102 Stat. 4181, 4469–70 (codified as amended at 8 Arizona v. United States, 132 S. Ct. 2492 (2012) U.S.C. § 1101 (2006)).

Beason-Hammon Alabama Taxpayer and Citizen Protection Act (2011) Ala. Laws Act 2011-535 (H.B. 56)

Brown, D. (2011) Why Padilla doesn't matter (much). *UCLA Law Review, 58,* 1393–1415.

Camins v. Gonzales, 500 F. 3d 872 (9th Cir. 2007).

Chin, G. J. and Holmes, R.W., Jr. (2002) Effective assistance of counsel and the consequences of guilty pleas. *Cornell Law Review, 87*, 697–742.

Communication from the Commission to the European Parliament, the Council, the Economic and Social Committee and the Committee of the Regions (2011) Communication on Migration, April 5. http://eur-lex.europa.eu/LexUriServ/LexUriServ.do?uri = CELEX: 52011DC0248:EN:NOT.

Eagly, I. (2010) Prosecuting immigration. *Northwestern University Law Review, 104*, 1281–1359.

Gabriel, T. (2011) Stance on immigration may hurt Perry early on. *NY Times*, September 23, 2011. http://www.nytimes.com/2011/09/24/us/politics/rick-perrys-stance-on-immigration-may-hurt-his-chances.html.

Garland, D. (2001) *The Culture of Control: Crime and Social Order in Contemporary Society*. Chicago: University of Chicago Press.

Gazz. Uff. 170 of July 24, 2009, *Legge 15 luglio 2009, n. 94, Disposizioni in materia di sicurezza pubblica*. Available at http://www.interno.it/mininterno/export/sites/default/it/assets/files/16/0189_legge_ 15_luglio_2009_n.94.pdf.

Georgia. *Illegal Immigration Reform and Enforcement Act of 2011*. 2011 Ga. Laws, Act 252 (H.B. 87).

Hakim, D. and Bernstein, N. (2010) New Paterson policy may reduce deportations. *NY Times*, May 3. http://www.nytimes.com/2010/05/04/nyregion/04deport.html.

Illegal Immigration Reform and Immigrant Responsibility Act of 1996 (1996) 110 Stat. 3009-546, 3009-627 to -628 (current version at 8 U.S.C. § 1101(a)(43) (2006)).

Immigration Reform and Control Act of 1986 (1986) 100 Stat. 3359, 3360 (codified at 8 U.S.C. § 1324a (2006)).

Kanstroom, D. (2000) Deportation, social control, and punishment: Some thoughts about why hard laws make bad cases. *Harvard Law Review, 113*, 1889–1935.

Kanstroom, D. (2011) The right to deportation council in Padilla v. Kentucky: The challenging construction of the fifth-and-a-half-amendment. *UCLA Law Review, 58*, 1461–1514.

Lamar Smith, Chairman of the US House of Representatives Judiciary Committee, Letter to the Editor. *Immigration Laws, NY Times*, Feb. 9, 2011. http://www.nytimes.com/2011/02/10/opinion/lweb10immig.html ('Waiting until illegal immigrants commit criminal offenses before deporting them places American citizens and legal immigrants in danger').

Legomsky, S. H. (2007) The new path of immigration law: Asymmetric incorporation of criminal justice norms. *Washington & Lee Law Review, 64*, 469–528.

Lydgate, J. (2010) *Assembly-Line Justice: A Review of Operation Streamline*. Chief Justice Earl Warren Institute on Race, Ethnicity & Diversity, University of California, Berkeley Law School. http://www.law.berkeley.edu/files/Operation_Streamline_Policy_Brief.pdf.

Massey, D. (2009) *Criminalizing Immigration in the Post 9/11 Era*. Points of Migration (Center for Migration and Development, Princeton University) September 1, 2009. Available at: mmp.opr.princeton.edu/databases/pdf/Massey_2009_Criminalizing Immigration in the Post 911 Era.pdf

Mitsilegas, V. (2003) *The European Union and Internal Security: Guardian of the People?* Basingstoke: Palgrave Macmillan.

Moore, J. (forthcoming) Minority overrepresentation in criminal justice systems: Causes, consequences, and cures. *Freedom Center Journal*. http://papers.ssrn.com/sol3/papers.cfm?abstract_id = 1919162.

Morris, M. (2009) Italy's immigrants despair at new laws. *BBC News*, July 27.

Motomura, H. (2006) *Americans in Waiting: The Lost Story of Immigration and Citizenship in the United States*. Oxford: Oxford University Press.

Motomura, H. (2008) Immigration outside the law. *Columbia Law Review, 108*, 2037–2097.

Office of Immigration Statistics, US Department of Homeland Security (2005) *2005 Yearbook of Immigration Statistics*.

Office of Immigration Statistics, US Department of Homeland Security (2006) *2006 Yearbook of Immigration Statistics*.

Office of Immigration Statistics, US Department of Homeland Security (2010) *2009 Yearbook of Immigration Statistics*.

Office of Immigration Statistics, US Department of Homeland Security (2011) *2010 Yearbook of Immigration Statistics*.

Olivares, K.M., Burton, V.S. and Cullen, F.T. (1996) The collateral consequences of a felony conviction: A national study of state legal codes 10 years later. *Federal Probation, 60*, 11–17.

Pacella, J.M. (2011) Welcoming the unwanted: Italy's response to the immigration phenomenon and European Union involvement. *Georgetown Immigration Law Journal, 25*, 341–375.

Padilla v. Kentucky, 130 S. Ct. 1473 (2010).

Pakes, F. (2004) The politics of discontent: The emergence of a new criminal justice discourse in the Netherlands. *The Howard Journal, 43*, 284–298.

Registration of Certain Nonimmigrant Aliens from Designated Countries, 67 Fed. Reg. 77, 642 (December 18, 2002).

Roberts, J. (2009) Ignorance is effectively bliss: Collateral consequences, silence, and misinformation in the guilty-plea process. *Iowa Law Review, 95*, 119–194.

Stumpf, J.P. (2006) The crimmigration crisis: Immigrants, crime, and sovereign power. *American University Law Review, 56*, 367–419.

Stumpf, J. P. (2008) States of confusion: The rise of state and local power over immigration. *North Carolina Law Review, 86*, 1557–1618.

Stumpf, J. P. (2009) Fitting punishment. *Washington & Lee Law Review, 66*, 1683–1741.

Stumpf, J. P. (2011) Doing time. *UCLA Law Review, 58*, 1705–1748.

Support Our Law Enforcement and Safe Neighborhoods Act (2010) ch. 113, 2010 Ariz. Sess. Laws 450 (codified in scattered sections of Ariz. Rev. Stat. Ann. tits. 11, 13, 23, 28, 41), as amended by Act of Apr. 30, 2010, ch. 211, 2010 Ariz. Sess. Laws 1070.

The Pew Charitable Trusts (2010) *Collateral Costs: Incarceration's Effect on Economic Mobility*. Washington: Pew.

Transactional Records Access Clearinghouse Immigration (2008) Surge in immigration prosecutions continues. http://trac.syr.edu/immigration/reports/188.

United States. *Immigration Marriage Fraud Amendments of 1986* (1986) 100 Stat. 3537, 3542 (codified at 8 U.S.C. § 1325 (2006)).

United States v. Brignoni-Ponce, 422 US 873 (1975).

United States v. Roblero-Solis, 588 F.3d 692 (9th Cir. 2009).

US Customs & Border Patrol (2005) DHS launches 'Operation Streamline II': Enforcement effort focusing on prosecuting and removing illegal aliens in Del Rio, Texas. US Customs and Border Protection News Release (Friday, December 16).

US Department of Homeland Security Fact Sheet (2006) *Secure Border Initiative Update 1* (August 23). http://www.dhs.gov/xnews/releases/pr_1158351496818.shtm.

US Department of Justice (2002) Memorandum from the Deputy Attorney General, Guidance for Absconder Apprehension Initiative, January 25. Available at http://fl.find-law.com/news.findlaw.com/hdocs/docs/doj/abscndr012502mem.pdf.

US Immigration and Customs Enforcement (2011) ICE arrests more than 2,900 convicted criminal aliens, fugitives in enforcement operation throughout all 50 states. News Release, September 28.

Van der Leun, J. (2010) *Crimmigratie*. Apeldoorn/Antwerpen: Maklu (inaugural lecture) (manuscript on file with author).

Van der Leun, J. and van der Woude, M. (2011) Ethnic profiling in the Netherlands? A reflection on expanding preventive powers, ethnic profiling and a changing social and political context. *Policing and Society*, 21, 444–455.

Van der Woude, M.A.H. (2009) Brede benadering terrorismebestrijding. *Openbaar Bestuur*, 11, 2–5.

8 Exporting risk, deporting non-citizens

Leanne Weber and Sharon Pickering

Introduction

At one level, deportation appears to be the logical and inevitable outcome of a rational legal system which has determined that an individual has no legal right to remain in a particular territory. It is a legal expression of sovereign will; widely understood as a legitimate and routine administrative act. In many cases 'voluntary' departures are made, no doubt involving varying degrees of reluctance, relief, regret and persuasion. But at other times the process of expulsion is characterized by resistance, fear and coercion. Observed at first hand, forced deportation reveals itself to be a process infused with human degradation and suffering. As reported by one sympathetic UK immigration officer: 'people struggle to go sometimes you know, and they're tied up and handcuffed and you think, well what happens to these people when they get back to their countries?' (Weber and Gelsthorpe, 2000: 93).

Many border control technologies have the capacity to cause death or serious harm by shifting risks onto illegalized migrants (Weber and Pickering, 2011). But forced expulsion expresses the sovereign power to exclude in its most immediate and visceral form. As Khosravi (2009: 40) has noted: 'Detention and deportation have become the bodily sanctions of the migration regime, producing a condition of "deportability" that threatens all migrants'. Between 2000 and 2006, to cite just one example, the Swedish government recorded 45,538 'voluntary returns' and 37,601 'forced returns' (Khosravi, 2009: 41). This figure is dwarfed by the 195,000 deportations per annum currently in the USA (Napolitano, 2010). Despite these large numbers, the violence and humiliation of forced deportation remains largely obscured behind a façade of legal rationality. The alternative term 'removal', which brings to mind the transportation of furniture or the neat surgical excision of a dangerous growth or unsightly blemish, seems expressly designed to mask the human dimension of deportation.[1]

Even so, the messy instrumental and expressive violence of forced deportations occasionally breaks through this legal and rhetorical veneer. This is the scene that confronted English press photographer Jessica Hurd when she boarded a commercial flight from Gatwick Airport to Vilnius in April 2004.

I got to my seat, some women were screaming at the back of the plane... It was too distressing not to intervene...I walked to the back of the plane.... The official on the girl's right appeared to have his hand on her neck. I am not sure if she was handcuffed at that point, though the woman behind her definitely was. The girl had tears streaming down her face and was obviously in a lot of distress. On the row behind her I looked more closely at the woman behind. She was an older woman, probably in her mid-thirties, also flanked by two security people. She had handcuffs on and was only wearing her underwear: bra and pants...I said, 'She has no clothes on!'... In front of her, there were three children (differing ages, about 10 years and under) sitting on the seats in front, looking very scared and shaken.... The female Immigration Officer went off briefly and returned. I asked again what she would do and she said she would take them off the plane, and she asked me to sit down.... The whole flight had to see the women being dragged back through the plane, one with only her bra and pants on. She was hunched over trying to preserve her modesty while she walked down the plane. She was still in handcuffs and being pulled from the front and pushed from behind.... After they left, an official came up to me and asked me what my name was. I asked why he needed to know. He said I had been "obstructing Government business".

(Granville-Chapman *et al.*, 2004, Appendix B)

In this chapter we subject the 'government business' of forced deportation to critical analysis. We discuss emerging trends across countries of the Global North and characterize deportation as an essentially transnational strategy for the exporting of risk. We then consider the risks posed by the process of deportation itself – firstly in relation to governments, but more crucially as experienced by those subjected to it.

Deportation as exporting risk

Organized deportation as a way of dealing with 'surplus' (Bauman, 2004) or 'nuisance' populations (Walters, 2002) has existed in various guises throughout human history – from ancient forms of individual exile and collective banishment (Gray, 2011; Walters, 2002); to the transportation of 'criminal classes' to the British colonies (Walters, 2002); and the recurring mass deportations of European Jews (Bloch and Schuster, 2005). At different times and locations these expulsion strategies have targeted both citizens and non-citizens, and have been variously directed towards abandonment, or continuing control with a view to punishment, the extraction of forced labour, and sometimes the deliberate infliction of death. Walters (2002: 279) associates the rise of contemporary forms of deportation with the process of governmentalization, namely the emergence of forms of governance designed to 'defend and promote the welfare of a nationally-defined population'.

We argue here that, under conditions of late-modernity, technologies of exclusion initially designed to protect the distribution of goods and resources within a territorially bounded polity, have become harnessed to the broader risk-reducing agendas of neo-liberal governments, who no longer interpret their duty towards their constituents through the provision of welfare, but govern largely through the production of community safety and the pre-emption of threats. Viewed through this lens, deportation comes to be seen, not just a routine exercise in legal rationality, but as a governmental device for the exporting of risk.

Deportation, globalization and risk

At a time when more of the world's population than ever before is on the move, the confluence of cross-border mobility and heightened risk perception has led to an intense focus on border controls across the Global North. Dauvergne (2008: 2) links border control so closely to globalization that she suggests that trends in migration law and enforcement 'function almost as a laboratory setting for testing globalization's hypotheses'. The same modalities of neo-liberal governance that generate punitive responses to domestic social problems also produce exclusionary tendencies in response to the unprecedented permeability of borders: 'Like being tough on crime, defending the border and protecting the nation from contamination by foreign elements also carries enormous political and symbolic capital' (Aas, 2007a: 292). As Jock Young (1999) has argued, societies driven by fear and insecurity become excluding societies. This may be observed at subnational level in manifold varieties of structural exclusion and through proactive policing strategies directed towards risky individuals in risky places. At the national level, we see governments across the Global North constructing categories of risky refugees and risky non-citizens 'in order to manage the insecurities caused by migration' (Khosravi 2009: 49). Anna Pratt also relates the rise in 'immigration penality' to the preoccupation of neo-liberal governments with risk-avoidance.

Official priorities are directed at the detection, detention, and deportation of the risky onshore refugee claimant rather than identifying and extending protection to refugees at risk. It is not that the objective of protecting genuine refugees has disappeared or that the corollary objective of excluding the risky was not previously present; rather, the humanitarian objective and the international legal obligation to protect refugees have come to be represented as a residual effect that is contingent in the first instance on the identification and exclusion of those who pose risks (Pratt, 2005: 217).

As Aas (2007b: 98) observes:

> Rather than creating "citizens of the world", the globalizing process seems to be dividing the world; creating and even deepening the "us" and "them" mentality – where the political and media discourse insists on the importance of protecting the national from the foreign.

Where possible, the border is defended pre-emptively in order, as Bauman (2002: 111) puts it, to 'steer clear of trouble by locking the doors against all those who knock asking for shelter'. If those who are locked out manage to find another means of entry, their immigration status thereafter assigns them to a 'risk class' which identifies them as ongoing objects of coercive control whose rights to stay are either non-existent or conditional (De Giorgi, 2006). Deportation therefore emerges as a key technology for dividing populations and protecting national territory. The internal border effectively operates to 'select, eject and immobilize' suspect individuals and surplus populations (Weber and Bowling, 2008). Bigo has described these exclusionary trends as the replacement of the 'panopticon' with the 'banopticon' (cited in Aas, 2007a: 288).

In addition to their value as governmental devices for risk reduction, coercive border practices also bear the hallmarks of sovereignty. As evidence of this, Pratt (2005: 219) notes that 'detention and deportation continue to display an affinity for spectacle and are still tied to the territoriality of the nation-state'. De Genova (2007: 434) refers to expressive forms of border performance as 'spectacle[s] of frontier policing'. The events witnessed and documented by Jessica Hurd amount to a degradation ritual which far exceeds actions that would normally be associated with a routine legal process. Other authors have proposed that deportation has a powerful symbolic value in reinforcing cultural, political and moral boundaries. Aas notes that 'the drawing of moral boundaries, a traditional concern of criminal law, is today performed not only through the discourse of punishment, but also through practices of banishment and expulsion' (2007b: 81). And Anderson *et al.* have argued that '[t]he act of expulsion simultaneously rids the state of an unwanted individual and affirms the political community's idealized view of what membership should (or should not) mean' (2011: 548). Alongside its significant symbolic value in marking the contours of morality, citizenship and belonging, deportation remains a distinctly embodied practice: 'By taking away the bodily pollution of an anti-citizen, the purity of society is preserved. Thus, removal of each anti-citizen can be seen as a worship of nationhood or a celebration of citizenship' (Khosravi 2009: 52).

Deportation as 'government business'

While they argue that democratic countries have traditionally considered deportation to be a 'last resort', Anderson *et al.* (2011: 551) note a 'prodigious rise' in the use of deportation by liberal democracies in the last 20 years and claim it is an 'international phenomenon'. In the face of unprecedented pressures for cross-border mobility, it seems that the 'government business' of forced deportation is booming. Gibney (2008) refers to this trend as the 'deportation turn'. Bloch and Schuster (2005) agree that deportation, along with other coercive aspects of border control such as detention and dispersal, have become normalized in contemporary Britain. In the Australian state of New South Wales, accompanying deportees is reported to be the most frequently registered extra-curricular employment for state police (Weber, 2011). In fact, forced deportation is properly seen, not *just* as government business, although it is clearly with governments that responsibility lies, but as an industry implicating a range of participants from police and immigration officials to international airlines and security staff. Khosravi (2009: 40) describes Sweden's deportation system as 'an enterprise involving transport companies, private security companies, five detention centres, deportation escorts, international networking (asylum attachés) and private expert companies'. 'Most pointedly,' argues Walters (2002: 266), 'we are reminded that private companies make money from this form of suffering. Deportation is business.'

According to Anderson *et al.* (2011: 547), the number of non-citizens 'leaving under the threat of coercion' doubled in the UK from 30,000 in 1997 to 68,000 in 2008, then remained relatively steady at 67,000 in 2009. The Obama administration has overseen the highest level of deportations in US history. The number of aliens returned or removed from the USA increased steadily from 114,432 in 1997 to 319,382 in 2007, representing a three-fold increase in just 10 years (Anderson *et al.*, 2011). According to Secretary for Homeland Security, Janet Napolitano (2010), her department increased their deportation rate by a further 70 per cent from 2008 to a total of 195,000 in the 2010 fiscal year. Gibney (2008: 146) reports increased expulsions also in the Netherlands, Germany, Canada and Australia, as a way of dealing with asylum seekers and non-citizens convicted of crimes. Figures published by Pratt (2005: 163) show deportations in Canada rose steadily from 4,798 in 1995 to a high of 9,165 in 2001, although remaining relatively low by world standards. More dramatic rises were recorded in Sweden. According to Khosravi (2009) deportations increased from 1,570 in 1999, to 10,434 in 2004, fell slightly, then rose again to over 10,000 in 2007. Relative to its population, Australia has historically maintained high levels of deportation, although its preoccupation with offshore controls has produced a slightly different pattern. According to Nicholls (2007: 146), deportations dipped in the mid 1990s when immigration authorities were directed to concentrate on dealing with asylum seekers arriving by boat, then increased to a peak of 26,000 over a two-year period from 2002 to 2004, but fell slightly thereafter to 10,501 in 2005–6 following scandals over the wrongful detention and expulsion of Australian citizens. Since then, the trend has once again been downwards, with 8,825 deportations recorded in 2009–10 (DIAC, 2010), roughly the same as the pre-2000 levels.

Against a general rise in the use of deportation, both the overall numbers and the groups that are targeted are subject to fluctuations according to political priorities and other exigencies. Noting which groups are deported, and on what grounds, gives some insight into the normative boundaries of citizenship, since those expelled are effectively labeled unfit for neo-liberal forms of citizenship based on merit (Zedner, 2010). This mentality underlies current strategies pursued by the Obama administration. The DREAM Act (standing for Development Relief and Education for Alien Minors) aims to increase deportations of undocumented immigrants, while at the same time extending the benefits of citizenship to those who entered the country before they were 16, and can therefore be construed as blameless (Napolitano, 2010).

From 2006, following political pressure in Britain about the release of 'foreign' prisoners into the community, legislation was passed to require that all non-British prisoners be routinely deported at the end of their sentence unless their expulsion would breach international obligations (Bosworth, 2011). Anderson *et al.* (2011) argue that the target of 4,000 deportations of foreign criminals by 2007 served an important symbolic function; but they note that rejected asylum seekers continued to be the largest category, accounting for 10,840 of 28,065 enforced removals in 2007. Khosravi (2009) associates the dramatic increase in removals in Sweden primarily with the harmonization of asylum policies in the EU and the consequent increase in rejections of asylum applications. The emphasis on deporting criminal offenders emerged as early as 1994 in Canada, when the 'Criminal First' Policy was announced in response to a highly publicized murder committed by a non-citizen (Pratt, 2005: 161). The policy had a significant effect on both deportation rates and the composition of excluded populations. Pratt reports that the proportion of all removals who were criminal deportees jumped from 15 per cent in 1993–4 to 37 per cent in 1995–6. However, it stabilized and fell back later in the face of rising numbers of failed asylum applicants, returning to 18 per cent by 1997. Notwithstanding the emphasis on terror suspects after 2001, asylum seekers emerge once again as the enduring target for expulsion. Despite the risk-related rhetoric about immigration offenders and dangerous others, asylum seekers, it seems, remain the easiest target for deportation programs across many jurisdictions (Gibney, 2008).

In Australia, the 'priorities matrix' which guides immigration enforcement practices places criminal deportees at the top, along with those who have committed systematic fraud against the immigration system, and unauthorized boat arrivals. No publicly announced quotas are set for removals and deportations. In fact, public announcements that large numbers of asylum seekers were being removed from the Australian mainland could undermine the contemporary myth of impermeable borders on which successive Australian governments have staked their credibility by acknowledging that unwanted arrivals have taken place. New provisions were introduced in 1999 to widen the scope for the Immigration Minister to cancel the visas of lawfully present non-citizens in the interests of community safety (Nicholls, 2007). Criminal deportations peaked in 2002–3 at 118, after being steady at around 60 to 70 over previous years (Nicholls, 2007, 155). The numbers fell away sharply thereafter due to a variety of legal and political challenges. While numbers remain low, the Department of Immigration has used deportation as a swift response to radio 'shock jocks' identifying serious criminals as having been born overseas, even when they have lived most of their lives in Australia.

Projects of mass deportation are highly racialized. The Dutch government rhetoric about the deportation of 'dangerous others' has focused on convicted criminals with Moroccan nationality, alongside calls for police surveillance of Antillean youths (Van der Leun and Van der Woude, 2011). In Japan, the population of 'illegal immigrants' was reduced by an astonishing 50 per cent in five years from approximately 220,000 persons in January 2004 to around 113,000 persons in January 2009, through a concerted deportation program primarily directed towards ethnic Koreans and Chinese (Namba, 2011). In some places, securitization has brought an added dimension and a particular urgency to deportation programs. In the aftermath of the September 11 attacks in the United States, the 10-year 'Endgame' plan was introduced to promote national security by ensuring the departure of all 'removable aliens' (De Genova, 2007, see also Sheik, 2008). This strategy fused the categories of non-citizen and terrorist within a highly racialized conception of those who were considered unfit for citizenship, focusing on young men from the Middle East.

Across countries, the use of deportation has been widely regarded as the integrity mechanism in the immigration framework. That is, deportation is the lever to redress what are regarded as anomalous outcomes or unacceptable risks in terms of allowing people to stay. When national governments reach for deportation they, on the one hand, use it as the sanction against visa breaches – in short a form of administrative punishment. And, on the other hand, they often use it to reduce threats to public perceptions of the migration program, in particular when the media identify law and order risks in relation to non-citizens.

Deportation as risky business for governments

While forced expulsion creates the illusion of unilateral power and control, to assert that this power is absolute would be misleading. Returning an individual to their place of origin necessitates bilateral negotiations which often fail (Walters, 2002). The nationality of undocumented individuals can remain a matter of endless dispute; states may be reluctant to accept the return of their citizens who have been absent for long periods, and who are seen to be returning with the taint of criminality or disloyalty; and situations in countries of origin may be so dangerous or disorderly as to preclude any possibility of return. One example of the latter is the failed attempt in 2009 by the UK government to expel a group of Iraqi asylum seekers (Bosworth, 2011). The Chief Inspector of Prisons in the UK has noted that '[s]ome of those we observed in detention had been dealt with by immigration authorities as though they were parcels, not people; and parcels whose contents and destination were sometimes incorrect' (cited in Youseff 2011: 12). Legal obstacles to forced expulsion can also arise on home soil, such as the longstanding antipathy between the former conservative Australian government and the appellate authorities over legal objections to the deportation of convicted non-citizens with strong family and community connections (Nicholls, 2007).

Bosworth (2011: 592) links these restrictions to criminological arguments about the limits of the sovereign state, noting that 'the forces of globalization restrict the capacity of the state to police and enforce its borders in a manner analogous to its equally impotent capacity to enforce crime control measures'. A 'deportation gap' (Gibney, 2008) which results when states prove unwilling or unable to expel non-citizens has been noted in Germany and the Netherlands, leading to rising detention populations (Broeders, 2010). On the other hand, Gibney (2008) argues that the UK government successfully overcame legal and practical barriers by shortcutting procedural justice, increasing the use of detention for those awaiting removal, and using more organized means of deportation such as charter flights for particular nationalities, backed up by bilateral return agreements.

Beyond the risk of failure, deportation also poses both financial and political risks for governments. Forced deportation requires a considerable infrastructure. The sharp increase in deportations from Sweden described by Khosravi (2009) necessitated a 70 per cent increase in the border enforcement budget. The recourse to secretive, jointly administrated charter flights by European Union has also proven to be expensive. European Race Audit (ERA) researchers reported that, of the €5,866 million allocated by the EU to so-called solidarity and management of migration flows for the period 2007–13, nearly €3,000 million is allocated to external border controls and returns (ERA, 2010: 2). And repeated financial crises have created further incentives to accelerate deportation programs as potentially cheaper options to the construction of more detention centres (ERA, 2010).

Deportations may also come at a heavy political cost. As argued by Anderson *et al.* (2011: 558): 'Although citizens may be broadly in agreement with government immigration policy and acknowledge the consequent logic of deportation, its actual practice can be deeply unsettling to a political culture that values physical integrity and individual rights'. Organized resistance movements may appeal to general human rights principles or to the particular value to the community of an individual threatened with deportation. On the other hand, unpopular groups such as foreign prisoners may be unable to mobilise community support, so there tend to be 'few qualms' about their deportation (Bosworth, 2011). Even so, deportation is still 'liable to generate conflicts amongst citizens and between citizens and the state over the question of who is part of the normative community of members' (Anderson *et al.* 2011: 547). The widely publicized deportations on 'character grounds' of individuals who have lived in Australia from early childhood (Grewcock, 2009; Nicholls, 2007) has drawn criticism from civil liberties groups and attracted some public sympathy, despite their criminal convictions. It seems at least some sectors of Australian society are prepared to accept that their apparent character deficits were 'made in Australia'.

Summarising the barriers encountered when seeking to deport non-citizens, Gibney (2008) identifies three main risks for governments: firstly that the target will be 'socially integrated' and therefore attract community support (a moral consideration); also that they will be 'lost' to the authorities and therefore be unavailable for deportation (a practical consideration), and finally that they will be available but will prove to be 'unreturnable' (a legal consideration). Despite these risks and obstacles, Walters (2002) notes that governments remain 'obsessed' with repatriation and expulsion as an apparent solution to the problems posed by neo-liberal globalization. Gibney (2008: 167) also acknowledges the continuing appeal of deportation, suggesting it 'reflects a new willingness and ability on the part of states to treat non-citizens in illiberal ways'. He concludes that the UK government has increased removals by finding innovative ways to stay marginally within normative expectations while streamlining processes in ways that mask the possibility for errors and hide the human impacts from public scrutiny. In the next section we reveal some of the human impacts of deportation and open them up for scrutiny.

The human risks of deportation

The harm to individuals arising from deportation may take the form of physical injury, psychological trauma, separation from family and community support, loss of livelihood and opportunities for education, to deep assaults on personal dignity and sense of belonging, the harm of which should not be understated. A young Iranian interviewed by Khosravi (2009: 53) who was 'deported back and forth between countries' said he 'felt himself redundant and unwanted'. The mentalities which underlie these practices reveal a 'vituperative quality pasted on the back of the rationale of control' which characterizes the responses of the 'included' to the perceived transgressions of the 'excluded' (Young 2003: 407). Deliberate humiliation tactics reminiscent of the spectacle witnessed by Jessica Hurd, were also identified by Khosravi in his analysis of deportation procedures in Sweden.

Those who have no travel documents are escorted by policemen to the embassy of their homeland in order to apply for a travel document. If they will not do this voluntarily, they are humiliated by being taken to the embassy forcibly, often in handcuffs and escorted by police in uniform. The authorities blame the deportees for any violence involved in this process and claim it is a consequence of their disobedience. In late October 2006, six uniformed policemen forced one young man to go to the Eritrean embassy wearing nothing but his underwear (Khosravi, 2009: 47).

Concerns about the physical and psychological risks associated with forced deportation are magnified when children are involved. Children may suffer the harm of being left behind, and may be traumatized by the experience of witnessing a parent's forced removal. They may be deported themselves, alone or with guardians, and may be exposed to the possibility of ill-treatment in transit. When they arrive at the place of return they face an uncertain future. Moreover, harm may also arise, not just for the adults and children who are, in fact, deported, but for those who live in perpetual dread of being taken into custody when they report to immigration authorities, or of having their home invaded by an early morning raid. Deportation practices can also generate wider social harm – from the schools and workplaces disrupted by the sudden disappearance of a colleague or classmate; the impact on affected minority communities in terms of their perceptions of the legal system and of their own social inclusion; to the message sent to the wider population, some of whom are willing to conclude that people who are so treated must be dangerous and undeserving.

While acknowledging these wider personal and social risks, we focus here on physical risks of injury and death arising directly or indirectly from forced deportation. Physical risks to the lives and well being of individuals may arise *during* the process of deportation, *following* deportation into situations of danger, and in *anticipation* of being forcibly returned to a country from which they have fled. The examples of harm in these three contexts that are outlined in the following three sections have been analysed in more detail elsewhere (Weber and Pickering, 2011).

Deadly deportations

Although certainly not the largest category, it has been observed that deaths during deportation are the fastest-growing category of border-related deaths in Europe (Fekete, 2009). The greatest risks arise from the inappropriate use of restraints and excessive force by private security guards or other law enforcement officers charged with escorting deportees who refuse, or have not been offered the opportunity, to make a 'voluntary' departure. The death by asphyxiation of 40-year-old Jamaican woman, Joy Gardner, in 1993, after police officers wound 13 feet of tape around her mouth, brought the violence of forced deportation to the notice of the British public. Ms Gardner, whose visa had expired in 1987, left behind a 5-year-old son who was born in England, and who witnessed his mother's violent death. A team of six immigration officers and police had been sent to their north London flat, which was occupied only by the mother and son. Joy Gardner's death at the hands of state officials came to symbolize wider concerns about the violence of forced deportation.

Forced deportation has now become an issue of great concern across Europe. The European Committee for the Prevention of Torture concluded in 2003 that deportation operations entailed a 'manifest risk of inhuman and degrading treatment' (CPT, 2003). The Committee specifically warned against prolonged application of body weight or bending the detainee forward, and urged an immediate ban on the use of gagging or other devices that could obstruct airways. They concluded that degrading practices such as preventing deportees from using toilet facilities, and forcing them to wear nappies violated Article 3 of the European Convention on Human Rights. The CPT also raised concerns about the mistreatment of detainees en route to or from airports[2] and stressed the importance of avoiding unnecessary anxiety by allowing deportees time to arrange their affairs – no doubt with the escalating practice of 'dawn raids' clearly in mind.

Across Europe, the imposition of removal targets, the instigation of bilateral agreements for the return of deportees, and the implementation of organized charter flights has had the effect of routinising forced deportations. In 2010, the United Kingdom reportedly operated charter flights to Afghanistan 'every other Tuesday evening under the codename Operation Ravel' (ERA, 2010: 5). Moreover, Fekete (2009: 3) argues that performance indicators for border police and security guards create a 'callous culture' which is conducive to violence. Accelerated legal processes aimed at expediting removals may also bring added risks to deportees by decreasing the quality of administrative decisions (ERA, 2010; Home Affairs Committee, 2003: 13). This increases the likelihood of deporting those in abject fear of return, who might be expected to exhibit more anxiety and resistance. A thematic review of detainee escorts and removals from the UK conducted by HM Inspector of Prisons in 2009 concluded that violent deportation methods could be unproductive, as well as individually unjustified, noting that 'in most cases the use of force did not assist removal, but in fact led to its abandonment' (HMIP, 2009: 6).

The death of Jimmy Mubenga in October 2010 on board British Airways flight BA77 drew attention to the personal and political risks of using commercial flights for forced deportation. The Angolan father of five had spent two years in prison for a serious assault, which proved to be a death sentence. After his time was served his leave to remain in the UK was revoked. Jimmy Mubenga died after passengers on board BA77 heard him shouting for 10 minutes or more that the G4S security guards were trying to kill him and insisting that he could not breathe. The three guards were questioned and released on bail, and media reports suggested that Scotland Yard was investigating a range of assault charges against other deportation escorts (Lewis *et al.*, 2010). Writing in the British newspaper, *The Guardian*, immigration adviser Anna Morvern (2010) spread the responsibility more widely, claiming it was time to 'look at ourselves and ask how we became a society that will now effect deportations by almost any means possible'.

Apart from a temporary ban on the use of restraints following the death of Jimmy Mubenga, the primary action taken by the Home Office was to decline to renew the G4S deportation contract (Lewis and Taylor, 2011). Responses to deportation deaths in other parts of Europe have shown a similar pattern of impunity and failure to ask fundamental questions about the deportation system. Of 12 documented deportation deaths in Europe, none resulted in a criminal conviction (Fekete, 2009: 4). The Spanish Government reportedly responded to the asphyxiation death of Osamuyi Aikpitanhi by recommending that resistant deportees be fitted with straightjackets and helmets. This was despite the fact that 'deportation helmets' designed to immobilize the lower jaw were banned in Germany in 1999 after contributing to the death of Sudanese asylum seeker Aamir Mohamed Ageeb (Fekete, 2009: 4). Regardless of the technical risks, these practices demonstrate a level of disregard for human dignity which would be hard to imagine if not for the fact that they are taking place, if not before our eyes, then at one small distance of remove.

The continuing risks of deportation

The risk of physical, psychological and emotional harm may not be over once a deportee arrives at their destination. In some cases this homecoming may signal the onset of even greater problems. Being transnational practices, deportation inevitably has transnational effects, which can include alienation from both societies. As Khosravi (2009) points out, deported individuals may not be returning 'home' – especially those who left as children. They may be treated with suspicion in their country of origin, stigmatized as failed migrants or worse, and may experience their return as a form of exile. According to Brotherton (2008), Dominicans expelled from the United States are often branded as troublemakers, regardless of the reason for their expulsion, and can be vulnerable to scapegoating and abuse from police after their return. Bowling (2010) also encountered negative responses amongst Caribbean communities to the return of criminal deportees from the United Kingdom. Even in the absence of criminal convictions, Sheik (2008) has argued that many Muslim men caught up in large-scale deportations from the USA in the security sweeps following the September 11 attacks were systematically criminalized following their return to Pakistan.

Most of them want to leave this episode in their lives behind them, yet they carry a deep sense of shame and guilt. The deportees have also been deeply affected by the physical and emotional abuse they experienced in prison and the lengthy deportation proceedings. Because some of them were imprisoned immediately after arriving in their home countries, they live in perpetual fear of further imprisonment (Sheik, 2008: 95).

Although documentary evidence is hard to find, refugee support groups often assert that serious harm befalls rejected asylum seekers who are returned to the country from which they have fled. This may occur in circumstances which vindicate the claims of persecution the individuals have made in their asylum applications or in situations of generalized conflict and violence. The very process of expulsion itself may create or magnify the suspicions of those in power. For example, the organization Pro Asyl documented several instances where Turkish Kurds were detained and tortured after being deported from Germany (Bloch and Schuster, 2005: 497). One Iraqi refugee who was recognized by the Australian government but only granted a temporary protection visa due to the irregular manner of his arrival, was killed following his forced return, reportedly because he was suspected of being a spy (Nicholls, 2007: 147). The Edmund Rice Centre followed the fate of a small number of rejected asylum applicants returned to Afghanistan by the Australian government in 2006, and reported that at least two were killed and two others had lost family members 'after they had returned to situations of lawlessness and reprisals' (Nicholls 2007: 147). Even so-called 'voluntary' returns, can have catastrophic consequences, where risk calculations made under extreme duress prove to be ill-founded. Fekete (2009: 5) reports that rejected asylum seeker Solyman Rashed was 'so ground down by his experiences in the UK' that he accepted 'voluntary' return to Iraq, where he was killed by a car bomb just two weeks after his arrival (Fekete 2009: 5).

Not only are immigration and asylum procedures implicated in *refouling* individuals to serious danger; deportation procedures themselves may expose individuals to additional risks. Khosravi (2009) found that the Swedish practice of tasking outposted 'asylum attachés' to verify the identities of undocumented deportees by visiting their villages, could greatly increase the risks they faced on return. He attributed failure to recognise these risks largely to faith in the efficacy of official refugee determination procedures in sorting genuine from false claims.

> They may be in even more danger after the deportation than before, particularly in countries such as Vietnam, where seeking asylum is itself a punishable offence ... [S]ince the asylum seekers' fear of persecution is rejected as

false, it is assumed that they will be in no danger if the authorities in countries of origin know about them.

(Khosravi, 2009: 51)

The Pakistani men deported from the United States who were interviewed by Sheik also reported a pervading sense of mistrust and some experiences of mistreatment that were exacerbated by the manner of their forced return.

For some, the ordeal was far from over even when they returned to their homelands. Some of the deportees were sent back with travel documents informing local authorities about their political asylum applications filed in the United States. These papers made the deportees appear suspicious to their home governments, and many underwent additional investigation, imprisonment, and even torture (Sheik, 2008: 99).

Vulnerable individuals, such as unaccompanied minors, may be at particular risk if they are deported without adequate arrangements for their ongoing care and protection. Along the US–Mexico border, the practice of summarily returning unaccompanied minors across the border, often into dangerous areas far from the child's home town, has attracted major criticism from NGOs. A study by a working group within the Mexican Congress found that 15 per cent of the 90,000 minors who were transported over the border from the United States in 2008 remained in the border areas to which they were returned, and did not travel back to their places of origin (Jimenez, 2009).

Anticipating risk

Fear of deportation, whether ongoing and pervasive, or triggered by the sight of approaching officials, can also lead to injury and death. After the formation of 'snatch squads' of immigration officials and police in the UK, a spate of 'balcony deaths' occurred due to desperate attempts to escape arrest (Weber and Bowling, 2004). These high-profile events, along with the desire of immigration authorities to avoid confrontations with supporters, may be behind the introduction of dawn raids. These commando-style tactics which rely on an 'element of surprise' (Gibney, 2008) were criticised by the UK Parliament's Joint Committee on Human Rights in 2007, and clearly run counter to the earlier advice issued by the Committee for the Prevention of Torture about allowing deportees sufficient time to prepare themselves for removal (CPT, 2003).

In Sydney, the death in 2004 of a Chinese man Seong Ho Kang, who was struck by a taxi as he fled from immigration officers during a workplace raid, also seems to have impacted on departmental procedures, as reported by this senior immigration official.

[I]t is our department's policy that we do not pursue people, and part of the reason for that is if a person is running they tend to run somewhat blindly and we don't want to chase them into a situation of danger where they are a danger to themselves and to others. So for example we won't chase – the police generally may.

(Weber 2012, forthcoming)

However, changed immigration enforcement procedures failed to stop the death by drowning in September 2006 of Malaysian national Wah Aun Chan who ran from police following a routine vehicle stop in rural South Australia (Weber, 2011). Although the coroners' report suggested no evidence that police had actively pursued Wah Aun Chan, it seems that his knowledge of their immigration enforcement powers was sufficient to persuade him to take risky evasive action.

The most desperate and tragic avoidance strategy, adopted by some people marked for deportation, is the taking of their own life. Ongoing uncertainty associated with precarious forms of migration status and fears surrounding impending deportation have been associated with high levels of stress and psychological disturbance (Mansouri and Cauchi, 2007; Steel, 2003). According to a report prepared by the Institute of Race Relations in the United Kingdom, deaths of asylum seekers in the community, particularly suicides, are increasing and averaging one known death a month (Athwal, 2010). Anticipatory suicide occurs within immigration detention centres and within the community, wherever individuals feel unable to deal with the fear of imminent or seemingly inevitable return. However, there is 'simply no way of knowing' how many self-inflicted deaths or incidents have occurred as a result (Cohen, 2008: 241).

Immiseration policies aimed at encouraging potential deportees to make 'voluntary departures' have been described as intended to 'break their will and resolve' (Fekete, 2009). Even so, the British Red Cross (2010: 19) found that '[m]ost refused asylum seekers feel safer being destitute and homeless in the UK than returning to their home country despite being at risk of violence and exploitation'. One rejected asylum seeker facing destitution told researchers that the consequences of forced departure were so intolerable that suicide would be preferable, saying: 'I have no hope. If I have to go back home I will kill myself' (British Red Cross, 2010, 25). Most suicides in Britain involve young men from Afghanistan, Iraq and Iran who are without family (Athwal, 2010).

Cohen has documented several cases in which the threat of deportation, coupled with various system and communication failures, resulted in suicides:

In one the victim was serving a sentence for travelling under a false passport and on being told he was to be moved to a different prison, apparently believed that he was going to be removed to his country of origin. No interpreter was used when he was given this information. In another case, the victim was served with a notice to quit his accommodation but believed that this meant his claim was lost and so killed himself. In fact he had been given refugee status but had not received the letter.

(Cohen, 2008: 243)

The arrival of official letters – sometimes misunderstood, and sometimes understood only too well – are often identified as a trigger for suicide. Dr Habuibullah Wahedy, a 46-year-old Afghan refugee, took his own life at home in South Australia after receiving a letter advising that his temporary protection visa was soon to expire (Weber and Pickering, 2011, Appendix 1). Letters of rejection were also associated with three suicides of asylum seekers that occurred in close succession between November 2010 and March 2011 in Australian Immigration Detention Facilities in Sydney, Queensland and Western Australia, involving 40-year-old Iraqi Ahmad al-Akabi, 20-year-old Afghan Miqdad Hussain, and 19-year-old Afghan Mohammad Asif Ata (Weber and Pickering, 2011, Appendix 1).

Although motives are not always known, some well-documented cases demonstrate that suicide may sometimes be perceived as the only way to spare loved ones from forced deportation. Khosravi spoke with an Afghan man who attempted suicide for this reason in 2009 while facing deportation proceedings in Sweden:

> I asked the man why he had attempted suicide. He said he thought that his death would help his children have a chance to stay. He assumed that the Swedish authorities would then believe that their fear of returning was genuine and well-founded. When all the documents he had offered the authorities were deemed not 'enough' to prove, in the eyes of the authorities, his and his family's suffering, he thought to attest to the authenticity of their case with his death. Not even his suicide attempt helped them.
>
> (Khosravi, 2010: 114)

On September 15, 2005 an Angolan man, Manuel Bravo, was motivated by the same altruistic desire to ensure that his 13-year-old son would be allowed to remain in England. He hanged himself in Yarl's Wood Immigration Removal Centre on the day of his thirty-fifth birthday, and the day that he and his son were due to be deported (Institute of Race Relations, 2006). While this did result in a stay of his son's deportation, lawyers at the time feared that deportation could still await the young man when he reached his eighteenth birthday.

Conclusion

The examples and patterns of deportation discussed in this chapter demonstrate that the exclusionary mentalities arising from the search for security and order under conditions of neo-liberal globalization are manifest at both local and transnational levels. Across the Global North, governments are engaging in the 'government business' of deporting unworthy, suspect or surplus non-citizens they deem to be risky. This in turn creates serious risks of injury, death and ostracisation for the men, women and children targeted for expulsion. While deportation can be thought of as a means of performing sovereignty through largely unchecked administrative power, it also creates political and financial risks for governments. The sovereign power to exclude produces only an illusion of control, and often amounts in practice to the transnational trading of real, supposed and indeterminate risks. It is an illusion of control that comes at a very high financial, political and – most importantly – human cost. The fact that this trade in human misery persists seems to reflect the 'vituperative quality', to return to Young's terminology, that is 'pasted on the back' of the seemingly objective and legalistic rationale of border control. The high human cost of forced deportation may give us cause for despair. But the possibility of increasing the political cost to governments through legal challenges and political activism creates some grounds for hope of an emerging, if still distant, 'cosmopolitanism from below' (Hudson, 2011: 130).

Acknowledgements

The theoretical basis for this chapter has been developed as part of an empirical research project Exporting Risk: The Australian Deportation Project, funded by an Australian Research Council Discovery Grant (DP110102453). The authors would like to acknowledge the invaluable research assistance of Helen Gibbon and Amanda Wilson, and the intellectual contributions of our fellow Chief Investigators Mike Grewcock and Marie Segrave.

Notes

1 In some jurisdictions the term removal applies in situations where expulsion is automatic or near-automatic while deportation is reserved for expulsions requiring a more protracted legal process, such as visa cancellation and subsequent appeals. In this chapter we use the terms interchangeably with a preference for deportation.
2 See Granville-Chapman *et al.* (2004) and Wistrick *et al.* (2008) for documented cases in the UK.

References

Aas, K. (2007a) Analysing a world in motion: Global flows meet 'criminology of the other'. *Theoretical Criminology*, *11*, 283–303.
Aas, K. (2007b) *Globalization and Crime*. London: Sage.
Anderson, B., Gibney, M. and Paoletti, E. (2011) Citizenship, deportation and the boundaries of belonging. *Citizenship Studies*, *15*, 547–563.
Athwal, H. (2010) *Drive to Desperate Measures*. London: Institute of Race Relations.
Bauman, Z. (2002) *Society Under Siege*. Cambridge: Polity Press.
Bauman, Z. (2004) *Wasted Lives: Modernity and Its Outcasts*. Cambridge: Polity Press.
Bloch, A. and Schuster, L. (2005) At the extremes of exclusion: Deportation, detention and dispersal. *Ethnic and Racial Studies 28*, 491–512.
Bosworth, M. (2011) Deportation, detention and foreign-national prisoners in England and Wales. *Citizenship Studies*, *15*, 583–595.
Bowling, B. (2010) Transnational criminology and the globalization of harm production. In: C. Hoyle and M. Bosworth (eds) *What is Criminology?* Oxford: Oxford University Press.

British Red Cross (2010) *Not Gone, but Forgotten: The Urgent Need for a More Humane Asylum System*. June. London: British Red Cross.

Broeders, D. (2010) Return to sender? Administrative detention of irregular migrants in Germany and the Netherlands. *Punishment and Society*, *12*, 169–186.

Brotherton, D. (2008) Exiling New Yorkers. In: D. Brotherton and P. Kretsedemas (eds) *Keeping Out the Other: A Critical Introduction to Immigration Enforcement Today*. New York: Columbia University Press.

Cohen, J. (2008) Safe in our hands? A study of suicide and self-harm in asylum seekers. *Journal of Forensic and Legal Medicine*, *15*, 235–244.

CPT (European Committee for the Prevention of Torture) (2003) 13th General Report on the CPT's activities covering the period 1 January 2002 to 31 July 2003, CM(2003)90, 10 September. European Committee for the Prevention of Torture and Inhuman or Degrading Treatment of Punishment. Available on line: https://wcd.coe.int/wcd/ViewDoc. jsp?id = 65161.

Dauvergne, C. (2008) *Making People Illegal: What Globalization Means for Migration and Law*. New York: Cambridge University Press.

De Genova, N. (2007) The production of culprits: From deportability to detainability in the aftermath of 'Homeland Security'. *Citizenship Studies*, *11*, 421–448.

De Giorgi, A. (2006) *Re-Thinking the Political Economy of Punishment: Perspectives on Post-Fordism and Penal Politics*. Aldershot: Ashgate Publishing.

DIAC (Department of Immigration and Citizenship) (2010) *Annual Report*. Canberra: Department of Immigration and Citizenship.

ERA (European Race Audit) (2010) *Accelerated Removals: A Study of the Human Cost of EU Deportation Policies, 2009–2010*, Briefing Paper No. 4, October. London: Institute of Race Relations.

Fekete, L. (2009) Europe's shame: A report on 105 deaths linked to racism or government migration and asylum policies *European Race Bulletin*. London: Institute of Race Relations.

Gibney, M. (2008) Asylum and the expansion of deportation in the United Kingdom. *Government and Opposition*, *43*, 146–167.

Granville-Chapman, C., Smith, E. and Moloney, N. (2004) *Harm on Removal: Excessive Force Against Failed Asylum Seekers*. London: Medical Foundation for the Care of Victims of Torture.

Gray, B. (2011) From exile of citizens to deportation of non-citizens: Ancient Greece as a mirror to illuminate a modern transition. *Citizenship Studies*, *15*, 565–582.

Grewcock, M. (2009) Conviction, detention and removal: The multiple punishment of offenders under Section 501 Migration Act. Paper presented at the *Australia and New Zealand Society of Criminology Conference*. Perth, Western Australia, 24 November 2009, available at http://ssrn.com/abstract = 1518185.

HMIP (2009) *Short Thematic report by HM Inspectorate of Prisons: Detainee Escorts and Removals – A Thematic Review*, August 2009. Available on line: http://www. justice.gov.uk/downloads/publications/inspectorate-reports/hmipris/Detainee_escorts_and_removals_2009_rps.pdf.

Home Affairs Committee (2003) *Asylum Removals, Fourth Report of Session 2002–2003*. HC654, House of Commons, London. Available on line: http://www.publications. parliament.uk/pa/cm200203/cmselect/cmhaff/cmhaff.htm.

Hudson, B. (2011) All the people in the world: A cosmopolitan perspective on migration and torture. In: C.M. Bailliet and K.F. Aas (eds) *Cosmopolitan Justice and Its Discontents*, 116–133. Oxford: Routledge.

Institute of Race Relations (2006) *Driven to Desperate Measures*. London: Institute of Race Relations.

Jiminez, M. (2009) *Humanitarian Crisis: Migrant Deaths at the US–Mexico Border*. American Civil Liberties Council of San Diego and Imperial Counties; Mexico's National Commission of Human Rights.

Khosravi, S. (2009) Sweden: Detention and deportation of asylum seekers. *Race and Class*, *50*, 38–56.

Khosravi, S. (2010) *'Illegal Traveller': An Auto-ethnography of Borders*. London: Palgrave.

Lewis, P. and Taylor, M. (2011) Jimmy Mubenga: Security firm G4S may face charges over death. *The Guardian*, 16 March. Available on line: http://www.guardian.co.uk/uk/2011/mar/16/mubenga-g4s-face-charges-death.

Lewis, P., Taylor, M. and Bowcott, O. (2010) Chaos over restraint rules for deportees. *The Guardian*, 27 October. Available on line: http://www.guardian.co.uk/uk/2010/oct/27/deportation-restraint-rules-chaos.

Mansouri, F. and Cauchi, S. (2007) A psychological perspective on Australia's asylum policies. *International Migration*, *45*, 123–150.

Morvern, A. (2010) Brutal deportations must stop. *The Guardian*, 15 October. Available on line: http://www.guardian.co.uk/commentisfree/2010/oct/15/deportation-jimmy-mubenga-borders.

Namba, M. (2011) 'War on illegal immigrants', national narratives, and globalisation: Japanese policy and practice of police stop and question in global perspective. In: *Policing and Society*, Special Issue 'Stop and Search in Global Context', (eds) L. Weber and B. Bowling.

Napolitano, J. (2010) How the DREAM Act would bolster our Homeland Security, 14 December. The White House Blog, available on line http://www.whitehouse.gov/blog/2010/12/14/how-dream-act-would-bolster-our-homeland-security.

Nicholls, G. (2007) *Deported: A History of Forced Departures from Australia*. Sydney: UNSW Press.

Pratt, A. (2005) *Securing Borders: Detention and Deportation in Canada*. Vancouver: UBC Press.

Sheik, I. (2008) Racializing, criminalizing and silencing 9/11 deportees. In: D. Brotherton and P. Kretsedemas (eds) *Keeping Out the Other: A Critical Introduction to Immigration Enforcement Today*. New York: Columbia University Press.

Steel, Z. (2003) The politics of exclusion and denial: The mental health costs of Australia's refugee policy. In *38th Congress of Royal Australian and New Zealand*. Hobart: College of Psychiatrists.

Van der Leun, J. and Van der Woude, M. (2011) Ethnic profiling in the Netherlands? A reflection on expanding preventive powers, ethnic profiling and a changing social and political context. In *Policing and Society*, Special Issue 'Stop and Search in Global Context', (eds) L. Weber and B. Bowling.

Walters, W. (2002) Deportation, expulsion, and the international police of aliens. *Citizenship Studies*, *6*, 265–292.

Weber, L. (2011) "It sounds like they shouldn't be here": Immigration checks on the streets of Sydney. In *Policing and Society*, Special Issue 'Stop and Search in Global Context', (eds) B. Bowling and L. Weber.

Weber, L. (2012) Policing a world in motion. In: *Borders and Transnational Crime: Pre-Crime, Mobility and Serious Harm in an age of Globalization*, (eds) S. Pickering and J. McCulloch. London: Palgrave.

Weber, L. and Bowling, B. (2004) Policing migration: A framework for investigating the regulation of global mobility. *Policing and Society, 14*, 195–212.

Weber, L. and Bowling, B. (2008) Valiant beggars and global vagabonds: Select, eject, immobilise. *Theoretical Criminology, 12*, 355–375.

Weber, L. and Gelsthorpe, L. (2000) *Deciding to Detain: How Decisions to Detain Asylum Seekers are Made at Ports of Entry.* Cambridge: Institute of Criminology, University of Cambridge.

Weber, L. and Pickering, S. (2011) *Globalization and Borders: Death at the Global Frontier.* London: Palgrave.

Wistrick, H., Arnold, F. and Ginn, E. (2008) *Outsourcing Abuse: The Use and Misuse of State-Sanctioned Force During the Detention and Removal of Asylum Seekers.* London: Birnberg Peirce and Partners, Medical Justice and the National Coalition of Anti-Deportation Campaigns.

Young, J. (1999) *The Exclusive Society: Social Exclusion, Crime and Difference in Late Modern Society.* London: Sage.

Young, J. (2003) Merton with energy, Katz with structure. *Theoretical Criminology, 7*, 388–414.

Youseff, S. (2011) *Yarl's Wood: A Case Study. Immigration Prisons: Brutal, Unlawful and Profitable*, March. London: Corporate Watch.

Zedner, L. (2010) Security, the state, and the citizen: The changing architecture of crime control. *New Criminal Law Review, 13*, 379–403.

9 Borderworld

Biometrics, AVATAR and global criminalization[1]

Ben Muller

Who is better at distinguishing truth-tellers from liars – a person or an artificial agent?

> (AVATAR Pamphlet, BORDERS: A Department of
> Homeland Security Center for Excellence and The University of Arizona)

Make a run for the border!

> (*Taco Bell* Advertisement, 1989)

Patrolled by Predator drones, radar blimps, dogs, and scanners, and US/Mexico border is now a state unto itself: Borderworld.

> (Hodge, 2011)

Introduction: from SB 1070 to 'Borderworld'

The increasing reliance on identification and surveillance technologies in contemporary border security provides an exemplary case of the complex interplay between globalization, securitization and criminology. Although technologies such as biometrics, surveillance and even artificial intelligence have longer and more diverse historical evolutions, the terrorist attacks on 11 September 2001 are highly significant (a point not lost on the paragons of the industry).[2] In response to these events, many states around the world have relied on these technologies as central components in their contemporary border security strategies. Not only are the genealogies of these technologies tied to the history of crime and law enforcement techniques (e.g. see Cole, 2001; Pugliese, 2010), but the prolific reliance on these technologies tells the story of the escalation of the global criminalization of borders and borderlands, even the securitization and criminalization of mobility itself, particularly post-11 September 2001.

By recounting the story of the emerging reliance on biometric and surveillance technologies in the borderlands of the Sonoran desert between Arizona, USA and Sonora, Mexico, and with some comparative elements raised by the controversial spring 2010 law, SB 1070, I argue that we are increasingly witnessing an emerging 'borderworld', wherein a vast array of techniques and technologies are similar across various borderlands throughout the world; in fact, borders and borderlands are increasingly rearticulated as techno-spaces. The reliance on biometrics and logics that are both coexistent and co-constitutive of these technologies and the categorizations that are enabled by such technologies have also enabled prolific reliance upon them; the related preoccupation with 'identity verification', or certification, as an essential part of border management and security; and, the ubiquitous escalation of discretionary state power, have all become hallmarks of this emerging 'borderworld'; crucial factors in the productive concealment of the politics of contemporary securitizing and criminalizing trends in border security.

Hollywood productions, corporate advertisements, and popular culture iconography of various sorts are replete with references to 'making a run for the border', equating the crossing of state or international boundaries with notions of freedom thereby highlighting the limitations of domestic law enforcement. In the 1969 film, *Butch Cassidy and the Sundance Kid*, the lead characters are finally pushed to flee to Bolivia, forestalling capture by US law enforcement. This long tradition depicting the close association of criminal activity and crossing borders to thwart law enforcement is a regular meme of popular culture and the popular imaginary; however, such handy references and tropes are not confined to popular culture. Although the events of 11 September 2001 were not framed as criminal actions, the focus on transnational criminality increased in the post-11 September 2001 context as all such transgressions beyond the gaze of the modern state were rearticulated as posing existential peril through the intersection of terror, transnational non-state actors, and Weapons of Mass Destruction. The role this has played in the securitization and criminalization of borders and borderlands is undeniable and worth examination.

As part of broader critical interventions in the examination of criminalization and globalization, this chapter focuses on the increasing reliance on surveillance and identification technologies in contemporary border security, particularly that of biometrics. Unpacking the application of these technologies at the border demonstrates the extent to which 'borderscapes' (see Rajaram and Grundy-Warr, 2007) are increasingly not only securitized, but also criminalized, and undeniably global. Beginning with a brief account of the immediate post-11 September 2001 developments in border security, the chapter moves on to unpack the nature of technologies such as biometrics and the specific story of AVATAR (Automated Virtual Agent for Truth Assessments in Real-time), an artificial intelligence kiosk funded by the US Department of Homeland Security. The development, testing, and increasing reliance on these technologies in the contemporary management of borders and the bodies that cross them, provides an illustrative case of the complex relations between globalization and criminology, and the extent to which borders and borderlands are transforming a techno-space I refer to as 'borderworld'.

The story of AVATAR requires distinct reference to not only the US case, but also the specifics of the borderlands of the Sonoran desert. The evolution of border security strategies by both US federal and Arizona state officials, the harrowing story of trans-border human trafficking, and dire humanitarian crises are all elements associated with this case. However, they form an incomplete vision of this rich and complex borderland. The limited account of this borderland and the evolution of AVATAR provides an instructive case study of the emerging reliance on biometrics and other technologies in contemporary border management, and the extent to which these accounts of local borderlands are simultaneously global stories of criminalization, securitization, and technological fetishism as constitutive elements of an emergent 'borderworld'. A significant element of this story, and in this analysis, is the Arizona legislation, Senate Bill 1070.

SB 1070 was passed by the Arizona legislature, and signed into law by Arizona Governor Jan Brewer on 23 April 2010. Perhaps more than anything, this piece of controversial legislation highlighted both the increasing securitization– criminalization nexus in contemporary border management, as well as highlighting the extent to which racial profiling was to play a large part in borderland security and law enforcement. As evidenced by the work of Pugliese and others, rather than challenging this trend, the introduction of biometrics emerged precisely in the midst of this milieu of racial profiling and geopolitical preoccupations at the border, often contributing to the solidification of these trends, and serving to conceal its own genealogical connections to racial and gender stereotypes (Pugliese, 2010: Muller, 2010). As Roger Hodge suggests, the 'reengineering' of Homeland Security on the borders has contributed to the emergence of a new state along the US/Mexico border he has designated 'borderworld' (Hodge, 2011). Moreover, the story of both the development and emerging reliance on particular biometric and surveillance technologies in the Sonoran desert borderlands along the Mexico/US border is not simply a story of trends in Arizona, or even the southern United States, but an account of global trends, and the emergence of a 'borderworld' wherein the borders and borderlands throughout many parts of the world are rendered more and more similar in so far as they are conceptualized and managed.

SB 1070 is symbolic of the emerging laws of 'borderworld', which dovetails well with the emerging reliance on biometrics, surveillance and artificial intelligence, a proliferation of scanning technologies and diverse law enforcement and security officials, as well as the ubiquitous unmanned aerial drones that inhabit the skies of 'borderworld'. Following the preoccupation with 'verification' that is systemic to biometrics, SB 1070 indicates that the verification of one's immigration status must be determined before one can be released from state custody. In other words, indeterminate status due to one not having documentation on one's person is for the first time in America just cause for incarceration following an encounter with state agents. Because the law fails to stipulate precisely how the determination and verification is to occur, law enforcement officials are granted extensive latitude in verifying that you are indeed who you say you are. In fact, SB 1070 indicates that: 'during any stop, detention or arrest, a police office[r] must try to determine a person's immigration status if the officer has reason to suspect the person is here illegally' (McCombs, 2010). Although leaving much discretion to the individual officers, as some experts note, this portion of the law to some extent compels police officers to inquire about immigration status, regardless of the nature of the lawful stop, detention or arrest, thus failing to prioritize laws and compel police to enforce all laws always. Along with this,

SB 1070 renders illegal the hiring, protecting, shielding, concealing, transporting and harboring of illegal immigrants.

Referring to what Andreas and Nadelmann (2006) call 'Policing the Globe', this chapter argues that such reliance on specific identification and surveillance technologies, used to support this move towards comprehensive transnational criminal law enforcement as an essential part of contemporary border management, tends to depoliticize these strategies (also see Deflem, 2010; Pickering and Weber, 2006). Despite being inconsistent with domestic and national priorities, particular notions of threat, risk, and danger are globalized vis-à-vis the reliance on particular surveillance and identification technologies. The widespread acceptance of the story of globalized crime, the war on terror, and the subsequent necessity of globalized crime control strategies, provides essential conditions for eliding certain political and economic interests, moral impulses, and ensures the export of certain historically and culturally distinct definitions of crime. The very notion that a technology developed with the challenges of a specific borderland in mind is easily testable and transferrable to virtually any other borderland in the world underscores the extent to which the *sui generis* aspects of particular borderlands gleaned from careful ethnographic analysis (see Donnan and Wilson, 1999) is of little consequence in contemporary border management and the new 'borderworld'.

This chapter begins with some discussion of the post-11 September 2001 developments in border security and border management. The complicated web which emerges between the reliance on particular technologies in border management, together with mutually constitutive and mutually reinforcing logics, such as the specific application of risk management, is not fully unpacked (see Muller, 2010). However, a brief account of this emergence is integral to the account of AVATAR and the Sonoran borderlands that follows, providing essential context to what is referred to below as a case study of one sight in the emerging 'borderworld'. Before engaging in this discussion, some brief methodological and theoretical baggage ought to be unpacked. The debt owed to the approach of Critical Security Studies, in particular, deserves comment. Together with the diverse scholarship found within International Political Sociology and surveillance studies, each of which grapples with interdisciplinary questions regarding law and order, criminology and globalization, and the diverse interplay between the diversification of state power(s) and its reliance on non-state actors, the essential contestable nature of security itself is situated directly at the root of much of this critical scholarship.

The legacy of 11 September 2001: risk management, biometrics and the criminalization–securitization nexus

Drawing on the work of Walker, Vaughan-Williams, in his engaging appraisal of border politics in his book of the same name (*Border Politics*), states 'the border is not where it is supposed to be' (2009: 14). In his introduction, Vaughan-Williams unpacks the central role the border and border politics plays in not acting simply as a limit, but rather as a concept which together with sovereignty frames the conditions of modern political life. That is, he centers the citizen, as well as the way 'global security relations are commonly conceptualised' (2009: 3), before finally moving to 'decenter our understanding of borders' (Vaughan-Williams, 2009: 15). Briefly unpacking this particular role in the context of Critical Security Studies (CSS) is essential here, so as to move forward with the 'denatured' account of security upon which this analysis rests.

Emerging most virulently in the post-1989 context, but drawing on critical literature that was revealed during the previous decade, CSS has become an influential and important discipline in a wide array of research areas (among others, see Balzacq, 2010; Booth, 2004; Fierke, 2007; Peoples and Vaughan-Williams, 2010). Moreover, CSS has become of particular importance to the contemporary study of borders. Historically, the border played a paramount role in understandings of security, as the essential (political) demarcation between friend and enemy[3] was reified at the border. Preventing the transgression of state borders was accepted as one of the most essential sites of international security. The revolutions across central and eastern Europe, heralded by the fall of Berlin Wall in 1989, and followed by the decline and break-up of the Soviet Union in the early 1990s marked not only the end of the Cold War, but for some the emergence of a world in which borders were becoming less relevant (Friedman, 2000). At the same time, however, there was a simultaneous resurgence of the academic study of borders and borderlands (see Anderson *et al.*, 2002; Donnan and Wilson, 1999). This contrast is one among many in the study of borders and security. Moreover, while the emergence of CSS in the 1990s, particularly regarding the study of borders, is significant, it is not to suggest that the conventional conceptions and articulations of borders and border security relying on historically dominant forms of threat and insecurity that had dominated the Cold War have vanished.

Regardless of changing nomenclature, managing borders and the bodies that cross them continues to be motivated by the transnational threat of terrorism and the sovereign breach, connoted by threats to the territorial integrity of the state. Coming at the end of a decade that some alleged was 'borderless' (Ohmae, 1999; Friedman, 2000, in contrast to Sparke, 2006, 2009), often under the auspices of homeland security, the response to the events of 11 September 2001 contributed to the intensification of border security and the overall increase of criminalizing and securitizing trends more akin to the Cold War dynamics of border (in)security. Closing borders was among a few of the initial predictable reflex reactions by the United States in response to the events of 11 September 2001. This move not only emphasized how essential cross-border flows were to the North American economy, but it also highlighted the extent to which the border would become an essential site in the emerging global war on terror (GWoT). Under the Bush administration, the United States consciously framed the actions and what were considered legitimate responses, as 'acts of war'; However, domestic terrorist threats on planes, trains, and certainly at national borders – virtual or otherwise – were to be considered criminal acts, and prosecuted under criminal law (on broader trends of law enforcement and policing in the war on terror, see Deflem, 2010). On top of exposing the relationship between criminalization and securitization, it also indicates the extent to which US border security norms would 'go viral' and in so doing go global.

Since 2001, borders have undergone a particular transformation. For purposes here, three key developments will be considered: the increasing reliance on risk management as a governing principle in border management; the increasing reliance on surveillance and biometric technologies to manage populations found in the borderlands; and, the contemporaneous intensification of securitizing and criminalizing trends at the border, specifically through increasing reliance on biometrics. A brief discussion of these trends provides context for the emerging reliance on and proliferation of surveillance and identification technologies, such as biometrics, and the extent to which there are mutually constitutive relations between what some have referred to as 'governing through risk' (Aradau and van Munster, 2007) and the complex relations between globalization and criminalization, which this chapter engages in the context of technology and border security.

The use of risk management (RM) in contemporary governance is widespread. In much the same way that Jonathan Simon's book, *Governing Through Crime*, explicates the emergence of a governance model based on law enforcement and crime prevention: distorting citizenship, debasing the welfare state, and fanning the fires of a politics of fear (Simon, 2007); Aradau and van Munster unpack the way in which 'governing through risk' has thrived in a post-11 September 2001 environment, placing threat assessment, imagined/imagining risks, danger, and catastrophe at the centre of contemporary security politics (Aradau and van Munster, 2007; also see Aradau and van Munster, 2011).

It almost appeared as if biometrics and surveillance were waiting in the wings for an event like 11 September 2001 to happen, thrusting them onto the stage of this new 'theatre' of border security. In an age of total information awareness (TIA), ubiquitous surveillance, and almost tacit acceptance of the troubling aspects of social sorting that accompany these technologies, data is increasingly treated as synonymous with security. This thirst to know and 'script' the body politic has anything but left the border untouched; in some senses, borders and borderlands have become the ground zero of these emerging strategies, obsessed with the preservation of sovereign power and an escalating criminalization of mobility itself.

The reliance on RM and 'governing through risk' at the border, as well as the wider commitment to neoliberalism, together with an underlying faith in technology, created the perfect storm for the increasing reliance on emergent technology in contemporary border management. In a mutually constitutive relationship, the reliance on surveillance and identification technologies both responded to concerns about the need to criminalize and securitize the borderscape, while also contributing to the intensified criminalization and securitization of borders and the bodies that cross them. The confluence of RM, the intensification of surveillance and its accompanying forms of 'social sorting' (see Lyon, 2003), as well as a ubiquitous reliance on biometric technologies, contributed to the securitization and criminalization of borders and the bodies that cross them. The emerging reliance on various forms of surveillance and biometrics in border security, together with a range of institutional changes, contributed to the shift from a customs and visa regime to a regime of surveillance and law enforcement. In light of these developments, such as the Smart Border Accord signed between Canada and the United States in December 2001, influential scholar Mark Salter asks: 'How smart can a border be?' (Salter, 2004). Of particular relevance to this chapter is the extent to which the global introduction of biometric and surveillance technologies in border and aviation security contributed to the globalization of American border norms – something Salter traces in terms of the role of the International Civil Aviation Organization and aviation security more generally (Salter, 2004, 2007, 2008). The reliance on biometric technologies came to form an essential portion of this emerging norm.

Most simply put, biometrics involves the digitization of physiological and physical attributes, ranging from the simple, such as fingerprints and retinal scans, to the more complex, such as facial thermography, gait analysis, and even DNA and brainwave biometrics. Reliant on what Cole points out is an increasingly archaic bodily notion of identification (Cole, 2001: 310), the underlying logic that supports biometrics and their alleged utility in criminal identification, remains relatively unchanged from early arguments in favour of fingerprinting (see Cole, 2001). However, similar to the history of fingerprinting, the development, evolution, and application of biometrics continues to be bound up in complex socioeconomic, legal, political and cultural networks that tend to ignore the persistently discriminatory, gendered and racially charged biopolitical categorizations that underpin the evolution of these identification technologies. As Pugliese notes insightfully,

> the biometric question is repeatedly made coextensive, in the biopolitical operations of biometric technologies, with *what you are* . . . the answer to the question "Who are you?" pivots on the specificity of a subject's embodiment and her or his geopolitical status. What you are – a person of colour and/or an asylum seeker – determines the answering of who you are.
>
> (Pugliese, 2010: 1–2)

In what Pugliese refers to as 'Identity Dominance' (Pugliese 2010), the central role of biometrics, particularly in their deployment, simultaneously reifies and conceals the racial and gendered categories that are solidified in the development of these technologies. Subsequently hidden is the subtle but powerful biopolitical and geopolitical power that lay behind the drawn curtain of prosaic accounts of technology. As such, the deep-seated commitments to particular strategies and categories of suspicion and criminal detection, securitization and geopolitics, even the definition of threats and insecurities themselves, are not simply better managed through the application of biometric technology, but rather are embedded in their development and cultivated through their deployment. In other words, rather than simply framed as the problem, in this case of border security, to which biometrics provides a solution, the complex socioeconomic, political, and legal context out of which these technologies emerge come to redefine the 'problem', in the case of the border, as one of 'identity management' (see Muller, 2009, 2010).

A central aim of biometric technology is verifying that *you are who you say you are.* As other researchers have demonstrated persuasively, this verification that attempts to solidify connections between the body and identity, have served as an important aspect of the building of the modern state and its colonial expansion (see Cole, 2001; Gates, 2005; Pugliese, 2010). Considering this, it is not surprising to see the continued use of these technologies in the theatre of war, specifically Iraq and Afghanistan in the post-11 September 2001 epoch (see Measor and Muller, 2010, 2011). As others have noted, the reliance on such identification technologies is about 'securing identity' in the widest sense possible. In what Pugliese's refers to as 'identity dominance', the use of biometric technologies on foreign populations during occupation, is precisely to identify, or 'over-code' existing identities with technologically visible ones (Measor and Muller, 2010), and 'surveil and capture targeted subjects' (Pugliese, 2010: 80). In similar ways, the increasing reliance on biometrics in border management has led to changing relations among the inhabitants of borderlands, in particular the mobile bodies that cross or intend to cross the border. As such, the introduction of biometric technologies functions in concert with the racial criminalization of immigrants noted by other observers (Provine and Doty, 2011), most clearly exemplified in legislation such as Arizona's infamous SB 1070, comes to full fruition with the application of specific technologies such as AVATAR.

'Borderworld': AVATAR and the politics of concealment

This section begins by introducing 'AVATAR'. As a technology developed largely by researchers at the University of Arizona for the management of local borders, it was nonetheless tested and developed with the help of global partners. Moreover, while SB 1070 is itself an Arizona law, it has remarkable similarities to emerging pieces of legislation across many US states and other jurisdictions around the world, and is the precise form of legislation that enhances discretionary state power in racially and ethnically intolerant ways, but tends to be concealed behind the smokescreen of technology. In this sense, the 'Arizona story' of the emerging reliance on specific biometric and surveillance technologies, its preoccupation with questions of verification and deception detection, and the increasing unbridled discretionary power of the state that is emerging there is simply a microcosm of global trends in what one might refer to as an emerging 'borderworld'. Not only are these emerging dynamics of interest here, but the extent to which the introduction, application and reliance on various surveillance and identification technologies in contemporary border management participate in the productive concealment of these politics is of particular note.

Before engaging in specifics, the general condition of the border and borderlands along the Mexico/US frontier which runs between Sonora, Mexico and Arizona, USA and the Sonoran Desert that overlays this space, deserves comment. Particularly in the past 5-10 years, the Sonoran borderlands have become infamous thanks in part to escalating media attention, focusing almost exclusively on the migration of undocumented people through this borderland. In January 2011, the Department of Homeland Security (DHS) announced the cancellation of the controversial and expensive 'Secure Border Initiative-Net' or SBI-Net, which entailed the construction at great cost of a virtual fence along the southern US border with Mexico. Even DHS realized the costs of such a technology far outweighed its alleged benefits; or, more likely that potentially cheaper technologies such as the prolific and escalated use of unmanned aerial drones along the Mexico/US border had come on line. At any rate, debates over the use of technology, reliant on rather caricatured, oversimplified conceptions of the borderlands, aptly describes much of what has occurred in the Sonora. The complex web of issues, not least being the economic issues related to the movement of undocumented migrants, but also: the separation of the Tohono O'odham Nation which straddles the border; the broad range of legitimate cross-border trade and commerce which has long been a part of this region's economic solvency; long-standing debates over water rights; and, increasing debates over matters such as SB 1070 and other state laws banning ethnic studies in public schools,[4] tend to be ignored in many one-dimensional accounts. Moreover, although a wide range of important local issues deserve attention, and make this a particularly interesting and complex borderland, popular accounts in the news media and elsewhere tend to boil these discussions down to simplistic accounts of security noted earlier. To this end, the attention and resources devoted to state legislation, notably SB 1070 is a case in point.

While much of the debate surrounding SB 1070 within the United States has as much if not more to do with state and federal competencies as it does with the overt racial profiling and discretionary state power advanced in SB 1070, the overall preoccupation with the 'verification' of identity as a key tool in securing borderlands has made it an exemplary case of global trends. Moreover, it also highlights the extent to which the emerging reliance on biometric technologies are coexistent and even mutually constitutive of criminalizing and securitizing trends at the border, towards a heightened interest in identity verification in a manner not hitherto considered even at national borders. Enter the AVATAR kiosk.

If the AVATAR kiosk is the new 'border guard' of the emerging 'borderworld', then this world looks like the dystopian vision in films such as *Sleep Dealer* (2009; also see Duran, 2010):

> [AVATAR] is an interactive screening technology designed to be on the front lines of border crossings and airports. Individuals would approach the AVATAR kiosk, scan their identification, answer a few simple questions, and then move on. Meanwhile, the AVATAR kiosk has used non-invasive artificial intelligence and sensor technologies to gauge suspicious behavior.
>
> (Warren-Pedersen, 2010)

As a doctoral student involved in the development of AVATAR quickly points out: 'Law enforcement would step in to work directly with individuals whose behavior has been flagged. "The goal is not to replace the person, but to augment law enforcement's ability to detect deception"' (Warren-Pedersen, 2010).

Moreover, the promotional literature provided by the creators of AVATAR underscores the fact that this is not intended to replace border guards, but rather, replace their inability to adequately detect deception. To some extent, AVATAR appeals to some common sense suspicions, nicely summed up by a journalist Hank Stephenson's account:

> On the way up to Tucson to check out the latest Department of Homeland Security technology, a virtual lie-detecting kiosk meant to rapidly screen deception and intent, I passed through the I-19 Border Patrol checkpoint.
>
> There I was stopped by a baby-fat-faced agent with rosy cheeks and stubble on his chin.
>
> "Are you a US Citizen?" he asked me.
>
> "Yes," I told him.
>
> "Go ahead," he said.
>
> How does he know if I'm telling the truth? I wondered.
>
> I was going to see AVATAR.... It's like a big ATM, but instead of conveniently taking care of your banking needs, a digital head appears on the screen and asks you questions, looks into your eyes, and listens very carefully, and monitors your every facial spasm, hand gesture and movement. Then it determines if you're lying.
>
> (Stephenson, 2011)

Stephenson's statement is an illustrative example of how the reliance on biometrics and surveillance technologies in border management has dramatic and wide-ranging effects. For the remainder of this section, I will outline both the manners in which the introduction of biometrics and similar technologies, such as AVATAR, simultaneously emphasize specific logics of border security and articulations of risk, threat, and insecurity, while at the same time, concealing and obfuscating critical issues such as the reliance on forms of ethnic and racial profiling and the escalating discretionary power of the state they provide.

In the case of Stephenson's description, the notion that deception is a key problem at borders – almost naturally – is embraced uncritically. As if it were pulled from the pages of the AVATAR promotional literature, the fundamental problem of border security – or what is increasingly termed 'border enforcement' – is reified in a mutually constitutive relationship between technology, the law, and security. As an almost shorthand for what I referred to earlier as the criminalization–securitization nexus, the centrality of 'border enforcement' also falls into Pugliese's notion of 'law as prosthetic', wherein the law is 'inextricably entwined with technology from its originary enunciation through the technology of language – enabl[ing] the disclosure of complex dynamics of power, disavowal and violence' (Pugliese, 2011: 931). In what might be framed as a sort of 'chicken–egg' problem, it seems increasingly clear that the technology is not simply applied to specific, predetermined problems with desired outcomes in mind, but rather, the specific articulation and application of technologies serve to reframe the 'problem' of border management – or border enforcement – and thus, also rearticulate what constitutes desirable outcomes. As such, there is a complex interplay between the role technology plays in rearticulating the border, borderlands, and the bodies that transit through them, and the ways in which the transformation of the border, borderlands, and 'border enforcement' into technology itself in the new 'borderworld', obfuscates and conceals the ramifications of escalating discretionary state power, and moves towards greater homogeneity in criminal law and law enforcement in response to the alleged globalization of crime (see Andreas and Nadelmann, 2006).

Into the charged political terrain of the Sonoran borderlands, characterized most notably by SB 1070 and its reliance on discretionary state power, the development of AVATAR at the University of Arizona in Tucson, Arizona, cannot be extracted from these charged politics. As noted in Stephenson's article: 'Unlike the rosy-cheeked Border Patrol agent at the I-19 checkpoint, AVATAR doesn't see race, doesn't play favourites and doesn't get tired' (Stephenson, 2011). Presented as the panacea to the problems of racial and ethnic profiling and the divisive politics ubiquitous in the Sonoran borderlands (again, embodied in the evolution and controversy surrounding SB 1070), AVATAR simply codifies and conceals its bias, cloaked in the cleanliness of technology. The extent to which the bias of the researcher and developer, and broader conceptions of power and difference are systemically built into the technology, are noted very clearly by the work of both Pugliese (2010) and Cole (2001). Such undergirding power dynamics are, however, altogether lost on the AVATAR's developers, promoters and those who feel safer in the cold embrace of such technologies. As AVATAR researcher Derrick indicates, the actual use of AVATAR is a few years off as testing is required to: 'see how it responds to kind of a dirty grimy environment, an uncontrolled environment, with people who aren't familiar with technology' (Stephenson 2011). Saturated in a colonial discourse of otherness and rife with stereotypes, Derrick's comment emphasizes the stereotypical assumptions of who poses a threat at the border from amongst the bodies that cross it. Unlike the exhortation by the 'Mother of Exiles' to 'Give me your tired, your poor, Your huddled masses yearning to breathe free, The wretched refuse of your teeming shore...' now agents of the American Republic identify migrants as dirty, grimy, and uncontrolled and contrast them with the clean control of technology. Moreover, Derrick's statement, almost reminiscent of Emma Lazarus' poem, *The New Colossus*, also suggests those who cross this border are likely to be primitive, as they are altogether unfamiliar with technology. Derrick goes on to say:

> We're not interested in replacing human screeners, but the goal is to make an objective rapid assessment... that's one of the advantages it doesn't have any biases. Every person regardless of how we try has prejudices, biases and

cognitive limitations. This is simply an objective look at the physiology of the person.

(Stephenson, 2011)

Critical questions raised during a public demonstration of AVATAR in November 2011 at the University of Arizona, attempting to tease out the extent to which AVATAR's developers are conscious of the sort of racial and ethnic bias that is systemic to the genealogy of biometrics (see Pugliese, 2010), were met with puzzled bemusement by the team of researchers present. The fact that AVATAR was tested by the European Union's border agency Frontex[5] along the Polish border was provided as an example of not only the implicit belief that all borders and borderlands are ultimately the same, but also as an example of the ethnically and racially unbiased approach to the development of this technology. However, the technologization of the border, borderlands, and the bodies that cross them in the new 'borderworld' is not only blind to its own gendered, racial and ethnically biased conceptualizations, but it also conceals the escalating exceptional sovereign power exercised across borderlands.

Throughout Stephenson's account of AVATAR, he contrasts it with his personal experience of the 'rosy-cheeked Border Patrol agent at the I-19 checkpoint' (Stephenson, 2011). While Stephenson's account naively plays into the unreflexive articulation of AVATAR as the solution to the alleged grimy, dirty, uncontrolled and almost chaotic realities of the borderland, in its rearticulation of the new 'borderworld', it also serves to forward its own gimmickry as a seductive smokescreen, concealing the extent to which the emerging 'borderworld' is not only known for its reliance on technology, but also the increasing reliance on discretionary state power and an undeclared state of exception. Notably, the fact that the checkpoint along the I-19 interstate highway is not at a port of entry, but approximately 26 miles from the border, is not even mentioned. Although much criticism of the I-19 checkpoint has come in the form of 'NIMBY'-type complaints, relating to human and narcotic traffickers using nearby residences as drop-offs, and skirmishes between border and law enforcement agents and traffickers occurring in the nearby community of Tubac, Arizona, some complaints focus on humanitarian and constitutional concerns raised (see Wagner, 2009). The extent to which the powers for search and seizure at the I-19 checkpoint are constitutional are murky at best, but at the very least, it demonstrates the broadening and widening of the discretionary power of the state, historically confined in liberal democratic states to the border itself. Moreover, following on broader political and philosophical arguments about the normalization of exceptional sovereign power (see Agamben, 2005), as the recent installation of license plate readers at the I-19 checkpoint indicates (Vandervoet, 2012), the permanence of the state of exception is increasingly unquestioned. The reliance on technologies such as AVATAR diverts attention from these deeply troubling political questions, and (re)articulates borders and borderlands as sanitized technological sites, where sovereign power is hidden behind the clean lines of the biometric scan, the infrared gaze of surveillance cameras, and the high-definition cameras of the aerial drone, where the conventional political considerations of legitimacy, authority and violence are recast in the fetishized techno-border of 'borderworld'.

Conclusion: the ABCs of borderworld

Although the unique aspects of the Sonoran borderlands were only minimally recounted and engaged here, this brief account nevertheless provides a persuasive reference to what is referred to as 'borderworld'. The increasing reliance on biometric technologies, together with a panoply of other identification and surveillance technologies, structured within a mutually constitutive relationship with escalating and broadening exceptional sovereign power, has become the shared dynamics of the emerging 'borderworld'. Under the auspices of the global war on terror, powerful states have pressured others towards greater globally homogenous criminal law enforcement, central to which is border enforcement. The account presented here has sought to engage the extent to which an increasing reliance on technology and the co-constitutive relationship with strategies of risk management and 'governing through risk', together with the broadening and widening exercise of discretionary state power, have flattened the important distinctions among the diverse borders, borderlands and the bodies that traverse them in the Sonoran Desert. This emerging 'borderworld' is a shorthand for the extent to which the external borders of the European Union, the Mexico/US border and virtual borders in airports across the globe are all increasingly similar, in so far as the logics, technologies and management strategies are governed by a series of commitments to technology, risk management and exceptional sovereign power that fail to take into account local and regional diversities. Particularly, through the rather truncated account of the Sonoran borderlands, this analysis has attempted to expose the critical role biometric and surveillance technologies play in concealing and obfuscating the troubling discriminatory politics that belie the clean and apolitical rendition of biometrics.

To expose this further, I engage in a brief 'ABCs of borderworld'. In this analysis, 'A' stands for AVATAR. Not only does this specific technology, and the story of its development and international testing, emphasize the global aspects and aspirations of its technological immodesty, but it underscores the role technology plays in transforming both the dilemmas associated with borders and borderlands, and their potential resolutions as a problem that is technological. The global nodes of criminal and border enforcement are easily linked through technology, and perceived risks, threats, and dangers have been reframed as technological considerations. Mobility is problematized in so far as it is unscripted, with humans transgressing such a technologized space, rearticulated solely through the biometric data they provide. The extent to which the application of technology and the subsequent rendering of 'borderworld' as a techno-space simply reifies existing differentiations based on class, race, and gender, is concealed by a discourse saturated with claims to objectivity, neutrality, and precision. This powerful discourse that accompanies the application of technologies such as AVATAR, and other biometrics and surveillance techniques, subsequently frames the imprecision, grimy and unscripted nature of the borderlands and the bodies transiting its space, as problematic. The technologically invisible and unknown, is dangerous, nefarious, criminal and insecure, as it is not technologically verifiable, and thus, runs up against the emerging 'borderworld'.

In the ABCs of borderworld, 'B' stands for borderlands. As an increasingly techno-political space, borderlands are at once problematized for their complexity and presented as a challenge to attempts at criminal and border enforcement, and at the same time, their differences are flattened by the transformation of borderlands vis-à-vis technology and 'governing through risk'. Imagined dangers, risk, and insecurities are rendered homogenous across the vast array of global borderlands, complimented by the universal enemy embodied in the subject of the 'terrorist;' thus, the diverse ethnography of borderlands is sidelined in favour of a unidimensional vision of the border as embodying the limits of authority, legitimacy, violence, and political subjectivity. With the integral aid of technology, discourses of deception detection, neutrality and objectivity replace the diversity of legal and illegal forms of exchange, services, and mobilities that characterize the diversity of borderlands throughout the world. As a technospace, the borderland becomes a site for the exercise of specific forms of identification and surveillance technologies and the deployment of exceptional state power well beyond its traditional locale at the limit of the political – the border. Rather than a thickened border, this proliferation of borders (Muller, 2010) belies the fecundity of borderlands for the violent potentialities and the capacity to know and tame technologically.

Finally, in the ABCs of borderworld, 'C' connotes the criminalization–securitization nexus. Although the war on terror is understood as a political engagement, acting as rationale for the military invasion of at least two nations, for Homeland Security and the border, questions of policing and criminal law enforcement are central. In many ways, the shift from notions of an emerging borderless world is rapidly replaced by strategies to 're-border' in often not so subtle ways.[6] Essential to these rebordering strategies were not only the neo-medieval border walls that proliferated (see Jones, 2012), but also the rapid and uncritical embrace of various forms of technology, notably biometrics. In this sense, 'C' might also stand for certification, and answering that 'you are in fact who you say you are' emerges as the preoccupation of border management strategies.

The total emergence of 'borderworld' is as yet incomplete. However, the increasing dominance of technologies such as biometrics in contemporary border management is escalating. The manner in which the reliance on such technologies dramatically changes border enforcement, shifting questions of defined crime and illicit activity to that which is technologically knowable and verifiable and that which is not increasingly makes suspects of us all. Technology has much to offer in terms of efficiency and reliability; however, the uncritical embrace of what it offers, and the false assumption that it has adequately bypassed complex concerns about racial, ethnic and gendered bias, that appear to complicate attempts to globally homogenize border enforcement, is a dangerous trend. The manner in which distinct borderlands have become 'borderworld' is equally troubling, as the introduction and application of biometric technology contributes to depoliticizing complex political considerations that are integral to both the salience and success of borderlands and the bodies that traverse these spaces.

Notes

1 Special thanks to Javier Duran and the University of Arizona for their support in carrying out some of the research necessary for the completion of this chapter, and for ongoing discussions on these matters. Also, the careful comments and suggestions on earlier drafts of this paper from John Measor, Francis Pakes and Tom Cooke contributed to this being a much stronger and clearer contribution. All inconsistencies and errors that remain are the sole responsibility of the author.
2 In their introduction to a seminal textbook on biometric technology, Woodward *et al.* (2003, xxiv) note: 'Following the September 11, 2001 terrorist attacks, the US government and other governments and organizations throughout the world became greatly interested in this emerging [biometric] human recognition system'.
3 In his book *The Concept of the Political*, Carl Schmitt outlined that the differentiation between friend and enemy is the ultimate political moment, drawing on his other work on sovereignty wherein he argues famously that: 'the sovereign is he who decides the exception.'
4 See Associated Press (2012).
5 According to its website, the purpose of Frontex is: 'Coordination of intelligence driven operational cooperation at EU level to strengthen security at external borders'. http://www.frontex.europa.eu/more_about_frontex/.
6 The prolific use of walls of various sorts along national borders since 11 September 2001 is an important case in point. On this development, see Jones 2012. Also see Andreas and Biersteker (2003).

References

Agamben, G. (2005) *State of Exception* (translated by Kevin Attell). Chicago: University of Chicago Press.
Anderson, J., O'Dowd, L. and Wilson, T.M. (2002) Introduction: Why study borders now? *Regional and Federal Studies*, *12*, 1–12.
Andreas, P. and Biersteker, T.J. (eds) (2003) *The Rebordering of North America: Integration and Exclusion in a New Security Context*. New York: Routledge.
Andreas, P. and Nadelmann, E. (2006) *Policing the Globe: Criminalization and Crime Control in International Relations*. Oxford: Oxford University Press.
Aradau, C. and van Munster, R. (2007) Governing terrorism through risk: Taking precautions, (un)knowing the future. *European Journal of International Relations*, *13*, 89–115.
Aradau, C. and van Munster, R. (2011) *Politics of Catastrophe: Genealogies of the Unknown*. London: Routledge.
Associated Press (2012) Tucson school district to dismantle its ethnic studies after state ordered to cut its funding. *Washington Post*, 11 January. Available on line: http://www.washingtonpost.com/local/education/tucson-school-district-to-dismantle-its-ethnic-studies-after-state-ordered-cut-in-its-funding/2012/01/11/gIQAnq2fqP_story.html.
Balzacq, T. (ed.) (2010) *Securitization Theory: How Security Problems Emerge and Dissolve*. London: Routledge.
Booth, K. (2004) *Critical Security Studies and World Politics*. Boulder, CO: Lynne Rienner.

Cole, S.A. (2001) *Suspect Identities: A History of Fingerprints and Criminal Identification*. Cambridge, MA: Harvard University Press.

Deflem, M. (2010) *The Policing of Terrorism: Organization and Global Perspectives*. New York: Routledge.

Donnan, H. and Wilson, T.M. (1999) *Borders: Frontiers of Identity, Nation and State*. Oxford: Berg.

Duran, J. (2010) Virtual borders, data aliens, and bare bodies: Culture, securitization, and the biometric state. *Journal of Borderlands Studies*, 25, 219–232.

Fierke, K.M. (2007) *Critical Approaches to International Security*. Malden, MA: Polity Press.

Friedman, T.M. (2000) *The Lexus and the Olive Tree: Understanding Globalization*. New York: Anchor.

Gates, K. (2005) *Our Biometric Future: Facial Recognition Technology and the Culture of Surveillance*. New York: NYU Press.

Hodge, R. D. (2011) How the US is reengineering homeland security on the borders. *Popular Science*, December. Available on line: http://www.popsci.com/technology/article/2011-12/how-us-reengineering-homeland-security-borders

Jones, R. (2012) *Border Walls: Security and the War on Terror in the United States, India and Israel*. London: Zed Books.

Lyon, D. (ed.) (2003) *Surveillance as Social Sorting: Privacy, Risk, and Digital Discrimination*. New York: Routledge.

McCombs, B. (2010) Experts go over SB 1070's key points. *Arizona Daily Star*, 2 May.

Measor, J.H.W. and Muller, B.J. (2010) Securitizing the global norm of identity: Biometrics, and *Homo Sacer* in Fallujah. In: B.J. Muller (ed.) *Security, Risk, and the Biometric State: Governing Borders and Bodies*. London: Routledge.

Measor, J.H.W. and Muller, B.J. (2011) Theatres of war: Visual technologies and identity in the Iraq War. *Geopolitics*, *16*, 389–409.

Muller, B.J. (2009) (Dis)qualified bodies: Securitization, citizenship and 'identity management'. In: P. Nyers (ed.) *Securitizations of Citizenship*. New York: Routledge.

Muller, B.J. (2010) *Security, Risk and the Biometric State: Governing Borders and Bodies*. London: Routledge.

Ohmae, K. (1999) *The Borderless World: Power and Strategy in the Interlinked Economy* (revised edition). New York: Harper Business.

Peoples, C. and Vaughan-Williams, N. (2010) *Critical Security Studies: An Introduction*. London: Routledge.

Pickering, S. and Weber, L. (eds) (2006) *Borders, Mobility and Technologies of Control*. The Netherlands: Springer.

Provine, D.M. and Doty, R.L. (2011) The criminalization of immigrants as a racial project. *Journal of Contemporary Criminal Justice*, *27*, 261–277.

Pugliese, J. (2010) *Biometrics: Bodies, Technologies, Biopolitics*. New York: Routledge.

Pugliese, J. (2011) Prosthetics of law and the anomic violence of drones. *Griffith Law Review*, *20*, 931–961.

Rajaram, P.K. and Grundy-Warr, C. (eds) (2007) *Borderscapes: Hidden Geographies and Politics at Territory's Edge*. Minneapolis: University of Minnesota Press.

Salter, M.B. (2004) Passports, mobility, and security: How smart can the border be? *International Studies Perspectives*, *5*, 71–91.

Salter, M.B. (2007) SeMs and sensibility: Security management systems and the management of risk in the Canadian air transport security authority. *Journal of Airport Transportation Management*, *13*, 389–398.

Salter, M.B. (2008) Imagining numbers: Risk, quantification and aviation security. *Security Dialogue*, *39*, 243–266.

Simon, J. (2007) *Governing Through Crime: How the War on Crime Transformed American Democracy and Created a Culture of Fear*. Oxford: Oxford University Press.

Sparke, M. (2006) A neoliberal nexus: Citizenship, security and the future of the border. *Political Geography*, *25*, 151–180.

Sparke, M. (2009) On denationalization as neoliberalization: Biopolitics, class interest and incompleteness of citizenship. *Political Power and Social Theory*, *20*, 287–300.

Stephenson, H. (2011) Are we telling the truth? Ask AVATAR! *Nogales International*, 11 February.

Vandervoet, K. (2012) DEA puttling license readers on Interstate 19. *Nogales International*, 9 January. Available on line: http://www.gvnews.com/news/dea-putting-license-readers-on-interstate/article_f94104d2-3b25-11e1-a51d-001871e3ce6c.html?mode = print.

Vaughan-Williams, N. (2009) *Border Politics: The Limits of Sovereign Power*. Edinburgh: Edinburgh University Press.

Wagner, D. (2009) I-19 checkpoint near Tubac angers locals. *The Arizona Republic*, 16 July. Available on line: http://www.azcentral.com/arizonarepublic/news/articles/2009/07/16/20090716checkpoint0716.html.

Warren-Pederson, L. (2010) AVATAR kiosk aims to automate, augment border enforcement. *Eller buzz*, Eller College of Management, University of Arizona. Available on line: http://www.eller.arizona.edu/buzz/2011/feb/avatar.asp.

Woodward, Jr., J.D., Orlans, N.M. and Higgins, P.T. (2003) *Biometrics: Identity Assurance in the Information Age*. Berkeley, CA: McGraw-Hill.

10 Globalization, mass atrocities and genocide[1]

Susanne Karstedt

> We may not know what absolute good is ... we may not even know what man or the human or humanity is – but what the inhuman is we know very well indeed. I would say that the place of moral philosophy today lies more in the concrete denunciation of the inhuman than in ... abstract attempts to situate man in his existence.
>
> (Adorno, 2001: 175)

> We may not be able to create democracies or constitutions. ... But we could do more than we do to stop unmerited suffering and gross physical cruelty. That I take to be the elemental priority of all human rights activism: to stop torture, beatings, killings, rape and assault and to improve, as best as we can, the security of ordinary people. My minimalism is not strategic at all. It is the most we can hope for.
>
> (Ignatieff, 2001: 173)

What is 'global' about genocide?

Nearly half a century separates the writing of Theodor Adorno and Michael Ignatieff, and their sober though not pessimistic perspective on gross human rights violations and cruelty. Both write under the shadow of genocide and mass atrocities. The Holocaust was central to Adorno's philosophy and social theory; for Ignatieff, the genocides in former Yugoslavia and Rwanda, as well as the failure of the international community to prevent or intervene, informed his analysis of the human rights project, and of what it could achieve. Both philosophers were confronted with the proliferation of mass atrocity and genocide in the second half of the twentieth century, as these spread through regions like Latin and Central America, and Africa, or what had been revealed about Stalin's Siberian camps and mass starvation in Ukraine at the time.

Indeed for many observers, the second half of the twentieth century as well as the start of the twenty-first century was a period during which mass atrocities and genocide became increasingly endemic and systematic in international relations (Shaw, 2011). Was the global increase of mass atrocities part of a complex process of globalization, and intricately linked to the mechanisms of globalization? Could specific processes of globalization be identified that characterized mass atrocities and genocide in the global age and post-modernity, in the same vein as Bauman (1989) had done for modernity and the Holocaust? Can we identify specific changes in the context, dynamics and structure of genocidal events that are distinct in the age of globalization and that set them apart from earlier periods? Do mass atrocities and grave human rights violations thrive on the inability of international criminal law and its instruments to globalize, as Nelken (2004: 381) stated for criminal law, and the inability of the global community to generate global and transnational instruments of intervention, protection and criminal justice?

Genocide and mass atrocities are global phenomena, and have always been. Harff (2003) identified 37 genocides and 'politicides' between 1955 and 2001 which took place in Europe, and across Asia and Latin America. During the first decade of the twenty-first century, events of mass atrocities in Africa and Asia have been added to this count with an estimation of more than a million victims of violence, violent ethnic cleansing and serious sexual violence. The twentieth century started with genocides in Africa – the genocide of the Hereros by the Germans, and in Asia – the massacre of the Armenians in Turkey, and in its first half saw the genocide of the European Jews by the German Nazi-State. Estimates for the victims of genocide and mass killings as distinguished from war deaths range from 60 to 150 million for the twentieth century alone (Valentino, 2004: 1), with most estimates at about 80 million, and some considerably higher (Rummel, 1998). For the second half of the twentieth century since 1945, estimates range between 9 and 20 million in more than forty episodes of genocide (Valentino, 2004: 255; Gurr, 1993). Genocide has been termed the crime of the twentieth century, and in many ways it epitomizes this 'age of extremes' (Hobsbawm, 1994; Bauman, 1989).

Genocide, politicide and 'democide' (Rummel, 1998) have been linked to global flows of power, goods and people long before the twentieth century. Rubinstein (2004) identifies periods and types of genocides, which all are part of the global expansion of powers, and imperial enterprise across the boundaries of nations and continents. This is evident for the period of imperial and religious genocide from the Roman Empire to the crusades and religious wars until the late Middle Ages. The period of colonial genocides from 1492 until the beginning of World War I signifies a different process of globalization, including trade and markets, as well as hegemonic projects. Across these periods and with the flows of potential perpetrators the focus and place of genocides shifted in and out of Europe to other continents in the course of the 'Europeanization of the globe' (Zimmerer, 2008), as well as during its 'De-Europeanization'. Mass atrocities during the second half of the twentieth century are linked to the process of de-colonization, as European powers retreated in wars of decolonization and left a legacy behind that was conducive to ethnic conflict and strife, and to the proliferation of civil wars on resources. The sweeping changes of international relations of power, emerging problems of national security in the wake of de-colonization as well as the end of the Cold War provided a context for nationalist/ethnic polices and a seedbed for ethnic cleansing, mass atrocities and conflicts.

Consequently, the contemporary global landscape of genocide and mass atrocities is defined by deep divisions that run between the Global North and South, and along post-colonial trajectories of dependence and influence, as several counts and lists of genocides and mass atrocities demonstrate (see Harff, 2003; Genocide Watch; Crisis Watch). The distribution of mass atrocities and genocidal events across the globe thus represents the asymmetrical contexts in which globalization operates and that it produces. Citizens in the Global South suffer from human rights abuses, war crimes and systematic sexual violence on a massive scale often at the hands of their governments, nearly unknown in the Global North. Contemporary genocides and mass atrocities contribute to flows of refugees from the South to the North, as well as within the regions of the Global South; they entail humanitarian crises and security problems across regions and for an increasingly connected global community. Even as the international community takes action to intervene, protect and to bring perpetrators to justice through its international organizations, legal instruments, and civil societies on an enhanced scale, its selective attention and that of international bodies continue to reflect the North–South divide, as evidenced by the differential attention and treatment of the simultaneous genocides in Yugoslavia and Rwanda (Melvern, 2010; Development Dialogue, 2008).

Genocides have been mostly defined as committed by a single perpetrator group or centre against a targeted single victim group. This genocidal relationship was facilitated by the development of the power of the modern state and its base in a national and ethnic group, and genocide therefore is often conceptualized as a state crime (e.g. Rothe and Mullins, 2008). Nation states thus became the seedbed of mass atrocities and genocidal events, as they were in a position to radicalize their populations. Contemporary genocides and mass atrocities have decisively changed their appearance, structure and dynamics. They are presently characterized by new patterns that have emerged across the past decades and that clearly set them apart from previous genocides and mass atrocities, in particular from the Holocaust of the European Jews. Contemporary mass violence is often embedded in trajectories of long-term conflict, and the majority of mass killings since World War II have been part of civil wars and ethnic conflicts (Natsios, 1997; Human Security Report Project, 2011). They typically occur beneath the level of the nation state and independently of its boundaries, and evolve in the environment, social formations and the complex actor configurations of 'extremely violent societies' (Gerlach, 2010; Karstedt, 2012).

Rather than being a 'mega-genocide' (Levene, 2005: 163) often these events are of a smaller scale and reiterated; few are massive with a large number of victims. As they follow the dynamics of the conflict, perpetrators and victims might change sides, certain groups and communities are repeatedly victimized, whilst others suffer less. The conflict in the region of Rwanda, Burundi and Congo is an exemplary case: between 1959 and 1996 Hutus and Tutsis changed place as victims and perpetrators several times. Under such conditions and in such environments, violence becomes 'multi-polar' (Gerlach, 2010: 149). Diverse groups of perpetrators participate for a multitude of reasons, ranging from state government forces to militias (for Darfur: Hagan and Rymond-Richmond, 2009), and engage in complex and shifting alliances. Perpetrators are located beyond borders, and recruited across borders. Various population groups become victims of massive attacks of physical violence, including mass killings, systematic sexual violence and enforced relocation, and mass violence oscillates between these different forms of violence; in several incidents of mass atrocities systematic sexual violence is the predominant type of violence. Mass participation in these events spreads across the boundaries of different groups and blurs the lines between different types of involvement and non-involvement as well as between the victimized and the persecuting groups. In these long-term conflicts involvement of groups is shifting, victimized and persecuting groups coalesce, communities are fragmented along different lines, and organized violent actors (e.g. paramilitary groups) become increasingly involved, whether encouraged and organized by state actors or other powerful actors. State actors engage in changing alliances with groups; a continuous characteristic is the engagement of military and paramilitary forces, as well as of the police in paramilitary action resulting in forced disappearances, widespread torture, and sexual violence. Genocide and mass atrocities are often linked to other criminal activity, including financial crimes, weapons and drugs trafficking or illegal exploitation of natural resources.

These changes in the nature of mass atrocity events which took place over the past decades have necessarily shifted perspectives and conceptualizations of genocide and mass atrocities. Genocide and genocidal events are seen in relational terms rather than as 'domestic' events (Scherrer, 1999) often spreading throughout regions and across borders. What happened in Rwanda in 1994 was preceded by genocidal violence in Burundi, and has subsequently set off mass atrocities in Congo. From this perspective, episodes of mass violence, often of a smaller scope and part of series of such events are included rather than marginalized. These are situated within the context of wider ranging conflicts and relations, either between groups within the borders of a state (or what is left of it), in border-crossing regions or between nation states (see Shaw, 2011). The shift away from a (nation) state-focused, domestic perspective also has questioned the use of established 'stage' or process models of genocide (e.g. Stanton, 2004). These models are based on a single and powerful perpetrator, actually the nation state, and a targeted group; they focus on the role of group pressure and power structures mostly within an environment of inter-ethnic conflict and discrimination. From the 'domestic' perspective inter-group relations were nearly exclusively conceptualized as state– and majority–minority relationships, and in terms of discrimination and racism, rather than in terms of complex and shifting alliances and long-term conflicts; boundaries between groups appeared as clearly defined rather than fluid and blurred, as they are in contemporary conflicts. Necessarily, this shifted the focus from rather vaguely defined macro-processes to the micro-dynamics of genocidal events and mass atrocities (Klusemann, 2010). In terms of prevention, the shift implied moving away from intervention into processes of discrimination at the macro- and state-level towards citizen-based response-systems 'on the ground' (Matveeva, 2006) and a culture of protecting civilians from atrocities from various actors, of which the state and its agents are but one (Lie, 2008).

What is the 'global' dimension of mass atrocities and genocide, and how is their changing nature related to processes of globalization, if at all? This chapter will address these questions in three steps: First, I will present recent conceptualizations which are better suited to guide criminological inquiry in the field. Second, I will analyse the development of mass atrocities and genocide during the past decades and relate these to processes of globalization. Finally, I will analyse in which ways the global community has responded to mass atrocities and genocide during the past decades, on the national, transnational and international level, and with various legal instruments.

Conceptualizing the crime of genocide from a global perspective

The international crime of genocide was established in a bold and path-breaking attempt at international law-making. It was legally defined in the United Nations Convention on the Prevention and Punishment of the Crime of Genocide in 1948, preceded by a resolution of the General Assembly proclaiming that 'genocide was the deprivation of the right to existence of a group in the same fashion that homicide was the denial of the right to exist of an individual' (Rubinstein, 2004: 308). This 'episode' of global law-making (Halliday, 2009) started an ongoing process, and resulted in what has been termed a global 'justice cascade' (Sikkink, 2011).

Acts that constitute genocide as detailed in the Convention include: killing members of the group; causing serious bodily or mental harm to them; deliberately inflicting conditions of life calculated to bring about their physical destruction in whole or in part; imposing measures intended to prevent births within a group; and forcibly transferring children of the group to another one. The Convention's definition is remarkable in two respects. First, it does not imply that genocide is the total destruction of a whole group; second, it includes a range of acts besides mass killings, and thus takes into account the *process character* of genocide.

It was not until the last decade of the twentieth century that the justice cascade developed momentum, and the international community established the requisite institutional framework, first with the International Tribunals for the Former Yugoslavia (Hagan, 2003) and Rwanda, and finally with the adoption of the Rome Statute of the International Criminal Court (ICC) in 1998, and its establishment in 2002 (Schabas, 2004). Indeed, the ICC and the international community have increasingly recognized the multi-faceted and multi-polar nature of genocide, war crimes and crimes against humanity. In 2008, the Security Council acknowledged systematic sexual violence and attacks as a war crime (UN Security Council, 2008). In 2005, the UN General Assembly affirmed that 'the international community has the responsibility . . . to protect populations from genocide, war crimes, ethnic cleansing and crimes against humanity' (UN General Assembly, 2005: 30).

The crime of genocide has been a contested and politicized concept since it was enshrined in the UN Convention, and it has been widely debated due to its strictly legal meaning and the often contested nature of cases (Schabas, 2010). It is instrumental in assigning individual responsibility to perpetrators in the realm of international criminal justice, and simultaneously used within the context of international relations and politics for purposes of risk assessment, early warning systems, and finally intervention by the international community. It is further used in advocacy, for righting historical wrongs like in the Armenian genocide, as well as for contemporary victims of mass atrocities. The inclusive and comprehensive approach taken by international justice as well as by regional and national judicial bodies testifies to the acknowledgment of the diversity of mass atrocities and grave human rights violations beyond the limits of the Convention, and thus to the recognition of the changing nature of genocidal events and the context in which they occur.

The convention has always been seen as too restrictive for scholarly research into genocide and mass atrocities; numerous definitions of genocide have been suggested which transcended the narrower limits of the legal definition in the convention (see e.g. Shaw, 2011; Alvarez, 2010). Criminologists have a particularly strong tradition of conceptualizing crime outside and beyond of legal definitions. The most prominent and successful example is the coinage of the term 'white collar crime' by Edwin Sutherland, which notwithstanding the numerous problems it poses for researchers, has made its way into the vernacular of many languages. The concept of state crime, which has no direct equivalent in law, has been applied to genocide: Green and Ward (2004: 2) define it as 'state organizational deviance involving the violation of human rights', and include genocide as an example of state criminality (see also Alvarez, 2010; Rothe and Mullins, 2008). However, conceptualizing genocide as 'state crime' reifies a particular type of 'domestic' genocide and historical period, which as outlined above has given way to more complex and diverse forms and types of mass atrocities. State-level processes are important in the evolvement of contemporary genocidal events and mass atrocities, but the state is hardly anymore the centre and single perpetrator of mass atrocities as it has been during the first half of the twentieth century, and as the terminology suggests. Rothe and Mullins (2008) therefore contextualize the state as perpetrator of mass atrocities within the environment of powerful corporate and global actors.

Two conceptual moves are presently adapting the legal and scholarly concept of genocide for the global context of the twenty-first century; both are explicitly addressing the emerging characteristics of mass atrocities and mass violence and the global context in which they take place. Christian Gerlach's (2010) term of 'extremely violent societies' as described above captures the diversity of victim and perpetrator groups, the pervasive nature of violence, the shifting alliances of violent groups and the fluid engagement of different groups. David Scheffer (2006, 2007), previously US Ambassador-at-Large for War Crimes Issues, aims at separating the political use of the term 'genocide' from its legal definition. He suggests to substitute it with the term 'atrocity crimes', and to define 'atrocity laws' as a new field of international law. He addresses in particular the needs of the international community to meet the challenges of multi-polar violence for its agenda of early response, intervention, and prevention. As the gap between the necessity of rapid response to such events, which often unfold at a fast pace as in Rwanda, and the 'slow motion' of international and national prosecution widens (see Braithwaite *et al.*, 2010), it is important to address 'precursors' to genocidal events without the preemptive usage of the highly contested legal term 'genocide'. Both terms – 'atrocity crimes' and 'atrocity laws' – recognize the diversity as well as the character and magnitude of the crimes that are adjudicated in international, hybrid and national criminal courts and tribunals. In the light of the responsibility of the international community to protect and to intervene, Scheffer aims at public dialogue and at 'shift(ing) the debate (in both legal and public discourse) during the early phases of such crimes... thereby standing a better chance of influencing the development of effective responses to massive death, injury and destruction' (2007: 92). In separating the legally burdened term of genocide from international political discourse and decision-making, it makes prevention and intervention independent of subsequent judicial decision-making, and (for the perpetrators) the looming risk of prosecution.

As the term 'atrocity crime' is applicable throughout the unfolding of conflicts and as risks increase that events of massive violence might occur, it is linked to the processual character of mass atrocities, both from a long-term and macro-perspective as well as from the micro-perspective of single events of mass atrocities. However, rather than being connected to the model of 'stages' in the development of genocide and mass atrocities, and long-term economic, social and cultural risk factors, precursors of atrocity crimes are events 'occurring immediately prior to and during possible genocide' (Scheffer, 2006: 232). These 'can point to an ultimate legal judgment of genocide' (Scheffer, 2006: 232); however, the final legal definition is not preempted by the term 'atrocity crimes'. For a global criminology the term captures the contemporary nature of mass violence and human rights violations; it allows for targeting actions that cause massive harm but only recently have been covered in national and international law like, for example, forced disappearances. As such the concept combines the 'merits of a unifying term' (Scheffer, 2007: 91) that enables public discourse, is easily understood by the public, and gives a focus to criminological discourse and inquiry, in the same way as the term white collar crime did more than half a century ago. It is an encompassing term that includes the crime of genocide without substituting it.

Globalization and genocide: empirical evidence and conceptual frameworks

Most observers of mass violence and genocide during the last decades of the twentieth century and even at the start of the twenty-first century would have agreed that the process of globalization coincided with or even was causally linked to a simultaneous exponential increase of mass atrocity crimes and genocide. Data on genocide collected by Harff (2003) and Genocide Watch (2010) show a more complex pattern. Harff counts 37 events between 1956 and 2002; the list of Genocide Watch comprises 161 events between 1945 and 2009. As these include double counting to provide for multiple perpetrator groups, only

149 countries are included in Figure 10.2. The death toll, however, is based on the total of 161 events. Accordingly, Figures 10.1 and 10.2 show slightly different trajectories for both genocidal events and the number of deaths. According to Harff, the main increase in mass violence and genocidal events takes place between 1960 and 1990, and subsequently subsides with the exception of the Rwandan genocide. Genocide Watch records a steady and, from 1985 to 1995, exponential increase of events, with a peak between 1995 and 2000. Since then, events decline, corroborating Harff's data. Both counts concur on a decreasing number of deaths since the beginning of the 1980s, a continuous development only to be interrupted by the Rwandan genocide.

The decline of mass atrocities and genocidal events coincides with a global decline of civil wars, and precisely the 'dramatic and unexpected decline in the number of civil conflicts that started in the early 1990s after three decades of steady increase' (Human Security Report Project, 2011: 5). This decline is most obvious for 'high-intensity civil conflicts' which account for the highest numbers of death and grave human rights violations, and mostly coincide with a range of mass atrocity crimes, even if not always genocidal events. They have remained at a low level with a net decrease since 1988 of nearly 80 per cent. These considerable changes went largely unnoticed during the decade of Rwanda, Somali and Bosnia, events that signified a series of mass atrocities and genocide coinciding with globalization. Whilst the overall number of conflicts generating mass

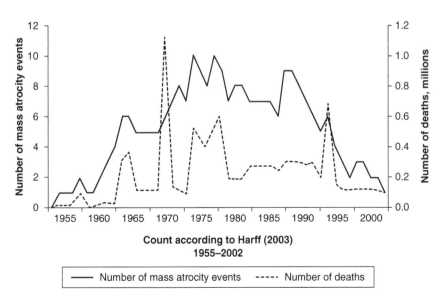

Figure 10.1 Genocide and mass atrocities, 1955–2002.

Source: Harff (2003).

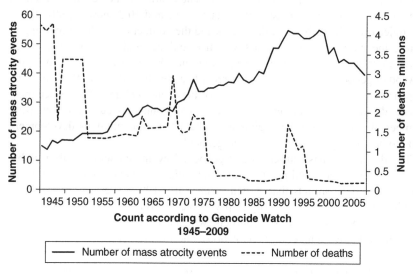

Figure 10.2 Genocide and mass atrocities, 1945–2009.

Source: Genocide Watch (2010): Genocide and Politicides since 1945.

atrocities decreased, these 'signal' events clearly established a link between globalization and mass atrocities and genocide fuelled by ethnic and religious strife
(e.g. Appadurai, 1998).

All evidence available suggests that when globalization took off after the Cold
War the number of mass atrocities and their death toll were already subsiding,
with the exception of major genocidal events both in Europe and Africa. In addition, in Latin and Central American countries like El Salvador, Guatemala or
Argentina, state-driven mass atrocity crimes and genocide were equally subsiding already at the end of the 1980s and in the early 1990s, as they were in Asia
(Karstedt, 2012; Human Security Report, 2010). The evidence raises three questions: Is there actually a legacy from the past that fuelled conflicts and mass atrocities? Were the major genocidal and mass atrocity events of the 1990s and in
the first decade of the twenty-first century related to specific characteristics of
the process of globalization at the time? And finally, do processes of globalization account for the decline, and if yes, which mechanisms are responsible?

The legacy of the past that reaches into the age of globalization and also
accounts for the North–South divide in the incidence of contemporary genocide
and mass atrocities is linked to post-colonial conditions and dependencies. They
created massive ethnic and religious tensions within and across the borders of
fragile states, as well as ethnic economic and social competition within these
states (Schaller, 2008; Zimmerer, 2008). The post-colonial legacy of categoriz-
ing ethnic groups and selectively investing particular groups with political and

economic power has been made responsible for the Rwandan genocide (see e.g. Long and Mills, 2008). Besides fuelling ethnic strife such categorizations have been identified as seminal in targeting Tutsi victims and their communities by Hutu perpetrator groups. They also have been identified as root causes in perpetuating economic inequality and competition among the rural population which fuelled the genocide in Rwanda (Verwimp, 2003). In the twenty-first century the genocide in Darfur is linked to colonial and post-colonial policies leaving in its wake weak states and governments (Hagan and Rymond-Richmond, 2009).

With regard to the processes of globalization, the political economy of globalization has been linked to the signal mass atrocity events of the 1990s and the beginning of the twenty-first century. Global neo-liberal policies as promoted and imposed by the World Bank, the International Monetary Fund (IMF) and core countries in the Global North are made responsible for the deregulation of markets, and the opening of local markets to international competition, thus weakening local producers and putting increasing economic pressure on them. As Rothe and Mullins (2008) point out, globalization enhanced the reliance on cash-crop economies with its unpredictable fluctuations. Simultaneously governments were forced to reduce public spending and generally to assume a smaller role. As these measures increased the conditions for violent conflict they were equally conducive to mass atrocities (Bendana, 2008). Neo-liberal doctrines as implemented through Structural Adjustment Programs by the IMF (Sassen, 2007: 150), exacerbated problems and strife in poor counties rather than alleviating them. Led by international finance institutions, these policies mainly benefited elites, while they destroyed living conditions for the rural population (Rothe and Mullins, 2008). It is precisely the mixture of opening markets, linking small farmers to the fluctuations of global commodity markets, privatizating the economy and reducing subsidy and welfare payments that characterize the global economy and the strategies of international agencies at the time. All processes have been identified as seminal factors that fuelled the crisis in Rwanda and its neighbouring countries, ultimately leading to the unfolding of the genocide (Rothe *et al.*, 2008). It is reasonable to assume that the global political economy of neo-liberalism was a decisive factor in a number of particular mass atrocity events during a limited period; the declining numbers of such events speak either to changes in the political economy of globalization and strategies of international financial institutions, or against a general and overall impact of the emerging political economy of globalization. Whichever route the potential impact of the global political economy on genocide and mass atrocity crimes takes, its main characteristic is the dominance of a consensus of strong global actors and the subsequent worldwide imposition of policies on poor and weak countries (Halliday and Carruthers, 2009: 6). Poor countries are more prone to violent conflict, and consequently, even if subsiding, mass atrocity crimes are more frequent in these than in other countries.

In which ways then might globalization have contributed to the decline of civil conflicts and mass atrocity events? The Human Security Report 2009/2010 identifies two major and decisive factors: an increase in income in the poor and conflict-ridden countries of the South and an 'upsurge in international activism' (2011: 6), ranging from peacekeeping initiatives and international intervention to sanctions and international criminal justice. Economic growth in the Global South has integrated previously weak economies and states into the global economy. As a higher level of integration strengthens states and governments (see Esty *et al.*, 1998) state capacities have increased with national incomes rising. States and governments are in a better position to address grievances, and offer political cooptation (Human Security Report Project, 2011: 5). This constitutes a distinctly different role for the state as perpetrator of mass atrocities and genocide in contrast to the first half of the twentieth century, when the powerful state machineries of totalitarian states were deeply implicated in genocide, with the Holocaust as the exemplary case. As the state strengthened in the course of modernity, it was provided with an array of 'achievements of modernity' that according to Bauman (1989) directly led to and supported the genocide of the European Jews. Whilst then a strong state took to 'final solutions' (Valentino, 2004), it is presently the weak state that engages in mass atrocities and genocide, and stronger states are more capable actors in prevention and intervention. However, in the major conflicts and mass atrocity events at the turn of the twenty-first century, state power also facilitated mass atrocities, as states closed their borders against any international intervention (Rothe *et al.,* 2009). In the age of globalization, mass atrocities and genocide take place at the cross-roads of local and international relations, and between local, international and global actors (Shaw, 2011; for Darfur, see Hagan and Rymond-Rychmond, 2009).

More importantly, the number of international mediation efforts, peacekeeping activities, disarmament, demobilization and reintegration operations as well as multi-lateral sanction regimes increased exponentially between the 1980s and 2008, as the number of conflicts and mass atrocities decreased (Human Security Report Project, 2011: 6, 61). A growing body of evidence (e.g. Doyle and Sambanis, 2006; Fortna, 2008, 2004; Braithwaite *et al.*, 2010) demonstrates that peacekeeping operations 'work' in terms of mediation, intervention and prevention. Globalization in many ways strengthened the international community and overall increased its capacity to act against conflict and mass atrocities, even in the light of massive failures as in Bosnia and Rwanda. In the following section we will explore in which ways the proliferation of criminal justice instruments and the 'justice cascade' (Sikkink, 2011) are linked to processes of globalization.

Globalization and 'the end of impunity': the proliferation of criminal justice

When asking what is actually 'international' or global about genocide, the apparent answer is that war crimes, genocide and crimes against humanity were internationally established, and the legal institutions that prosecute these crimes are part of and linked to international organizations (Shaw, 2011; Rothe and Mullins, 2006). The 'justice cascade' that started at the end of the 1980s constituted a major strand of the upsurge of international activism. The emergence of international criminal justice is intricately linked to the dynamics of globalization, and has shaped and enhanced the notion of the responsibility of the global community to protect the vulnerable against genocide and crimes against humanity (UN General Assembly, 2005). In this process the genocides in former Yugoslavia and Rwanda were seminal events in the proliferation of international criminal justice and prosecution of genocide and crimes against humanity on a global scale after it had been dormant during the Cold War. The impact of contemporary globalization becomes visible in global law-making, intervention and criminalization of genocide and crimes against humanity, and it is here where we can identify links with globalization proper. The emergence, propagation and stabilization of norms and institutions to combat genocide and crimes against humanities can be deemed one of the most important instances of the creation of global standards, norms and values in the latter half of the twentieth century, and these are presently at the core of global law-making (Halliday, 2009). The past two decades have witnessed the emergence of a global normative consensus on the necessity of prosecuting and adjudicating atrocity crimes, and the establishment of an international institutional framework to address these crimes. This is epitomized in the worldwide and consensual demand of an 'end to impunity', even confirmed by the African Union in a statement otherwise highly critical of the International Criminal Court (African Union, 2012). The 'culture' involved and the normative standards it promotes has a world-wide basis and is built up in recursive processes of law-making (Halliday, 2009; Meyer *et al.*, 1997). The power of the global normative discourse is demonstrated by the world success of a recent video on YouTube, in which Hollywood celebrities called for the extradition of Joseph Kony, the leader of the Ugandan Lord Resistance Army.

This normative consensus emerged as a result of major structural changes and shifts of power on the global stage, and was embedded in a global discourse on the 'end of impunity' for these crimes and the powerful perpetrators. Importantly, these processes were linked to the emergence of new local, regional and global models of justice designed for transitional processes across the globe. Structural changes, global discourse and model diffusion complemented each other in what Sikkink calls the 'justice cascade' (2011). They did not start from the global level and trickled down, but emerged first at the national and local level, predominantly as Truth and Clarification Commissions in Latin America, and the regional Inter-American Court of Human Rights. Since then, international, local and regional justice systems have been involved in the global proliferation of procedures to put perpetrators of mass atrocities on trial. Networks, norm and policy diffusion had a major role in establishing the consensus, which then in processes of 'recursive global law making' (Halliday, 2009) generated pressures on states to commit and to bind themselves to the global project of international criminal justice (Simmons and Danner, 2010).

Figure 10.3 demonstrates the two seminal characteristics of the proliferation of proceedings against perpetrators of genocide and other atrocity crimes. It starts with nearly two decades of national proceedings, and since the 1990s a slow

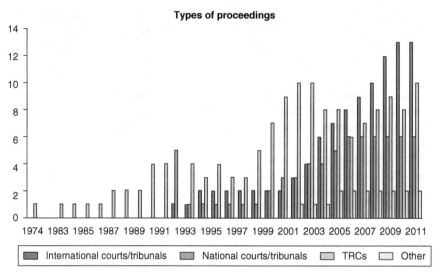

Figure 10.3 Proceedings against mass atrocity crimes and crimes against humanity: international and national courts, tribunals and Truth Commissions.

Source: Own data collection; based on all incidents included in Harff (2003) and Genocide Watch;
TRC: all types of Truth Commissions; other: Khulumani Support Group class-action lawsuit (South
Africa, 2002–); Disarmament, Demobilisation and Reintegration Programme (Colombia, 2005).

increase of international and international/hybrid proceedings can be observed,
which takes off into exponential growth with the start of the twenty-first century.
It is important to note that the increase in international procedures is preceded by
an upsurge of Truth and Reconciliation Commissions, as well as proceedings in
national courts. The distance between the global and the local has narrowed in
the endeavour to end impunity. As particularly weak and vulnerable states have
signed up to the Statute of Rome, international criminal justice might provide a
potentially useful tool for these states to reduce violence (Simmons and Danner,
2010; see also Fortna, 2008). Non-governmental organizations that operate locally
and internationally put pressure on states, as they bring their local knowledge of
mass atrocity crimes into the international sphere. However, as Figure 10.4 shows,
much of the increase in proceedings before international courts is owed to the protracted nature of such proceedings, which becomes visible in the 2000s.

Does the global proliferation of local and international prosecution of perpetrators of atrocity crimes and genocide, as well as gross human rights violations,
have an impact on the frequency and severity of such crimes? As Sikkink (2011)
judges on her international and encompassing data base, it does on human rights
violations in general. Claims are made by the ICC that their indictments in
Uganda reduced violence and restarted peace talks (Rothe and Mullins, 2008:
141). Whether the mechanism is deterrence or the adoption of and socialization

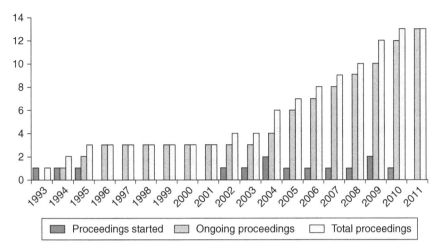

Figure 10.4 Prosecution of international crimes: international proceedings.

Source: Own data collection.

into normative standards cannot be decided; however, both mechanisms broadly work as controls on the use of massive violence and the engagement in mass atrocity crimes by all actors in a violent conflict, and it might be particularly effective with regard to state actors who are more visible and more vulnerable on the global stage. International criminal justice is operating in an international order of sovereign nation states, and consequently in a system of power and domination, with balance of power and networks of security; weak states where contemporary mass atrocities happen, in many ways emulate this international anarchic system (Halliday, 2009; Karstedt, 2011).

The exclusive authority of the nation state over its territory, jurisdiction and its system of criminal justice is key in understanding the problems and tensions that the prosecution of mass atrocity crimes encounters. The tensions that arise between the nation state as 'the occupant of a role' (Meyer *et al.,* 1997) and a particular space in the international system on the one hand, and its authority over its own territory and jurisdiction on the other, shape the face of international criminal justice. As members of the normative culture of 'world society' (Meyer *et al.,* 1997), nation states will implement human rights regimes, or will adopt international criminal justice instruments; however, actual prosecution and extradition is left to the nation state and subject to its interests in the domestic as well as international sphere. International criminal justice and its bodies have been accused of biased prosecution and targeting the Global South, of criminalizing conflicts and leaders in particular in African states (Bendana, 2008; African Union, 2009). The international community has been blamed for highly selective attention to ongoing mass atrocities, and its differential and discretionary willingness to protect and intervene (Melvern, 2010). The ICC's president has called the court 'a judicial institution operating in a political world'; in this he acknowledged the role of political pressure and powerful actors in forcing nation states to prosecute and extradite offenders to international criminal justice, and how these shape the procedures and outcomes of international criminal tribunals. The crime of genocide and the arena of international criminal justice illuminate the paradox of globalization: the proliferation, acceptance and impact of standards and norms that constitute a 'world society' on the one hand, and the role of nation states within a system defined by political, economic and even normative power and competition on the other.

We can assess the proliferation of the adoption and socialization of the normative standards of international criminal justice by measuring impunity. We take as baseline all cases of mass atrocity crimes between 1945 and 2011 as listed by Harff (2003) and Genocide Watch (see above, Figures 10.1 and 10.2). The first measure of impunity is the number of cases that have not been prosecuted, brought to trial or before a tribunal or truth commission, in contrast to those that have been. As such we include international and local procedures as well as all types of transitional justice in the widest sense. A second indicator of impunity is based on those cases that have been brought to trial and measures the interim period between the end of the conflict and the start of proceedings (if proceedings start during the conflict, the interim period is zero). A third measure is based on all cases, including those with absolute impunity, and measures the total period of immunity. Table 10.1 shows the results for regions, as the overlap between end of conflicts, resurgence of conflicts and start of proceedings makes it impossible to calculate meaningful indicators for decades.

The leading role of Latin American countries in the proliferation of justice and ending impunity is clearly visible, if we leave Europe with its small number of cases aside. Asia has the worst record of impunity, with only 15 per cent of the cases prosecuted (column 2), followed by Africa. Nonetheless, the Americas and specifically Latin America have the longest overall periods of impunity

Table 10.1 Mass atrocity crimes, genocide and impunity, 1945–2011

	(1) *Total number of mass atrocities*	*(2)* *Number and % of proceedings*	*(3)* *Average interim period of impunity (proceedings) Years*	*(4)* *Number and % of cases of impunity*	*(5)* *Average interim period of impunity (all cases)*
Africa	56	38% (21)	1.6	62% (35)	16.7
Americas	16	43% (7)	4.3	57% (9)	22.9
Asia	68	15% (10)	4	85% (58)	20
Europe	6	67% (4)	3.5	33% (2)	8
All	146	31% (49)	2.8	69% (104)	18.8

Sources: Own data collection; ICC, http://www.icc-cpi.int/; ICTY, http://www.icty.org/; JIP (Justice in Perspective), http://www.justiceinperspective.org.za/; SCSL (Special Court for Sierra Leone), http://www.sc-sl.org/; USIP (United States Institute of Peace), http://www.usip.org/

(column 5), as it took slightly longer for proceedings to start, if they started at all. As Latin American countries and proceedings had a pioneering role, this might account for the longer time that elapsed between the event and the start of proceedings (column 3). For Africa the shortest interim period of impunity is recorded before proceedings start; this is presumably due to the fact that most conflicts in Africa were rather recent, and proceedings started as a result of the proliferation of international criminal justice during the past decades. As the Human Security Report 2009/2010 (2011) records, most conflicts in Asia that involved mass atrocities subsided before the 1980s; since then they have more than halved. Most of the conflicts ended before international criminal justice re-emerged, and perpetrators were not and have not been prosecuted; most of the more recent cases have been subjected to some kind of procedures, and a country-by-country analysis demonstrates that Asia has witnessed a break with the past of impunity over the past two decades (not shown).

Globalization, cycles of violence and cycles of norm-making

The dynamics of globalization coincide with cycles of violence and cycles of international norm-making. Deaths from one-sided, i.e. state, violence were lowest in 2008, notwithstanding an explosion in intra-state conflicts, mainly in two countries (Kenya and Pakistan), after a long period of decline (Human Security Report Project, 2011). As much as certain characteristics of the global political economy might have been causal in the genocide and mass atrocity crimes in the African region, the emerging structure of globalization at least coincides with globally declining figures of genocidal and mass violence events. More important, globalization enhanced a cycle and *longue-durée* period of international and global law-making against genocide and mass atrocity crimes, which had started decades earlier. However, globalization certainly gave it momentum, and reduced the level of impunity. International criminal justice engages a multitude of local and global actors in networks that are decisive in bringing perpetrators to justice and doing justice to victims of such crimes (Turner, 2007). Besides the proliferation of justice, the global community increasingly adopts responsibility for preventing genocide and atrocities crimes and bringing perpetrators to justice, and the international and global instruments to achieve the aims of the UN Genocide Convention are considerably strengthened. Presently, international action against genocide and mass atrocities is trapped in the gap between the urgency to respond rapidly to the fast pace in which mass atrocity crimes evolve, and the 'slow motion' of peace-building and international criminal justice, which often leaves victims disappointed and distrustful. Innovative routes addressing these challenges imply a shift from global and macro-level political intervention to the activation and empowerment of social forces on the ground. The extent to which global structures and discourses influence and produce international criminal justice and the prosecution of atrocity crimes can only be measured in outcomes on the ground, in less violence, more peace, reconciliation and mediation, and justice for perpetrators and victims.

Note

1   I am particularly grateful to Michael Koch, University of Bielefeld, for research and graphic design.

References

Adorno, Th.W. (2001) *Problems of Moral Philosophy*. Cambridge: Polity Press.

African Union (2012) *Press Release 002/2012*. Addis Aababa, 9 January.

Alvarez, A. (2010) *Genocidal Crimes*. London: Routledge.

Appadurai, Arjun (1998) Dead certainty: Ethnic violence in the era of globalization. *Development and Change, 29*, 905–925.

Bauman, Z. (1989) *Modernity and the Holocaust*. Ithaca, NY: Cornell University Press.

Bendana, A. (2008) Is there a south perspective on genocide? *Development Dialogue, 50*, 281–291.

Braithwaite, J., Dinnen, S., Allen, M., Braithwaite, V. and Charlesworth, H. (2010) *Pillars and Shadows: Statebuilding as Peacebuilding in Solomon Islands*. Acton, ACT: ANU E Press.

Development Dialogue (2008) *Revisiting the heart of darkness: explorations into genocide and other forms of mass violence*. Special Issue, *Development Dialogue, 50*.

Doyle, W. and Sambanis, N. (2006) *Making War and Building Peace*. Princeton, NJ: Princeton University Press.

Esty, D.C., Goldstone, J.A., Gurr, T.R., Harff, B., Levy, M., Dabelko, G.D. and Surko, P.T. (1998) *State Failure Task Force Report*. Phase II Findings. Working Papers, 31 July, University of Maryland.

Fortna, V. (2004) *Peace Time*. Princeton, NJ: Princeton University Press.

Fortna, V. (2008) *Does Peacekeeping Work?* Princeton, NJ: Princeton University Press.

Genocide Watch (2010) *Genocide and Politicides Since 1945*. http://www.genocidewatch. org/genocide/genocidespoliticides.html [04.03.2012].

Gerlach, C. (2010) *Extremely Violent Societies*. Cambridge: Cambridge University Press.

Green, P. and Ward, T. (2004) *State Crime. Governments, Violence and Corruption*. London: Pluto Press.

Gurr, T.R. (1993) *Minorities at Risk: A Global View of Ethnopolitical Conflicts*. Washington, DC: United States Institute of Peace Press.

Hagan, J. (2003) *Justice in the Balkans: Prosecuting War Crimes in the Hague Tribunal*. Chicago: University of Chicago Press.

Hagan, J. and Rymond-Richmond, W. (2009) *Darfur and the Crime of Genocide*. Cambridge: Cambridge University Press.

Halliday, T. (2009) Recursivity of global normmaking: A sociolegal agenda. *Annual Review of Law and Social Science, 5*, 263–289.

Halliday, T. and Carruthers, B.G. (2009) *Bankrupt: Global Law Making and Systemic Financial Crisis*. Stanford, CA: Stanford University Press.

Harff, B. (2003). No lessons learned from the Holocaust? *American Political Science Review, 97*, 57–73.

Hobsbawm, E. (1994) *The Age of Extremes: A History of the World 1914–1991*. New York: Michael.

Human Security Report Project (2011) *Human Security Report 2009/2010*. Simon Fraser University, Canada.

Ignatieff, M. (2001) *Human Rights as Politics and Idolatry*. Princeton, NJ: Princeton University Press.

Karstedt, S. (2011) Exit: The state, globalisation, state failure and crime. In: D. Nelken (ed.) *Comparative Criminal Justice and Globalization*. Dartmouth: Ashgate.

Karstedt, S. (2012) Extremely violent societies: Exploring the dynamics of violence and peace. *European Journal of Criminology*, *9*, 499–513.

Klusemann, S. (2010) Micro-situational antecedents of violent atrocity. *Sociological Forum*, *25*, 272–295.

Levene, M. (2005) *The Meaning of Genocide*. London: I.B. Tauris.

Lie, J. (2008) *Protection of Civilians, the Responsibility to Protect and Peace Operations*. Oslo: NUPI.

Long, B.S. and Mills, A.J. (2003) Globalization, postcolonial theory and organizational analysis: Lessons from the Rwanda genocide. *Critical Perspectives on International Business*, *4*, 389–409.

Matveeva, A. (2006). *Early Warning and Early Response: Conceptual and Empirical Dilemmas*. The Hague: ECCP.

Melvern, L. (2010) *A People Betrayed: The Role of the West in Rwanda's Genocide*, 2nd rev. edition. London: Zed Books.

Meyer, J.W., Boli, J., Thomas, G.W. and Ramirez, F.O. (1997) World society and the nation state. *The American Journal of Sociology*, *103*, 144–181.

Natsios, A. (1997) *US Foreign Policy and the Four Horseman of Apocalypse: Humanitarian Relief in Complex Emergencies*. Westport, CT: Praeger.

Nelken, D. (2004) Globalisation and crime. In: P. Kennett (ed.) *A Handbook of Comparative Social Policy*, 373–382. Cheltenham: Edward Elgar.

Rothe, D. and Mullins, C.W. (2006) *Symbolic Gestures and the Generation of Global Social Control*. Lanham, MD: Lexington Books.

Rothe, D. and Mullins, C.W. (2008) Genocide, war crimes and crimes against humanity in Central Africa: A criminological exploration. In: A. Smeulers and R. Havemann (eds) *Supranational Criminology: Towards a Criminology of International Crimes*. Antwerp: Intersentia.

Rothe, D., Mullins, C.W. and Sandstrom, K. (2008) The Rwandan genocide: International finance policies and human rights. *Social Justice*, *35*, 66–86.

Rothe, D., Ross, J.I., Mullins, C.W., Friedrichs, D. *et al.* (2009) That was then, this is now, what about tomorrow? Future directions in state crime studies. *Critical Criminology*, *17*, 3–13.

Rubinstein, W.D. (2004) *Genocide*. London: Pearson Longman.

Rummel, R.J. (1998) *Statistics of Democide*. Muenster: Lit.

Sassen, S. (2007) *A Sociology of Globalization*. New York: W.W. Norton.

Schabas, W.A. (2004) *An Introduction to the International Criminal Court*, 2nd edition. Cambridge: Cambridge University Press.

Schabas, W.A. (2010) Commentary on Paul Boghossian: The concept of genocide. *Journal of Genocide Research*, *12*, 91–99.

Schaller, D. (2008): Colonialism and genocide – Raphael Lemkin's concept of genocide and its application to European rule in Africa. *Development Dialogue*, *50*, 75–94.

Scheffer, D. (2006) Genocide and atrocity crimes. *Genocide Studies and Prevention*, *1*, 229–250.

Scheffer, D. (2007) The merits of unifying terms: 'Atrocity Crimes' and 'Atrocity Law'. *Genocide Studies and Prevention*, *2*, 91–96.

Scherrer, C.P. (1999) Towards a theory of modern genocide. *Journal of Genocide Research, 1*, 13–23.

Shaw, M. (2011) From comparative to international genocide studies: The international production of genocide in twentieth century Europe. *European Journal of International Relations*. Published online 11 May 2011 ejt.sagepub.com/content/early2011.

Sikkink, K. (2011) *The Justice Cascade*. New York: W.W. Norton.

Simmons, B. and Danner, A. (2010) Credible commitment and the international criminal Court. *International Organization, 64*, 225–256.

Stanton, G.H. (2004) Could the Rwandan genocide have been prevented? *Journal of Genocide Research, 6*(2), 211–228.

Turner, J.I. (2007) Transnational networks and international criminal justice. *Michigan Law Review, 105*, 985–1032.

UN General Assembly (2005) *World Summit Outcome*. UN Doc. A/RES/60/1. http://www.un.org/Docs/journal/asp/ws.asp?m=A/RES/60/1.

UN Security Council (2008) Resolution 1820 (2008). UN Doc. S/ RES 1820 (2008).

Valentino, B.A (2004) *Final Solutions: Mass Killing and Genocide in the Twentieth Century*. Ithaca, NY: Cornell University Press.

Verwimp, P. (2003) The political economy of coffee, dictatorship and genocide. *European Journal of Political Economy, 19*, 161–181.

Zimmerer, J. (2008) Colonialism and the holocaust – towards an archeology of genocide. *Development Dialogue, 50*, 95–124.

11 Parochialism and globalisation

The rise of anti-immigration parties in Europe

Francis Pakes

Globalisation is subject to talk of extremes. Whereas bestselling authors like Friedman discuss globalisation in highly beneficial terms (e.g. Friedman, 1999, 2005), others, like Nobel-prize winner Stiglitz (2002) refer to it as an 'unmitigated disaster for many' in the way it currently plays out. Much is made of the benefits of globalisation but within criminology the focus is understandably most likely to be on its adverse consequences (e.g. Nelken, 2011; Waquant, 2009; Brown, 2011), and to be sure, these are varied and many. For the purposes of this chapter an apt description of globalisation is provided by Sjolander: 'Globalisation needs to be understood (...) as an economic, political, social and ideological phenomenon that carries with it unanticipated, often contradictory and polarizing consequences' (Sjolander, 1995: 604). By now this is a familiar characterisation. Rather than conceiving of globalisation as a singular, one-way flow towards global connectivity, Giddens in fact already in 1990 referred to it as a set of dialectic and contradictory processes.

Globalisation is often discussed in the evocative terminology of 'flow': flows of money, opportunity, industry and culture. Friedman in fact puts it nicely: 'people, information, money, and technology all flow around the globe in a rather chaotic set of disjunctive circuits that somehow bring us all together' (Friedman, 2008: 111). Bude and Dürrschmidt (2010) argue that movement is the essence of globalisation. We are being told that the paradigmatic experience of contemporary society is 'rapid mobility over long distances' enabled by 'new forms of long-distance transportation and travel' (Lash and Urry, 1994: 253). The imagery is one of effortlessness enhanced by a discourse of unlimited consumerist choice. Although this imagery is vivid and seductive the ubiquity of borders and the intensity of border control puts paid to any notion or true borderlessness, in particular when it comes to the movement of people (see also Friedrichs, 2011). Flow therefore is mainly a disembodied flow of notions, cultures, and not least, finance. For embodied travel the same rules do not quite apply. According to Friedman (2008), the extent of immigration is simply not such that you could conceive of it as a signifier for a state of borderlessness. The more graphic counterargument of course is the re-emergence of borders (Lyon, 2005), the burgeoning industry associated with them, and the harm that industries, technologies and policies intended to keep the unwanted out, bring (see Pickering and Weber, this volume, Stumpf, this volume and Muller, this volume). These are examples of contra flow, or movements of de-globalisation Bude and Dürrschmidt (2010) that seem particularly strong in relation to human movement and most particularly to what Aas (2007) called 'dangerous mobilities'.

Düvell (2006: 199) refers to a 'migration paradox' constituted by the growing discrepancy between mobility as a technical possibility on the one hand and attempts at political governance that effectively immobilise large groups of people on the other (Salter, 2009). As the possibilities and appetite (or perhaps more poignantly, desperate need) for travel increases, walls and fences become higher and border control, at least in many cases, intensifies. This essential tension between openness and closedness, has been phrased and rephrased many times, perhaps with most currency by Friedman in 'the Lexus and the olive tree' (Friedman, 1999) where the car brand Lexus represents a global perspective (cars can be manufactured, marketed and sold anywhere) whereas the olive tree represents locality as a tree is literally rooted in time and place. It also, in a way, manifests itself in the distinction between parochialism and cosmopolitanism. That certainly is a theme that has come to pervade discussions on globalisation in our discipline (e.g. Van Swaaningen, 2011, Hudson, 2008). On the one hand the increased mobility of people, money, ideas and goods and enhanced exposure to diversity could bring about a sense of self that transcends time and place, a cosmopolitan identity in which, as it were, the world is your oyster. On the other hand, globalisation can be frightening, disturbing as it does our sense of place, culture and community. That fear mobilises. One of the most visible manifestations of this is in efforts to stem some of globalisation's most disturbing processes which include the movement of people deemed to be unwanted or dangerous.

In this chapter I want to look at one particular expression of parochialism in the face of globalisation, the emergence of neo-nationalist, populist, anti-immigration political parties across a number of Western European countries including Belgium, Denmark, the Netherlands, Sweden, France and Austria. Rydgren (2005) refers to these as a family of parties. They include the Austrian FPÖ (*Freiheitliche Partei Österreichs*), mostly associated with its long term leader, the deceased Jörg Haider. The party was led by Haider until 2005 when a split occurred and the Alliance for the Future of Austria (*Bündnis Zukunft Österreich, BZÖ*) was founded, a party that arguably is somewhat more moderate. Haider led the latter party until his death in 2008. Another prominent example is the Danish People's Party (*Dansk Folkeparti*) under leadership of Pia Kjærsgaard. The family can also count Geert Wilders' Party for Freedom (*Partij voor de Vrijheid*) in the Netherlands as a member as well as the Sweden Democrats (*Sverigedemokraterna*) and also the Flemish Interest (*Vlaams Belang*, a reincarnation of the *Vlaams Blok*, Flemish Block) in Belgium. They are characterised by populism on the one hand and a strong anti-immigration position on the other. In addition, they share notions of anti-Islam, anti-elitism, an anti-European Union stance and a strong law and order agenda.

The family archetype is the French *Front National* whose first electoral success was achieved as early as 1982 when Jean-Marie Le Pen, *pater familias* and long-term leader (until 2011 when his daughter Marine Le Pen took over) won a seat on the council of Paris's twentieth *arrondissement*, an area in the East of the city. Further electoral gains followed in the subsequent years, in European and general elections making the *Front National* a force to be reckoned with within French political and social life. The *Front National* embodies the two stances that were to characterise this family of parties as a whole. The first is anti-establishment populism. Le Pen referred to the leading parties as the 'gang of four' and in the early years railed against a media boycott. It cemented the party's positioning as that of an outsider aiming to shake up a tired, self serving and out of touch political elite. The other is a strong stance of anti-immigration which nowadays particularly focuses on Muslims or Arabs conflating notions of ethnicity, culture and religion with otherness, dangerousness and risk.

Although Rydgren (2005) refers to these collectively as extreme right political parties, it could be, and has been argued that the essence of these parties' programmes and its electoral appeal lies in its anti-immigration policies and rhetoric. Arzheimer (2008) undertook a social survey in 22 European countries and found that voting for anti-immigration parties is mainly driven by intense feelings of anti-immigrant sentiment. Thus, rather than to interpret the electoral success as a protest vote, immigration is the key issue that drives electoral success. Anti-immigration parties may therefore as apt a characterisation although it must be conceded that 'immigration' and the processes and groups associated with it are far too multi-faceted to cover the simplistic policies proposed and sentiments frequently expressed. Much vitriol is directed at asylum seekers for instance, and similarly ethnic minorities who are neither foreigners nor immigrants are frequently targeted. Nevertheless, I will adopt the terminology of anti-immigration parties, despite its obvious shortcomings. In this chapter I want to briefly sketch the key ingredients of such parties and chart their electoral success. Their influence on issues of immigration and other aspects of criminal justice policy will be discussed subsequently and finally, we look at the wider meaning of the rise of these parties in terms of views and sentiments on globalisation in relation to flow and contra flow of human movement.

The phenomenology of anti-immigrant parties: a sketch

The family of anti-immigration parties is characterised by populism, anti-elitism and anti-immigration policies that are justified by pointing to ethnic, cultural or religious difference so that any growth of a 'non-native' population would put some nationalist essence at risk. But the similarities in how these parties operate go much further than that. It is clear that the rise of such parties is much furthered by a vocal and highly visible figurehead. They include Jean-Marie Le Pen in France, Geert Wilders in the Netherlands, Pia Kjærsgaard in Denmark and Jörg Haider in Austria. Anti-immigration parties seem to rely more on the persona of the leader than on party infrastructure or grass roots support. This is most particularly the case for Geert Wilders, leader of the Dutch Party for Freedom. Although technically a political party, it has Geert Wilders as its sole member.

Thus, whereas there are Members of Parliament, employees and volunteers, there is no grass roots movement in the sense of a party membership. This has repercussions for funding in the absence of state subsidy and raise issues of financial transparency and dependency.

This leader needs to create a persona that can command the trust of a part of the electorate that tends to distrust public figures. For them to credibly assume the position of relative outsider and to provide a haven for disenfranchised voters they require an identifiable set of skills. The first skill involves use of language. It is frequently referred as non-parliamentarian: simple and straightforward on the one hand and more pugnacious and swashbuckling rather than administrative and legalistic, on the other. It is essential that anti-immigrant parties set themselves apart in tone and content from the political mainstream yet remain sufficiently moderate to acquire or maintain a degree of respectability (Rydgren, 2005). The latter consideration puts limits on the extent to which confrontational and offensive language can be used. The spokesperson needs to find that balance between sounding refreshingly different, regularly communicating outrage at certain trends or events but at the same time tempering that outrage to ensure that mainstream voters are not put off.

At the same time, anti-immigration parties need to be able to be taboo-breaking. In many instances, not least in Denmark and the Netherlands, immigration as a political or social issue was anathema for decades after World War II. Where it was discussed it was within the confines of far-right movements with Nazi or fascist sympathies or associations. The far right had been associated with militarism, racism, fascism and anti-democracy and after World War II and had become largely marginalised with only very few exceptions across Europe. In order to be able to gain any level of electoral success, present day anti-immigration parties need to demonstrate a clear break with the past. Today they present themselves persistently as democratic, do not espouse violence and generally do avoid strong versions of racism. Instead, anti-immigration talk is couched in terms of incompatible or inferior cultures and threats to the country's social cohesion, values and public services. Obviously, immigration, Islam, asylum seekers and ethnic minorities are *ad infinitum* associated with crime, disorder and unacceptable strain on and misuse of public resources. But hard talk of racism is usually avoided and with it talk of violence or the expression of anti-democratic sentiments. Instead, the image-building of the leader tends involve a narrative of a decent person, not a career politician who seeks to save the country from being overrun by immigrants which threatens the native culture and the social fabric. It is important for the leader to further that message at every opportunity. Danish People's Party's leader Pia Kjærsgaard provides a paradigmatic quote that shows emotive language, a common touch, anti elitism and a distrust of official sources and academia alike, in relation to crime, violence and immigration:

> I'm sure that the usual group of criminological experts will soon be badgering us with their statistics – in an attempt to downplay the problems and lull the minister to sleep. But many of us began to disregard the statistics a long

time ago, we only need to look out of the window, walk the streets or read the papers and watch television in order to realize that things are getting out of hand. It cannot go on for any longer. We will simply not take it anymore.
(Scharff-Smith, 2012: 44)

De-association with racism, and even more so fascism and Nazism is of primary importance. Several of the parties in the family are continually surrounded by debate whether their thought, parts of it or the undercurrents beneath it, can be characterised as racist. This debate frequently occurs in the media, the internet, and occasionally in Parliament or in court. Certainly the *Front National* in its early days was associated with comments that belittled the Holocaust or were otherwise deemed as anti-Semitic. Jean-Marie Le Pen was convicted more than once for such offences. The same to an extent applied to Jörg Haider in Austria, son of members of the Austrian national-socialist party whose anti-Semitic associations led the Israeli government to issue a statement further to the election of Haider as governor of the *Bundesland* or state of Carinthia in the South, one of nine states within Austria, in the South. It led to a political storm across the European Union and Israel proceeded to recall its ambassador. The leaders of more recently established parties do not tend to carry any baggage involving anti-Semitism. Instead, Wilders is strongly pro-Israel and visits the country frequently. Pia Kjærsgaard has also been noted for pro-Israel positions. It is perhaps noteworthy that Marine Le Pen, the daughter of Jean-Marie and new leader of the *Front National* has recently spoken more positively about Israel as well. Where Islam has emerged as the key ideological enemy of the anti-immigration parties, the position towards Israel has changed and the saying 'an enemy of an enemy is a friend' does seem to apply.

The newer generation of parties and party leaders are desperately keen to not be branded as, or to brand themselves as racists and seek to defend themselves robustly at any opportunity. That has not stopped public debate or legal action, as the Court case against Wilders in the Netherlands in 2011 testified, for incitement of racial hatred. Part of the case against Wilders was his comparison of the Koran with Hitler's book *Mein Kampf* and his reference to Islam was fascist. It led, in the end, to an acquittal. Conversely, Pia Kjærsgaard took an opponent to Court in Denmark for libel after allegedly having been branded a racist. The Court did not rule in Kjærsgaard's favour. The *Vlaams Blok* fought a verdict of racism and discrimination all the way to Belgium's high court but to no avail. In the aftermath the movement re-emerged as *Vlaams Belang* (Flemish Interest).

A further skill frequently evidenced is the framing of incidents and events. International events are to be 'translated' into local immigration issues and similarly, local incidents are frequently elevated to national emergencies if they fit an anti-immigration or anti-Muslim frame. Wilders is certainly adept at both (Pakes, 2010). It has been argued that the *Fatwa* declared against writer Salman Rushdie in 1989 furthered the cause of the *Front National* in France as it allowed Le Pen to frame the prevalence of extremist views within Islam to counteract any claims of extremism on his own account. The murder of Pim Fortuyn in the Netherlands in 2002 has served as both legitimisation and inspiration for Geert Wilders. Fortuyn led a populist party that in 2002 suddenly rose to popularity on an anti-immigration and anti-Islam ticket. Fortuyn was assassinated by a self-proclaimed environmental activist just prior to the 2002 general elections. This allowed for the argument that 'the bullet came from the left' to be put forward relentlessly. That mantra represented a crucial act of framing. It furthered the argument that it was the political left, embodied in the Labour Party that allegedly treated Fortuyn unfairly on the one hand and as the main culprit with regards to laxity on issues of immigration and integration, on the other. In such a fashion, key incidents frequently help raise the profile of these parties as they embed their interpretation of such events into their grand narrative. In an age of demise of the 'grand ideological narrative' (Fukuyama, 1992) the threat of Islam and immigration serve as a handy umbrella-type substitute for anti-immigration parties: rather than being dismissingly framed as 'single issue' parties, the argument furthered is that immigration is actually to blame for a wide range of problems that can all be solved by restricting it. In addition, framing helps to identify local adversaries, such the Dutch Labour Party, depicted as appeasing tea-drinkers that have abandoned the plight of the working classes. Geert Wilders refers to Labour as the Party for Arabs. It illustrates a strategy of highlighting processes of de-alignment along traditional cleavages in society such as on the basis of class or income. With the portrayal as the Labour Party as the Party for immigrants the new cleavage of foreigners versus 'natives' gains salience.

In Denmark the Westergaard cartoon controversy has been said to put the wind in the sails of the Danish People's Party (The Economist, 2006). The outlet *Jyllands-Posten* printed a number of cartoons by Westergaard featuring the prophet Muhamed in 2005 which led to, more or less manufactured, outrage in many places in the Middle East. The newspaper *Politiken* from the same publishing stable also published a cartoon and subsequently apologised. It was seized upon by Pia Kjærsgaard to highlight that Islam must be seen as a threat to Western/Danish values and that grovelling apologists are treasonous sell-outs. It helps sell the story of global threats and at the same time furthers the salience of local enemies.

A further desirable attribute for an anti-immigration party leader is to be able to portray themselves as a political outsider. They need a common touch, and an *imago* of a decent citizen alarmed by developments surrounding immigration and integration who has adopted a stance that sometimes is akin to a mission to fight it. Wilders certainly uses the word 'mission' a lot, and discusses his work almost in crusading terms. On order to do this, it is important to avoid the ways of a career politician, a much distrusted figure in their constituency. In terms of personal background, Kjærsgaard has a past as a home carer and is not tainted by having been part of the 'elite' political establishment. She is therefore well placed to adopt the position of a concerned citizen to fight ostensibly on behalf of native Danes. Wilders, on the other hand, broke away from Liberal Party VVD in 2004 and is undeniably a career politician. Both Le Pen and Haider had far right associations from the onset. That has served as an obstacle in three ways. The first is the general distaste of the electorate to vote for single issue parties associated with violence and fascism that takes time and energy to overcome. The second is that these associations have frequently prompted mainstream politics and on occasion the mass media to ostracise or ignore the parties. In Belgium the so-called *cordon sanitaire* (quarantine) was applied around the *Vlaams Blok* in order to isolate it, a consensus that the party would be largely ignored in terms of cooperation, and would not form part of any coalition at any political level (Damen, 2001). The third is that such associations complicate the recruitment of political talent.

Electoral success

What most, but not all anti-immigration parties share is electoral success. Wilders' Party for Freedom gained 15.5 per cent of the popular vote in the 2010 Dutch general elections, which led to 24 seats in the Dutch 150-strong Parliament. After protracted negotiations, the Party for Freedom supported a coalition government that took power consisting of Christian Democrats (CDA) and Liberals (VVD). This is a minority government relying on Wilders' party for support, which has been written into the coalition agreement. Until recently the Danish People's Party was in a similar position. In 2007, Pia Kjærsgaard's party gained 13.8 per cent of the vote in the Danish general election. It also ended up offering vital support for the liberal–conservative coalition in power. In 2011, however, the party suffered a slight downturn in the general election, gaining 12.3 per cent and losing three seats. The new government led by Social Democrat Helle Thorning-Schmidt has no involvement from the Danish People's Party.

The rise of the *Front National* goes back to the 1980s. After some notable electoral success in local and European elections, the *Front National* won 9.8 per cent of the vote and 35 seats in the National Assembly in 1986. Its electoral heyday as far as general assembly elections was concerned was in the 1990s with the party achieving 15.3 per cent of the vote in 1997. Although never ultimately successful the party has a history of vigorous campaigning in the French presidential elections in which Le Pen pulled over 5.5 million votes (over 17 per cent) in the presidential election second round in 2002. Although the complexities of the French electoral system account for the fact that the party in fact boast very few elected representatives, Marine Le Pen certainly is one to watch for the French presidential elections in 2012 and in early 2012 polls in the order of 15 per cent.

In the 1990s the FPÖ, the Freedom Party of Austria regularly pulled over 20 per cent of the votes in the general elections for the National Council and even 26.9 per cent in the 1999 general elections. Its electoral fortunes seem to have waned as the percentage of votes gained were 10 per cent (2002), 11 per cent (2006) but 17.5 per cent in 2008, suggesting something of a revival. However, the heyday of the movement in Austria remains strongly associated with Haider despite his death in a car crash in 2008.

In Sweden, anti-immigration parties have long remained marginal but in 2010 the Sweden Democrats managed to acquire seats in parliament after achieving

5.7 per cent of the vote, up from 2.9 per cent in 2006. The parliamentary threshold in Sweden is 4 per cent. The party's increased success has been ascribed to distancing itself from fascist and military associations in the past under the leadership of Jimmie Åkesson, since 2005. Rydgren has argued that the Sweden Democrats' origin in and connections to the fascist movement has hampered their earlier efforts to create a respectable facade (Rydgren, 2010).

Although there are exceptions it is clear that in many countries anti-immigration parties have become a force to be reckoned with in political life. In Austria, Denmark and the Netherlands they have been in, or propped up, national governments. They have gained seats in local elections and sometimes in European elections, and have seized important political posts such as Haider as Governor of Carinthia. These are unambiguous signs of success. In addition, Widfelt (2010) argues, these parties have become legitimate. They have lost the pariah status of earlier incarnations and *cordons sanitaires* has been punctured. The Dutch Party for Freedom's ideological predecessor, Pim Fortuyn's party actually entered government in the Netherlands in 2002. Thus, we can summarily say that across many countries in Western Europe anti-immigration parties have become rather *salonfähig* and what is more they have become influential in a variety of ways.

Local and wider effects

It is clear that in several countries, the effects of the success of the anti-immigration parties has gone well beyond simply giving a voice to the 1 in 6 voters or so with strong anti-immigration views. The parties have achieved an increased politicisation of issues of immigration, and increased its salience. They seem to have pulled traditional conservative or medium right parties further to the right in order to compete for the votes of those cast adrift. That is particularly apparent in immigration law and practice (see also Engbersen and Broeders, 2010) where we have seen genuine transformations. Earlier in the book we have seen the vivid descriptions of Borderworld by Ben Muller, as well as issues of crimmigration (Stumpf) and of deportations (Pickering and Weber). It can easily be seen how such transformations can be furthered by governments incorporating or pandering to anti-immigration party rhetoric and policy. As the rise of anti-immigration parties rather coincides with these developments, they provide insight into the political capital gained by pursuing them.

In Denmark, Hedetoft (2003) argues that already in the 1990s immigration had become a focal point in general election with all major parties proposing a tightening of immigration laws and policing, such as in the areas of family unification and the immigration of foreign partners or spouses (e.g. Rubin, 2004). Denmark now has the toughest immigration laws in the European Union. Rytter (2010) explains that the 2002 immigration law was a watershed moment. It sought to define Danishness in certain terms, essentialism at its finest, but already in 1999 integration requirements and further restrictions on family unification had been put in place. Welfare payments were reduced whereas deportation possibilities were extended. After a centre-right government came into place in 2001, immigration policies were further tightened. The general legal right to family reunification was removed. Rules about permanent residence and citizenship have been made stricter. Prospective citizens now must sign a statement of loyalty to Danish society and fundamental legal principles and values in Denmark before applying for citizenship. The bar with regards to command of the Danish language has been raised several times since 2002. Consequently, the number of naturalisations has reduced quite sharply (Rubin, 2004). Incidentally, the Danish People's Party seemingly booked a symbolic victory with the re-instatement of border controls between Denmark and Sweden in 2011 although any such moves, which would be contrary to the EU Schengen Agreement, have been kicked into the long grass by the new government.

In the Netherlands, we have also witnessed increased requirements on acquiring citizenship which involves a language requirement but also a civic integration requirement. The 2010 government agreement co-signed by Wilders lists a substantial reduction of immigration as a stated aim. To that end, several EU treaties and EU migration directives need to be renegotiated, as does the Association Treaty between the EU and Turkey in relation to restrictions on immigration from Turkey (Groenendijk, 2011). Wilders has stated that a reduction of immigration from non-Western countries of 50 per cent needs to be achieved.

The reinstatement of border controls is an oft-voiced aim. Wilders's Party for Freedom asked parliamentary questions to this effect in April 2011. Le Pen has been said to applaud Denmark's efforts to seek to reinstate border controls and in the past has suggested the same should have happened in France, in 2007. The *Vlaams Belang* also has advocated border controls, for reasons of security and to combat Islamic influence in Belgium. Interestingly, the *Front National* had added the ambition of economic protectionism to its wish to reinstate border control so as to protect the French from products from 'low wages countries'. In the Netherlands, Wilders wanted border controls to 'stem the tide of thousands of North Africans' who gained entry into Italy in 2011, a population movement associated with unrest in Libya and Tunisia as part of the Arab Spring. Stemming the tide is very much an overarching motive of anti-immigration policies and rhetoric. What is more, the rhetoric is increasingly translated into policy.

There is similarity of influence in many other areas as well. What is at present emerging across these parties is the expression of anti-global-finance sentiments, strong opposition against the European Union in general, its enlargement in particular and most specifically the accession of Turkey, and an emerging agenda on the strengthening of social care provision, at least for the 'deserving' parts of the population. In addition to that, harsher sentencing across the board and a reduction of judicial discretion seem to be part of any anti-immigration party manifesto.

Whereas the communalities between the parties in the party family are easily established, that should not obscure a great deal of difference. There is a difference in salient issues, structure and operation. In many other policy areas disparities can be vast and are probably rooted in local or national policy configuration issues, what Savelsberg (2011) calls national sediment. The *Front National* is ardently anti-abortionist (Rydgren, 2005). This is in contrast to the Dutch and Nordic anti-immigration parties. Wilders in the Netherlands has emerged as somewhat of a champion of gay rights and seeks to highlight the extent of violence and abuse directed at homosexuals. The party does seem to be popular amongst gay men (according to a survey undertaken by the gay magazine *Gay Krant* (2010)) but at the same time, it has been found that the average Party for Freedom voter has more negative attitudes towards homosexuality than the rest of the population. Paradoxically, a month earlier the very same magazine reported a statement by a Party for Freedom council candidate who argued that HIV-positive patients should be cattle-burned. Generally the Party's attempt to seize ownership of gay issues is best viewed as part of a campaign to conflate anti-gay aggression with Moroccan perpetrators. That furthers the narrative of Muslim intolerance to Western values such as in relation to sexuality. Similarly, Pia Kjærsgaard has pushed the issue of gang rape up the agenda with the argument that this was an unheard of crime in Denmark prior to the advent of Muslim immigrants. Recently, several anti-immigration parties have sought to brand themselves as champions of women's rights. Perhaps the emergence of female leaders such as Pia Kjærsgaard and Marine Le Pen has facilitated this transition. Historically, anti-immigration parties are male dominated and characterised by a macho and action-oriented culture. Modern anti-immigration parties have moved away from this. On the one hand, they emphasise a cultural rather than a military threat and on the other hand, they highlight issues such as the role of women in Islamic societies and frame issues of domestic violence in terms of cultural and religious disparities. In the Netherlands, the coalition governmental agreement lists, for instance the establishment of a registration procedure for 'culturally determined domestic violence and child abuse' (*Regeerakkoord*, 2011, page 9). It highlights that this conflation has now found its way into governmental objectives. Thus, whatever type of crime or problem can be associated with immigrants has gained salience, be it gay bashing, gang rape, domestic violence, truancy or antisocial behaviour forcing governments with or without involvement of anti-immigration parties to find ways of addressing these issues.

The ostensive taming of globalisation

It is instructive to look for the causative patterns of these highly nationalist movements in global developments. The context of globalisation upon the rise of these parties is not difficult to discern. Profound changes involve the shift from industrialisation to post-industrialisation, the rise of neo-liberalism and economic, political and cultural globalisation. The result in terms of constituency consists of processes of dealignment and realignment or in other words the emergence of new social bifurcations and stratifications. It has certainly created a group of voters who perceive a threat to their identity, who have become discontented with traditional parties and politicians to represent their interests, and whose traditional frames of reference seem insufficient to understand current society. These circumstances provide both political opportunity and constituency. The electorate is less faithful to parties traditionally deemed to represent certain segments of society. In addition, traditional parties have been criticised for failing to foresee this alienation or to prepare for the emergence of immigration as a key political issue. The anti-immigration parties have emerged as taboo breakers and agenda setters through the politicising of issues of immigration and integration. From there is it has been profitable to link many issues to the overarching issues of immigration and ethnic minorities. Immigration therefore has come to present something resembling a grand narrative, the single tangible threat that politics must tackle (Aas, 2007). Leaders of these parties at one time or another may have described their work as a mission or calling, to highlight the grandness of both their work and the issues on which is it focused which helps to distinguish themselves from mainstream 'technocratic' and elitist political leaders.

The precise status of the rise of anti-immigrant parties is contested. It is contested whether they enhance or challenge democracy and whether they are a result of, or a remedy against alienation in society. What is clear is that part of the electorate is swayed by the promise that globalisation can be tamed. This ostensibly can be done by promising to tackle the most visible and tangible globalisation processes, such as immigration, that are perceived as an economic and security but probably mainly as a cultural threat.

From this perspective anti-immigration parties are both harbingers of hope and merchants of fear. They further the myth that you can have your global cake and eat it. The parties tend to promise that social problems will simply disappear when immigration is controlled, that isolation should bring both security and prosperity and that budget cuts and austerity measures further to the global financial crisis would never have been necessary in a land without foreigners. For those without the skills to succeed in a globalised world, the offered mixture of outrage and nostalgia is undeniably seductive. What it tells us about globalisation is that its counter forces carry much weight, both in an emotional and in a political sense. It is important to appreciate the sentiments of that constituency.

The dialectics of globalisation are in particular fought out through such platforms. At the same time we must also acknowledge a further level of contradiction. Despite their nationalist outlook, there is something intense international about these parties. Geert Wilders' website is in English, for instance. He travels the world for public speaking and, no doubt, fundraising. Marine Le Pen of the French *Front National* travelled to Lampedusa, an Italian island off the coast of Tunisia to investigate and discuss immigration problems there. These are just two examples. It therefore seems that these leaders talk national but think international. Although they fight globalisation through furthering neo-nationalist sentiments at the same time they emerge as a globalising force themselves.

A more insidious set of processes relate to what has on occasion been referred to as the criminalisation of Islam or perhaps the securitisation of Islam (Cesari, 2009). National constitutions and European legislation will put paid to any direct attempts to criminalise religion per se, but there are processes at work that may hint at something akin to the criminalisation of Islam, or so it has been claimed. More acute analysis of these processes is certainly in order but a few remarks here may highlight the effects of parochialism through anti-immigration parties and their wider influence. First, citizens of the Islam faith may find themselves under increased surveillance (Spalek and Lambert, 2007) perhaps even hyper-surveillance, often justified and legitimised through anti-terrorist policy and legislation. Second, there is something of a process of seeking to constrain the expression of faith or culture. That includes measures such as banning religious clothing such as the burqa in France and the Netherlands and restraints on the building and operating of mosques, and restrictions on ritual slaughter. The latter was a hotly debated issue in Parliament in the Netherlands where the Upper House quashed a law to that effect that had already passed Parliament. Finally, there is the racialisation and re-prioritisation of conduct associated with minority groups, in particular Muslims. These include domestic violence, gang rape in Denmark and violence against homosexuals in the Netherlands. It is unclear to what extent such processes constitute anything like a concerted effort that we may call the criminalisation of Islam. However, the risk of alienation, as Cesari (2009) and Spalek and Lambert (2007) argue, is substantial. It also shows that the contradictions of globalisation are real in its effects. The rise of anti-immigration parties threatens to bring out the exclusion and demonisation of large groups of society. This represents a threat to justice which is of grave concern and should be of grave concern to criminology. We must be vigilant. The interests of fairness and justice are served by vigilance and close scrutiny of such developments. That certainly is one challenge offered by globalisation to the field of criminology.

References

Aas, K.F. (2007) *Globalization and Crime*. London: Sage.

Arzheimer, K. (2008) Protest, neoliberalism or anti-immigrant sentiment: What motivates the voters of the extreme right in Western Europe? *Zeitschrift für Vergleichende Politikwissenschaft*, *2*, 265–280.

Brown, D. (2011) The global financial crisis: Neo-liberalism, social democracy, and criminology. In: M. Bosworth and C. Hoyle (eds) *What is Criminology?* Oxford: Oxford University Press.

Bude, H. and Dürrschmidt, J. (2010) What's wrong with globalization? Contra 'flow speak' – twards an existential turn in the theory of globalization. *European Journal of Social Theory*, *13*, 481–500.

Cesari, J. (2009) *The Securitisation of Islam in Europe*. European Union: CEPS.

Damen, S. (2001) Strategieën tegen extreem-rechts: Het cordon sanitaire onder de loep. *Tijdschrift voor sociologie*, *22*, 89–110.

Düvell, F. (2006) Irregular migration: A global, historical and economic perspective. In: F. Düvell (ed.) *Illegal Immigration in Europe, Beyond Control?* New York: Palgrave MacMillan.

Economist (2006) Reaping the whirlwind: Denmark's cartoon crisis has one clear benefi-ciary – the far right. *The Economist*, 16 February.

Engbersen, G. and Broeders, D. (2010) Fortress Europe and the Dutch donjon: Securitization, internal migration policy and irregular migrants' counter moves.

In: T.-D. Truong and D. Gasper (eds) *Transnational Migration and Human Security.* New York: Springer.

Friedman, J. (2008) Global systems, globalization, and anthropological theory. In: I. Rossi (ed.) *Frontiers of Globalization Research: Theoretical and Methodological Approaches.* New York: Springer.

Friedman, T.L. (1999) *The Lexus and the Olive Tree.* New York: Farrar, Straus and Giroux.

Friedman, T.L. (2005) *The World is Flat.* New York: Farrar, Straus and Giroux.

Friedrichs, D.O. (2011) Comparative criminology and global criminology as complementary projects. In: D. Nelken (ed.) *Comparative Criminal Justice and Globalization.* Farnham: Ashgate.

Fukuyama, F. (1992) *The End of History and the Last Man.* New York: Free Press.

Gay Krant (2010) *PVV het populairst.* Available on line: http://www.gk.nl/?id= 9&bericht = 8446.

Giddens, A. (1990) *The Consequences of Modernity.* Stanford, CA: Stanford University Press.

Groenendijk, K. (2011) From assisting to requiring integration: Selective citizenship policies in the Netherlands. In: OECD (ed.) *Naturalization: A Passport for the Better Integration of Migrants?* OECD: OECD Publishing.

Hedetoft, U. (2003) 'Cultural transformation': How Denmark faces immigration. Open democracy forum. Available on line: www.opendemocracy.net/content/articles/PDF/ 1563.pdf.

Hudson, B. (2008) Difference, diversity and criminology: The cosmopolitan vision. *Theoretical Criminology*, *12*, 275–292.

Lash, S. and Urry, J. (1994) *Economies of Signs and Space.* London: Sage.

Lyon, D. (2005) The border is everywhere: ID cards, surveillance and the other. In: E. Zureik and M.B. Salter (eds) *Global Surveillance and Policing.* Cullompton: Willan.

Nelken, D. (2011) *Comparative Criminal Justice.* London: Sage.

Pakes, F. (2010) Global forces and local effects in youth justice: The case of Moroccan youngsters in Netherlands. *International Journal of Crime, Law and Justice*, *38*, 109–119.

Regeerakkoord (2010) *Concept Gedoogakkoord VVD-PVV-CDA.* Available on line: http:// www.parlement.com/9291000/d/pdfs/gedoog2010.pdf.

Rubin, L. (2004) Love's refugees: The effects of stringent Danish immigration policies on Danes and their non-Danish spouses. *Connecticut Journal of International Law*, *20*, 319.

Rydgren, J. (2005) Is extreme right wing populism contagious? Explaining the emergence of a new party family. *European Journal of Political Research*, *44*, 413–437.

Rydgren, J. (2010) Radical right-wing populism in Denmark and Sweden: Explaining party system change and stability. *SAIS Review of International Affairs*, *30*, 57–71.

Rytter, M. (2010) 'The family of Denmark' and 'the aliens': Kinship images in Danish integration politics. *Ethnos*, *75*, 301–322.

Savelsberg, J.J. (2011) Globalization and states of punishment. In: D. Nelken (ed.) *Comparative Criminal Justice and Globalization.* Farnham: Ashgate.

Salter M.B. (2009) Borders, passports, and the global mobility regime. In: B.S. Turner (ed.) *Handbook of Globalization Studies.* London: Taylor & Francis.

Scharff-Smith, P. (2012) A critical look at Scandinavian exceptionalism: Welfare state theories, penal populism and prison conditions in Denmark and Scandinavia. In: T. Ugelvik and J. Dullum (eds) *Penal Exceptionalism? Nordic Prison Policy and Practice.* London: Routledge.

Sjolander, C.T. (1995) The rhetoric of globalisation: What's in a wor(l)d? *International Journal*, *51*, 603–616.

Spalek, B. and Lambert, B. (2007) Muslim communities under surveillance. *Criminal Justice Matters*, *68*, 12–13.

Stiglitz, J. (2002) *Globalization and Its Discontents*. New York: W.W. Norton.

Van Swaaningen, R. (2011) Critical cosmopolitanism and global criminology. In: D. Nelken (ed.) *Comparative Criminal Justice and Globalization*. Farnham: Ashgate.

Wacquant, L. (2009) *Punishing the Poor: The Neo-liberal Government of Social Insecurity*. Durham: Duke University Press.

Widfeldt, A. (2010) A fourth phase of the extreme right? Nordic immigration-critical parties in a comparative context. *NordEuropa Forum*, *20*, 7–31.

Index

T - #0077 - 090119 - C0 - 234/156/10 - PB - 9780415643528